The Color Bind

THE COLOR BIND

*California's Battle to
End Affirmative Action*

Lydia Chávez

UNIVERSITY OF CALIFORNIA PRESS
BERKELEY LOS ANGELES LONDON

University of California Press
Berkeley and Los Angeles, California

University of California Press, Ltd.
London, England

© 1998 by
The Regents of the University of California

Library of Congress Cataloging-in-Publication Data
Chávez, Lydia, 1951–
    The color bind : California's battle to end affirmative
action / Lydia Chávez.
        p. cm.
    Includes bibliographical references and index.
    ISBN 0-520-20687-8 (cloth : alk. paper). —
    ISBN 0-520-21344-0 (pbk. : alk. paper)
    1. Affirmative action programs—California. I. Title.
HF5549.5.A34C484   1998
331.13'3'09794—DC21   97–13397
                                                        CIP

Printed in the United States of America
9 8 7 6 5 4 3 2

The paper used in this publication meets the minimum
requirements of American National Standard for
Information Sciences—Permanence of Paper for Printed
Library Materials, ANSI Z39.48-1984.

Life is not a level playing field, and I am most grateful for having started mine in the lap of a wonderfully supportive family that now extends beyond my siblings, Manuel, Andrea, Robert, Susana, and Martin, to their spouses and children.

My parents, Geraldine and Manuel, continue to create a climate—enriching, engaging, and generous—in which it is hard to fail. This book is dedicated to them.

Contents

Acknowledgments

I am indebted to the help of many. Sandra Salmans read every chapter and offered invaluable editing and advice on small and large editorial questions. She and Barbara Wright inspired and encouraged me throughout the two years that I worked on this book. My colleagues at the University of California and elsewhere—patient and exacting readers—included Teresa Paloma Acosta, Marty Baron, Sandy Close, Doug Frantz, Tom Goldstein, Susan Rasky, Orville Schell, Peter Schrag, Tony Platt, Sharon Rosenhause, and my editor at the University of California Press, Naomi Schneider. All took time out from their busy lives to make this a better book. Others—Cynthia Gorney, Cecilia O'Leary, and Judith Romero—fed, consoled, and urged me on. Tona Vides was unfailing in her efforts to make my life sane. My aunt and uncle, Alex and Nadine Chaves, opened their home to me in Southern California and, after long days of reporting, offered their good company.

Mark Rabine helped in every way imaginable—researching and attending events that I could not make because of my teaching responsibilities. He read countless drafts and, with humor and patience, endured endless conversations about affirmative action and the campaign. My daughters, Geraldine and Lola, lived through two years of having their mother at the computer for too many weekends. They did so patiently and, when necessary, with creative revolt.

I also want to thank the Silk family. Leonard Silk was the economics columnist at the *New York Times* when I was just starting out. He generously took the time to make me and other young reporters feel welcome and connected. After Leonard's death his family and friends established the Leonard Silk Fellowship Award, and this project was the first the fellowship chose to support.

Finally, I want to thank Professor Penn Kimball, who reached out when it counted most.

Preface

In November 1994, after a tumultuous and divisive campaign, Californians approved their state's Proposition 187, an initiative that promised to end public education and medical care for undocumented workers and their families. I had watched the campaign closely and was curious to see if the anti-immigrant sentiment it fomented succeeded in discouraging undocumented workers from coming to California. After the election, I took a trip to the Salinas Valley. To walk through those fields of lettuce was to experience the disconnect between politics and reality. Proposition 187 was as ephemeral as an early morning fog. What remained after it burned off were muddy fields filled with scores of undocumented workers and farmers eager to employ them.

I wrote an op-ed piece for the *New York Times* about my visit to Salinas. As I worked on it, I found myself more and more intrigued by how the immigration issue had been packaged to maximize its political velocity. Proposition 187 stirred up voters' fears about immigration, making serious discussion of an already complex problem next to impossible. Proposition 187's success wasn't just about Governor Pete Wilson's campaign savvy in exploiting the tangible problem of illegal immigration, and it wasn't just a knee-jerk racist reaction by voters. The promoters of 187 had a whole initiative "infrastructure" at their disposal—an infrastructure that, unlike the legislative process, was splendidly suited to offering voters simplistic solutions providing little change in policy.

It wasn't long before I began reading about Thomas Wood and Glynn Custred, two Bay Area academics who were intent on putting the California Civil Rights Initiative (CCRI) on the state ballot. Their initiative promised to take an issue that the courts had wrestled with for decades—the use of race and gender in state affirmative action programs—and put it to a popular vote.* By doing so they would once again focus Californians on the explosive issues of race and inclusion and put both at the center of the state's political debate. I felt that CCRI would be at least as important to California and the country as Proposition 187, and I decided to chronicle the initiative—the story of its authors, the struggles and conflicts of getting it on the ballot, the campaign for it, and the efforts of those who opposed it.

California is often on the cutting edge of political trends. The tax revolt, the environmental movement, and the immigration debate all began here. Although the courts have so far blocked Proposition 187's implementation, the anti-immigrant sentiment it embodied and inflamed has influenced federal legislation on welfare and immigration. So I believed that the final vote on CCRI would define the national debate on affirmative action. CCRI's historical importance was also compelling. If CCRI made it onto the ballot—a fact that was much more in doubt than the hyperbole in November 1994 suggested—it would be the first time that a sizable portion of the American public voted directly on a civil rights measure. If passed, it would dramatically change a thirty-year-old civil rights policy in the country's most populous state, a development that was likely to influence federal legislation and state ballot initiatives elsewhere. This was a watershed and well worth documenting.

---

*Unless otherwise noted, the term *affirmative action* refers to programs that take race and gender into account. These represent the vast majority of affirmative action programs. As noted in this book, CCRI's sponsors argued that they favored affirmative action that did not take race and gender into account, but in internal memos they acknowledged they would be hard-pressed to name any such existing programs.

I came to this project with a journalist's desire for a good story and a beneficiary's stake in a system that was suddenly in jeopardy. My enrollment at the University of California, Berkeley, and Columbia University's Graduate School of Journalism, and my employment at the *Los Angeles Times,* the *New York Times,* and the Graduate School of Journalism at the University of California, Berkeley—all were assisted either directly by affirmative action programs or indirectly by the receptivity toward minorities and women that those programs fostered. I continue to see the importance of affirmative action for all of the students I teach. There are, however, already many books that argue for or against affirmative action. This is not one of them.

Instead, in writing this book I wanted to understand why a linchpin of the civil rights movement became unpopular and politically vulnerable. My reaction to Thomas Wood, Glynn Custred, and Ward Connerly—the prominent black Californian who was CCRI's most effective advocate—was not hostility but curiosity. How did they arrive at their decision to undo affirmative action, and how would they, and the politicians who endorsed their initiative, wage their campaign? I was equally interested in how the opponents of CCRI would argue their case. Few can deny that by 1994 preferences had become unpopular with a substantial number of Americans and political debate made it difficult to distinguish for many the difference between preferences and affirmative action. Could those political leaders who still supported affirmative action make a compelling case for continuing it? Could they defend affirmative action in a way that was inclusive and addressed the concerns of white voters? Or would they become defensive and moralistic, much as Democrats had become several years earlier when taunted by conservatives about the "L word"?

While race is often just a subtext in discussions about crime, welfare, and illegal immigration, it lies at the heart of the debate on affirmative action. Without these programs, how would the United States bring into the fold people long shut out of mainstream America? Would alternatives to affirmative action be discussed? And could a long overdue conversation about race and inclusion take place under the klieg lights of a presidential campaign?

It was my hope that a book would answer some of these questions. As I began covering the first portion of the CCRI campaign—the process of getting the initiative onto the ballot—I began to see a secondary purpose. Although there have been many studies of the initiative process, I have found no book that chronicles an initiative campaign from beginning to end. Inasmuch as the ballot measure is a political tactic that has become increasingly popular in California and elsewhere, voters need to closely scrutinize the dynamic of the "popular" referendum. I hope that this book about a specific initiative campaign will serve as a case study.

Most campaign books are dominated by unattributed quotes. My training as a journalist and my concern for credibility made me determined to get on-the-record interviews. My interviews with both sides of the campaign were carried out with the understanding that the book would not be published until after the election. As a result, participants were extremely candid. I was given access to polling material and to internal documents and memos from both sides of the campaign. These documents were not intended for public consumption, and they provide additional insight into the strategies and motivations of the different players.

To understand the campaigns and the issue of affirmative action, I interviewed hundreds of sources in California, Washington, DC, and elsewhere. I followed the key players to meetings, debates, and fund-raisers. I watched and listened as the campaign's main participants experienced and talked about a campaign and an issue that sometimes seemed out of their control—changing their moods, predictions, and alliances. Months before the vote, the victory of CCRI was a foregone conclusion, but little else about the campaign was predictable. Everyone made and lost political bets.

Lydia Chávez
Berkeley, California

1

Origins

Canon and Culture Wars on Campus

As an anthropologist, I know that when you've got
diversity, you've got a problem, which means that
you've got to come up with ways to deal with it in
the most realistic way possible.

GLYNN CUSTRED
co-author of CCRI

The 1994 midterm elections represented the biggest loss for an
incumbent president since 1946, when Harry Truman lost
fifty-five Democratic seats. When the last vote was counted,
the Republican Party had ended the Democratic Party's forty-
year hold on Congress, gained eleven new governorships to
hold a majority for the first time in twenty-four years, and top-
pled such liberal Democratic icons as New York governor
Mario M. Cuomo and Texas governor Ann Richards. The as-
cending star was a conservative Georgian named Newt
Gingrich, but the real celebrities of the 1994 election were the
white males who put Gingrich and his fellow conservatives
into office.[1] Some 63 percent of them had voted for
Republicans, and suddenly they—like the Christian right before them and the soccer moms who would follow—became
the group that politicians most wanted to please.[2]

What did white males want and who knew how to deliver
it? Analysts didn't have to look far for an answer. California

governor Pete Wilson, near political death a year earlier, had found new life in his 1994 reelection campaign by turning voter attention to illegal immigrants: "they" crowded "our" schools and hospitals and cost the state billions of dollars. Wilson had defined his campaign by championing Proposition 187, a citizen-initiated ballot measure that promised to deny health and education benefits to illegal immigrants. Wilson was for it—some $2 million worth of advertising had made that clear—and his opponent, Kathleen Brown, was against it. In the end, voters—especially white men—agreed with Wilson. In the post-election prognosticating, Wilson's use of Proposition 187 became a blueprint for those looking to attract these voters. Immigration and Proposition 187 had worked in 1994. What issue and initiative would work in 1996? Enter Glynn Custred and Thomas E. Wood, two San Francisco Bay Area academics.

At the end of 1994 their initiative appeared to be the proverbial right-place, right-time proposal. Their California Civil Rights Initiative (CCRI) promised to end the use of race and gender preferences in state employment, contracting, and education. In 1994 this meant the end of nearly all state affirmative action programs, and at that moment such a proposal was the answer to the prevailing but not necessarily accurate political buzz. White males voted, white males hated affirmative action, and therefore, according to the crude popular logic of the moment, any politician wanting to win in 1996 had better be ready to pounce on affirmative action. That the initiative would be on the California ballot made the proposition all the more terrifying for the Democrats. California had fifty-four electoral votes—more than any other state—and in 1994 the electoral arithmetic showed that President Bill Clinton could not return to the White House without those votes. That math sent political analysts into high gear. Affirmative action, they predicted, would become the "mother of all wedge issues," creating a split between a candidate's supporters. In this case, affirmative action was viewed as a policy that would put white voters—especially white males—in opposition to minority and liberal voters, thereby dividing the Democratic Party and finishing Clinton off for good.

No two people were more surprised than Custred and Wood. They too were white and male, but their initiative did not stem from flash-in-the-pan anger. Nor was it concocted by strategists striving to find the consummate wedge issue. If their timing looked perfect, it appeared so only in retrospect. Custred, fifty-five, and Wood, forty-seven, had been working in obscurity for two years. They had already failed once to get CCRI on the ballot, and they still had much to learn about politics. The developments that moved Custred and Wood to write and promote an initiative to end affirmative action had been smoldering on U.S. college campuses for years. Custred, a professor of anthropology, watched these events unfold at suburban California State University, Hayward. Wood observed them from the outside looking in.

They were an odd couple. Custred, a disarmingly open man with a ready smile, had the affable demeanor of a Little League coach who values fun over winning. He was tall with a pleasant bulk. His eyes, an almost translucent light blue, would have given a different man an icy effect. He used words like "stuff" when he referred to new academic currents and "dumb stuff" when he disagreed with an idea.[3] He taught at a state university where he had a comfortable retirement guaranteed. Like a number of San Francisco Bay Area professionals in need of less expensive housing and good public schools, Custred lived in Walnut Creek, a largely white suburb connected to the more urban East Bay by a tunnel running through the Diablo Hills. Until the late 1980s, Custred's world revolved around his German-born wife and daughter and son on one side of the Caldecott Tunnel and his job twenty miles to the south, in Hayward.

Wood, who wore wire-rimmed glasses and, at his most casual, a blazer and khakis, may have looked the consummate preppy, but he didn't fit in anywhere. As a child, he had preferred the library to the playground. His father's career as an Air Force officer had taken the family to Southern California,

Iran, France, and Germany by the time Wood arrived in Berkeley to study philosophy in the late 1960s. Even after he graduated with a doctorate in philosophy in 1975, he continued to spend hours in the library reading everything from *Newsweek* to journals on linguistic theory, and then switched on his computer to read or write for hours more. His attention to detail bordered on the neurotic. Some mornings, he told Custred, Wood woke up before the alarm went off in his small Berkeley apartment, wondering if something he wrote the night before needed another comma. Twenty years after receiving his doctorate from U.C. Berkeley, Wood was still struggling financially. He had held a few temporary teaching jobs and then dropped out of academia to study meditation. Later, he worked for the Federal Reserve Board as a researcher during the day and wrote books on Sanskrit texts at night. But nothing jelled. Wood began to blame trends beyond his control for his failure to move beyond the margins of the academy.

Multiculturalism, Hayward, and the Campus Culture Wars

If Wood observed changes on U.S. campuses from the sidelines, Custred witnessed them from his lectern at Hayward State. During his first years of teaching, Custred taught students who shared his white working-class roots. In the fall of 1976, five years into his teaching career, 63 percent of the freshman who enrolled at Hayward were white; some 20 percent were African American; 8 percent were Asian or Filipino; and 5 percent were Latino. When school opened in the fall of 1994, Custred faced a class that looked decidedly different: 34 percent were Asian or Filipino; 18 percent were African American; 16 percent were Latino; and only 24 percent were white. A similar change in the racial and ethnic mix had evolved on other state campuses.[4] These changes had little to do with affirmative action and everything to do with more permanent demographic changes. The state universities accepted all high school seniors who finished in the top third of the state's high school graduates, and all but one campus had space for all its eligible applicants.[5] Increasingly, however, applicants were nonwhite. California was inching toward the time near the year 2000, when, demographers predicted, it would become the first state in which white residents were a minority.[6] In Custred's classroom, this reality had already come to pass.

For his part, Custred wasn't bothered by the new students: he found them as uneven in potential as the all-white classes he had taught twenty years earlier. "I have noticed that a lot of the minority students are just not with it," Custred said. "But then we get some who are not only with it but are right at the top. We get a lot of white students who are not prepared either."[7] Nonetheless, the new students would trigger other changes that would begin to grate on Custred.

In the spring of 1979 Robert Portillo, the special assistant to the president of Hayward State and its director of the Employment Affirmative Action Program, predicted that half of the school's tenure-track faculty would retire in the next decade. "It is vital to recognize this and to begin taking steps to insure appropriate minority representation in our faculty ranks," he wrote.[8] Some of the new faculty recruits arrived at Hayward eager to explore new ways of tackling old disciplines. One new current was to look at history, literature, and other fields from a multicultural perspective. They felt that teaching students about the world required including different points of view—black, Latino, and Asian as well as Anglo-Saxon.

Barbara Paige, who had a doctorate in philosophy from U.C. Berkeley, and Gayle Young, who had a doctorate in communications from UCLA, were among the new faculty members enthusiastic about broadening Hayward's curriculum. In 1985 they codirected a three-year state grant to help their colleagues "mainstream the cross-cultural perspective" into their courses. Unlike many grants, this one caught the administration's attention. At seminars attended by the provost, guest scholars encouraged literature professors to add black writers like Alice Walker and Toni Morrison to their reading lists. The scholars suggested that history professors include the experience and viewpoints of blacks, Latinos, and women. As an anthropologist, Paige, who is black, befriended Custred. The two had different African American intellectual heroes— Custred quoted conservatives like Shelby Steele, while Paige was more likely to cite Henry Louis Gates, Jr.—but Custred enjoyed the debate. "He said he had always been vilified and that at least he could talk to me," Paige said.[9]

Others warned Paige that Custred was unfriendly to the minority faculty, but she took him at his word when he said he wanted to participate in the grant and invite an anthropologist to lecture on multiculturalism. When Custred's guest trumpeted what Paige viewed as traditional anthropology and ignored multiculturalism, Paige said, "My mouth dropped. I felt that he had been disingenuous, that he was a closet racist." Custred could not recall the incident and said only that he "wasn't very interested in" what Paige and Young were doing. "We felt like we were doing multiculturalism anyway," he explained.[10] Although Paige felt blindsided by Custred, the three-year grant she helped direct at Hayward produced little controversy. If some disagreed with the effort, they did so privately. When the grant ended in 1988, a group of faculty interested in keeping multiculturalism alive at Hayward founded the Center for the Study of Intercultural Relations. "We could see that we were dealing with a very long journey," said Young, who is white. "Other academics were not going to jump on this like scientists jumped on the discovery of DNA."[11]

From the outset, Custred was skeptical of the multicultural scholars. They had, he said, a romantic view of the world. "The model they had was a nice, ethnically diverse neighborhood in a big city where everyone is happy and everyone dances around the Maypole," he said. "As an anthropologist, I know that when you've got diversity, you've got a problem, which means that you've got to come up with ways to deal with it in the most realistic way possible."[12] Custred believed that to live in harmony, Americans had to find common ground.[13] This clashed with the multiculturalists, who were intent on defining and celebrating the uniqueness of ethnic Americans. To many professors interested in multiculturalism, Custred's common ground was limited to traditional Western values and traditions.

By 1989 Hayward's embrace of multiculturalism had begun to nettle Custred. When the new Center for the Study of Intercultural Relations organized a conference—Hayward's first national conference—entitled "The Inclusive University: Multicultural Perspectives in Higher Education," Custred objected. "I could see this moving in a direction I didn't like," Custred said.[14] When he complained, his dean suggested that he participate. It was a mistake. Custred felt like a classics professor among pop culture enthusiasts. He represented tradition and they considered themselves on the cutting edge of a new discipline. He presented a paper defending standard English; his fellow panelists wanted to explore the value of black English. Custred's paper, Young said, was "well reasoned, well thought-out," but, she acknowledged, "there was not much tolerance for his argument."[15] Custred found listening to their papers equally torturous. "I was there listening to some of the most god-awful things you can imagine," he said.[16]

It wasn't a conference alive with open debate. Many of those who attended were under attack at their own universities, and they attended the gathering to find friends and share war stories. Most didn't want to analyze multiculturalism; they wanted to celebrate it. It is impossible to say what would have happened if everyone had been more civil, but they weren't. Custred was ostracized. There was a sense among the conference's participants that they were "agents of change" and Custred represented the status quo. Custred could have lived with the reputation of being unfashionable, but the debate on multiculturalism had a more cutting subtext. "What

we didn't realize," Young said, "is that we were not just dealing with intellectual issues, but with emotional issues. We
were asking what it means to be an American, what it means
to be an educated person. We were saying that whiteness was
constructed to keep people down and no matter how softly
you say this, it's hard to take."[17] For his part, Custred was less
offended personally than he was intellectually: "I just found it
terribly misguided," he said.[18]

The slights at the conference were compounded by other developments at Hayward. In the past, the administration's efforts to increase minority faculty had resulted mostly in the
hiring of white women. The pool of minority applicants wasn't
as large, and Hayward's intentions to hire more were complicated by the competition from other universities. Nonetheless,
in 1989 the administration decided to double its efforts.
Blacks, Latinos, or Asians in any field could apply through the
administration's main office, and their applications were sent
to the different departments for consideration. This meant that
departments could add to their faculty numbers without waiting for someone in their department to retire. In effect, the
university set aside jobs for minorities. This, too, upset
Custred. To him, the set-aside trod on individual rights; it favored candidates because they were part of a racial or ethnic
group and discriminated against others for the same reason.

As a child growing up in Birmingham, Alabama, during the
1940s, Custred had seen the evils of lumping individuals into
groups. He was one of three children in a working-class family. Until after World War II, his father worked in the tin mills
as a speed controller, watching over the machines that turned
metal into sheets. The young Custred noted early on how his
fellow whites in Birmingham treated blacks as a separate
species and, for a while, he accepted that view. But as Custred
experienced the world, he began to question the notion that
blacks were altogether different from whites.

When the war ended, Custred's father took a job as a sales-
man for the Alabama Gas Corporation, and Custred some-

times accompanied his father on business calls. His world, he said, opened on those trips. The young Custred discovered black families who lived much like his own family: two parents living in a neat but modest home and struggling to survive. "I was quite surprised," Custred said, recalling the visits. "I thought, 'God, they're no different than we are.'"[19] Custred's family moved on to Vincennes, Indiana, in the year before he entered high school, but every Thanksgiving and for two weeks every summer, they returned to Birmingham, and Custred watched the changes embroiling the South. These experiences and others, he said, informed his belief that it was wrong to sweep individuals into groups. The set-asides, he felt, did exactly that. As a result, when the set-asides were announced at Hayward, Custred organized the anthropology department to decline to participate. "He considered it racist," said Paige.[20]

Other developments troubled Custred as well. When the budget crisis hit California in 1990, it looked like Hayward might announce layoffs; recent hires—minorities and women—would be among the first to go. But Terry Jones, a black tenured professor, and others found a clause in the union's rules that would permit the administration to circumvent the seniority system to retain faculty who offered something unique to the university. A faculty member's racial or ethnic identity, Jones argued, could be construed as unique. Hypothetically, Custred could have been laid off at Hayward so that a junior member of the faculty—a woman or a Latino or black who had just been hired—could stay on. Again, Custred organized his department. "I said, hell, that's fine and dandy, but the problem is we have this union understanding and this would adversely affect the anthropology department." The battle in Hayward's academic senate was fierce. "They just screamed their bloody heads off," Custred recalled. "People got hysterical."[21] In the end, layoffs proved unnecessary, but Custred was becoming more active.

Although Hayward's educational battles received little notice in the media, the same wars were making national news at places like Stanford, Berkeley, and the University of Michigan. Until the 1980s, students had protested actions taken in Washington—notably the country's involvement in Vietnam. Now the tables had turned, and Washington was reacting—volubly—to actions on campus. An intellectual debate was becoming a national political issue. When Stanford University began discussing the possibility of including new ethnic writers in its core humanities course, U.S. Secretary of Education William Bennett ridiculed the proposed changes. "They are moving confidently and swiftly into the late 1960s. And why anybody would want to do that intentionally, I don't know," he said, adding that some at Stanford were being intimidated by the "noisiest" of their colleagues.[22] The *Wall Street Journal* weighed in with an editorial accusing Stanford of riding "the main hobby horses of today's political left—race, gender and class."[23] What should have been a pedagogical debate became political.

In fact, Stanford was talking about only a handful of new writers and, in the end, the changes were modest. The freshman Western civilization course was renamed Culture, Ideas, and Values, and the eighteenth-century autobiography of the African slave Olaudah Equiano, readings from the Koran, and Mary Wollstonecraft's 1792 book on women's rights joined Homer, Machiavelli, and Freud on the reading list. A new section, entitled Europe and the Americas, used classics such as *Uncle Tom's Cabin* or *Democracy in America.* The conservative U.C. Berkeley philosopher John Searle wrote in the *New York Review of Books* that "reports of the demise of 'culture,' Western or otherwise, in the required freshman course at Stanford are grossly exaggerated."[24] Referring to the most innovative of Stanford's sections of Culture, Ideas, and Values, he concluded: "If I were a freshman at Stanford, I might well be tempted to take 'Europe and the Americas.'"[25]

The canon had survived. But new intellectual camps had formed, and some of the heavyweights were firmly aligned against change. Allan Bloom, an academic from the University of Chicago, had already risen to fame in 1987 with his book *The Closing of the American Mind,* and Dinesh D'Souza would follow in 1991 with his attack on the new trends in education in *The Illiberal Education: The Politics of Race and Sex on Campus.* A group of prominent scholars, including Jeane Kirkpatrick and James Q. Wilson, formed the National Association of Scholars in 1988 to ensure a "reasoned scholarship in a free society." The Princeton-based group billed itself as "the only American academic organization dedicated to the restoration of intellectual substance, individual merit, and academic freedom in the university." To multiculturalists, those were code words used to defend the Western canon and to attack affirmative action. But it was language to which Custred responded favorably: he helped form a California chapter—the California Association of Scholars, or CAS.

There was much to do. The California State Assembly, concerned that minority students were being left behind in higher education, considered legislation in 1991 to ensure that the freshman classes at the state's public colleges and universities reflected the ethnic composition of the class that graduated from the state's public high schools. A similar bill had been approved by the Democratic-controlled Assembly in 1990 but had been vetoed by Republican Governor George Deukmejian. The California Association of Scholars immediately opposed the 1991 measure, which was introduced in March by Assembly Speaker Willie Brown. Brown's bill called for "educational equity," which as defined by the bill meant that the students and faculty at public schools and universities must reflect the diversity of the state.[26] In addition, it called for "enhanced success at all educational levels so that there are similar achievement patterns among all groups regardless of ethnic origin, race, gender, age, disability or economic circumstance."[27] To ensure that the bill's vision was carried out, it also held faculty and administrators accountable. The CAS argued strongly against such provisions, stating that students seeking admission to college and faculty applying for teaching positions should be judged on the basis of their qualifications as individuals, not by their race, color, or sex. The Brown bill was vetoed by Governor Pete Wilson.

As Custred became involved in these debates, he began to develop his arguments against affirmative action and, to do this, he did what all academics do: he went to the library. For many, the history of affirmative action begins with the Civil Rights Act of 1964, so Custred looked it up. He read it once, and then he read it again. He was delighted. Title VII, the section on equal employment opportunity, says: "It shall be an unlawful employment practice for an employer (1) to fail or refuse to hire or to discharge any individual or otherwise to discriminate against any individual with respect to his compensation, terms, conditions, or privileges of employment, because of such individual's race, color, religion, sex, or national origin."

"I thought, 'Hey, there's nothing wrong with this,'" he recalled. "It just wasn't being enforced."[28] He photocopied the act and took it home. Far from promoting affirmative action that took race and gender into account, the Civil Rights Act, by Custred's reading, actually prohibited it. He began toying with the idea of a statewide initiative. In his mind, taking race or gender into consideration violated the 1964 Civil Rights Act. Custred wanted to write an initiative that would end programs that he viewed as discriminatory against white males and others who were not considered underrepresented minorities.

Wood Goes Job Hunting

While Custred was in the throes of academic politics in the late 1980s, Thomas Wood was looking for work. It was a quest that had problems from the start. Berkeley's philosophy department went all out for its newly minted Ph.D.'s but was less willing or able to help alumni who had been out of the field for several years. And even for its new graduates, the job market was tight.

"We were one of the best schools at placing our Ph.D.'s, and we were happy if we placed half of our Ph.D.'s in tenure track positions,"[29] said Bruce Vermazen, chairman of the philosophy department at U.C. Berkeley. Wood's search had another obstacle, according to Anita Silvers, the secretary-treasurer of the Pacific division of the American Philosophical Association. Few jobs existed in Wood's field, the philosophy of religion.[30]

Wood's job search might have been forgotten altogether if he had not mentioned it in late 1994, when a *Washington Post* reporter asked if he had ever encountered reverse discrimination. "I was once told by a member of a search committee at a university, 'You'd walk into this job if you were the right gender,'" Wood told the reporter.[31] Reporters ferreted out the details of that incident on their own; when some discovered it was San Francisco State University, they confronted Wood. He refused to comment. The school, Wood insisted, wasn't important. The important issue, he argued, was that a member of the search committee felt it was legitimate to tell a white male that he was unlikely to be considered. Imagine, he said, if a committee member had said that to a female or black prospect. "For me, it's a legal question," Wood said. "The law said you can discriminate against some, but not against others."[32]

It was only in a 1995 memo to his CCRI colleagues that Wood offered an explanation of his experience at San Francisco State.[33] The memo raises questions as to whether Wood had ever been discriminated against by anyone. Wood wrote in the memo that even before he had sent in his application to the university, he ran into San Francisco State philosophy professor Anatole Anton in a Berkeley computer store. Anton, Wood noted, was dismayed when he discovered that Wood wanted to apply for the job. "He then proceeded to tell me quite candidly that the department had decided that it needed a diversity hire and that it had already found a black woman who looked promising. 'Well, Tom,'" Wood wrote that he was told by Anton, "'it sounds to me as though you would just waltz into this job if you were the right gender.'"[34]

Undaunted by Anton's warning, Wood applied and he landed on the short list of candidates, according to his memo. The interview, he reported in the memo, went badly. "A number of individuals seemed icily adversarial." When he suggested that he would also like to teach a course in parapsychology, the committee was unimpressed. "There was widespread reaction in the room that this was a preposterous suggestion," he wrote.[35]

Anton, who in 1996 was working to oppose CCRI, said he could only vaguely recall the meeting Wood described. He failed to remember any specific remarks to Wood and said he would have deferred to Jacob Needleman, the head of the search committee.[36] Needleman declined to talk about the incident, but James Syfers, who served as philosophy department chair at the time, said that no one remembered Wood and that he had not been one of the two finalists. The school keeps tape recordings of final interviews, and though they have tapes of the two finalists, they have no tape of an interview with Wood. "No one remembers Tom Wood at all," Syfers said. "I think you can say this with authority: he was not a serious candidate." To Wood's charge that the university was looking for a diversity hire, Syfers said, "We were just looking to find the best person we could find." Budget constraints had prevented the department from hiring anyone in more than fifteen years, and it had no minorities on the faculty in the late 1980s. The committee ended up hiring a black woman who went by only one name—Tandeaka. She left S.F. State after one year to take a fellowship at Stanford University.

Although Wood applied elsewhere, no job offers materialized, and he continued to pick up part-time jobs. One of them sent him to U.C. Berkeley's library at Boalt Hall School of Law to research mediation law. Soon he found his way to the stacks where the multivolume history of the U.S. Supreme Court's 1978 *Bakke* decision was housed. After the medical school at the University of California, Davis, had rejected Allan Bakke, a white applicant, in 1973 and again in 1974, Bakke had challenged their admissions policy, which set aside sixteen slots for minority students. "It was a fascinating tale," said Wood. "I would go back and forth, seeing the merits of both sides, but in the end Allan Bakke had the stronger case." Wood agreed with Justice Lewis Powell, who wrote the majority opinion, that Davis had violated the equal protection clause of the Fourteenth Amendment by setting aside sixteen slots for underrepresented minorities. Powell ruled that such quotas were unconstitutional, that all applicants had be to considered in the same pool. But Powell also said that race could be considered as a factor in admissions. Here, Wood disagreed. He felt that any use of race ultimately discriminated against other applicants. Wood's position was not difficult to reach since Powell's decision was cautionary. He warned that "racial and ethnic distinctions of any sort are inherently suspect and thus call for the most exacting judicial examination."[37] Powell, however, agreed with and underscored the argument that the university's goal of creating a diverse student body was clearly a "constitutional permissible goal."[38] Offering the Harvard College program as a model, Powell said that "race or ethnic background may be deemed a 'plus' in a particular applicant's file, yet it does not insulate the individual from comparison with all other candidates for the available seats."[39]

Whereas Wood chose to read the Powell decision as restrictive, most university and college administrators read it more broadly. "The crucial fact about *Bakke*," wrote Robert Post, a professor of law at Boalt Hall School of Law at U.C. Berkeley, "is that Powell did not end his judgment with a simple declaration of unconstitutionality. He took the unusual step of appending to his opinion the affirmative action plan of Harvard College, which Powell said he would find constitutional. The Harvard Plan celebrated the diversity of individuals, but it also specifically noted that the value of ethnic and racial diversity could be attained only through an admission process that paid 'some attention to numbers.'"[40]

The *Bakke* decision came long before Wood began his job hunt in the late 1980s. He became convinced, however, that his failure to find a permanent place in academia might have had something to do with affirmative action. He chose to ignore the reality that white males, who represented 75 to 80 percent of all new graduates in philosophy between 1985 and 1990, were in fact filling the majority of the 2,790 job openings during those years.[41] Instead, his experience at San Francisco State University became the focus of his attention, and affirmative action became the explanation for his inability to find a tenure-track job. Much later, he would write a memo to CCRI's Los Angeles office underscoring the initiative's connection to discrimination against white males. "The white male backlash story does not serve our interests (though on the other hand, of course, if we're honest we can't deny that the issue is largely about discrimination against white males)."[42]

Two events in 1990 were of particular interest to Wood. One was the success of Proposition 140, which limited the number of terms a state legislator could serve. "It gave me an idea that the same thing could be done with affirmative action," he said.[43] Then in December, he opened a copy of *Newsweek* that discussed the academic battles over Western civilization courses, such as the one at Stanford, and the backlash against political correctness. "Is this the new enlightenment on campus or the new McCarthyism?" the cover story's headline asked.[44] "Opponents of PC see themselves as a beleaguered minority among barbarians who would ban Shakespeare because he didn't write in Swahili," *Newsweek* reported. "Outnumbered they may be on some campuses, but they are also often the most senior and influential people on their faculties."[45] Of particular interest to Wood was *Newsweek*'s story on Theodore S. Hamerow, described as "a wispy, white-haired professor of German and European history" at the University of Wisconsin, who, at the age of seventy, had become a "Don Quixote figure, the chairman of the campus branch of the National Association of Scholars, whose reason for existence is mortal combat with the windmills of PC."[46] The NAS chapter was "preparing to issue a statement denouncing what it calls minority-hiring quotas being imposed by the university's administration."[47]

Wood called the National Association of Scholars to ask if there was an affiliate in California. By the end of 1991 he had hooked up with Custred.

The First Initiative: 1992 to November 1994

In many respects, Custred and Wood were the kind of citizens California Governor Hiram Johnson of the Progressive Party had in mind in 1911, when he lobbied to include in the California state constitution a voter's right to propose and enact laws by collecting enough signatures to put an initiative on the ballot.[48] Both Custred and Wood were nonpartisan, well-educated citizens who were angry about policies they felt were unjust, and in 1992 they had no strong ties to any one party—Custred was a registered Independent, and Wood had only recently changed his registration from Independent to Republican. What Governor Johnson had long ago failed to foresee was that few initiatives make it onto the ballot without the help of paid signature gatherers and the money of special interest groups.[49] The bottom line was that in 1992 it cost about a million dollars to put an initiative on the ballot. Custred and Wood were about to learn this the hard way.

They began their efforts by calling a few people with an interest in politics whom they knew, or whose names they knew: former L.A. County Supervisor Pete Schabarum, who had managed the successful campaign for term limits (Proposition 140); and Stanley Diamond, at U.S. English, a Washington-based group that promoted English as the country's official language and helped to pass a 1986 "English only" ballot measure in California. Custred had met Diamond a few months earlier at a national conference in Washington. Both Schabarum and Diamond recommended Reed and Davidson, a Los Angeles law firm that specializes in election law and represents some of Orange County's most influential political

donors, as well as some major conservative political action
committees. They also recommended Louis W. M. Barnett, a
Wilson appointee to the state Unemployment Appeals Board
with many contacts and enough political savvy to know that
an anti–affirmative action initiative was something the state's
Republicans could get behind. "Initially, I thought they were
well intentioned and not very politically astute," said Barnett.
"They needed to hook up with various political organizations
that were affected—people who have an interest in the
issue."[50] Another early advisor to Custred and Wood was
Michael Arno, the president of American Petition Consultants,
a firm that had put some two hundred initiatives, many of
them backed by conservative interests, on the ballot. Arno's
advice was similar to Barnett's: "I told them to go to the
Republican Party."

Custred and Wood hesitated. At that time, they didn't know
any Republicans with enough clout to raise the issue, and they
were determined to make it nonpartisan. So instead of poli-
ticking in 1992 and 1993, they focused on writing the initiative. The language would be fine-tuned from 1992 to 1995.
Opponents would later claim it had been the brainchild of
countless focus groups, but its most eloquent section—the
part that drove civil rights leaders into a fury—came from
Custred's initial visit to the library. In his reading of the Civil
Rights Act of 1964 and Wood's familiarity with polling data on
affirmative action and preferences, they found the linguistic
equivalent of a sure thing.

In crafting this section, Custred and Wood drew inspiration
from a 1979 U.S. Supreme Court decision involving another
angry white man; that decision had, ironically, upheld affirmative action. In 1974 Brian Weber, a white Louisiana steelworker, was turned down for a place in a new training program
at a Kaiser plant in Gramercy, Louisiana.[51] Under pressure
from federal regulators, Kaiser Aluminum and Chemical
Corporation and the United Steelworkers of America had set
up training programs to increase the number of minority

workers in skilled jobs. At that time in Gramercy, blacks made up 39 percent of the local labor force, but held only 2 percent of the slots for craftsmen.[52] To remedy this imbalance, half the training program slots were set aside for minorities. When two blacks with less seniority than Weber won places in the training program, Weber filed a reverse discrimination suit, arguing that the preferential treatment given to blacks violated Title VII of the Civil Rights Act of 1964.[53]

The Supreme Court ruled against Weber. Justice William J. Brennan, Jr., stated that private employers have an "area of discretion" and can use preferential programs "to eliminate conspicuous racial imbalance in traditionally segregated job categories." Brennan argued that one could only interpret the meaning of Title VII's ban on discrimination by considering the intentions of the law's congressional authors. Even though Democrats such as Hubert Humphrey had sworn that the new act would never permit preferential treatment, Brennan concluded otherwise. The act, he wrote, "intended to improve the lot of those who had been 'excluded from the American dream for so long,'" and it would be ironic if it were read as a "prohibition of all voluntary, private, race-conscious efforts to abolish traditional patterns of racial segregation." Title VII bars the government from requiring employers to give preferential treatment, he continued, but "the natural inference is that Congress chose not to forbid all voluntary race-conscious affirmative action." The decision infuriated constitutional experts with conservative leanings. "A lot of legal scholars see the *Weber* decision as an illegitimate departure from the intent of the Civil Rights Act," said Eugene Volokh, a law professor at UCLA. So did Wood and Custred.

In addition to reading *Weber,* Wood, a dedicated researcher, had also looked at the polls. They showed that if voters tended to support affirmative action, they hated quotas and loathed preferences.[54] When asked in a Gallup poll in April 1991, for example, if quotas were necessary to accomplish fairness in education, hiring, and promotion, whites opposed them by 59 percent.[55] The dislike of preferences was even greater. When asked if qualified blacks should receive preference over equally qualified whites, 72 percent of all white voters said no and 42 percent of all black voters agreed with them.[56] Wood also looked at a new book, *The Scar of Race,* by Paul M. Sniderman and Thomas Piazza. While noting a 1988 Harris poll that showed 55 percent of the whites polled favoring affirmative action, the authors concluded, "The idea of quotas and preferential treatment is the reef on which affirmative action founders."[57]

As they read about the debate over *Weber* and looked at the polls, Custred and Wood came up with the key for what would be the first clause of the California Civil Rights Initiative. It would not focus on affirmative action but on "preferential treatment" based on race and gender. It, however, would not address other preferences, such as those for military service, disability, socioeconomic status, and special athletic or artistic abilities. The initiative read: "Neither the State of California nor any of its political subdivisions or agents shall use race, sex, color, ethnicity, or national origin as a criterion for either discriminating against, or granting preferential treatment to, any individual or group in the operation of the State's system of public employment, public education, or public contracting."[58] If the Supreme Court could interpret the Civil Rights Act of 1964 as permitting voluntary preferential treatment, Custred and Wood intended to set everyone straight by rewriting and clarifying the state constitution.

In 1993 Wood and Custred began to circulate a wordier version of this clause. By then, Wood finally had steady work: the California Association of Scholars had hired him as its executive director. He now had access to a multitude of prominent professors interested in the issue of affirmative action, and over the next two years he would spend hours on the phone with them discussing the initiative's language. "The nice thing about giving advice to him," said Richard Epstein, a law professor at the University of Chicago, "is that he actually listened."[59] Epstein, a Libertarian who in the end disagreed with the initiative because it only masked what really needed to be done—in his mind, the University of California system should be privatized—proved to be a lively intellectual sparring partner. Ultimately, however, perhaps Epstein's biggest contribution was to suggest that Wood call Epstein's colleague Michael McConnell, an advocate of school prayer who had one bit of advice: leave religion out of the initiative. McConnell advised Wood: "I believe that inclusion of the term 'religion' could be taken to outlaw legitimate religious accommodations, for example, allowing state employees to take unpaid leave for celebration of religious holy days or allowing religious employees to deviate in unobtrusive ways from a uniform requirement."[60] "The effect of inclusion would primarily be to create confusion and possibly to interfere with the protection of free exercise of religious rights." Custred and Wood agreed, and as a result, religion was left out.

Lino Graglia, a well-known professor of constitutional law at the University of Texas, Austin, and the author of a 1976 book on busing, *Disaster by Decree,* advised Wood to limit the initiative to race. Graglia warned him, "When you include sex, you run into a lot of problems that you don't run into with race."*[61] Wood and Custred refused, and their argument on the issue went on until late 1994. Both authors explained their reasons for including gender in long memos to Larry Arnn, the president of the Claremont Institute, who would later become the initiative campaign's first chairman. Custred's two-page memo, which lists seven points, stressed the fairness issue. "Removing gender from the initiative, when for the last thirty years it has been intimately linked with race and ethnicity, would suggest hypocrisy and a lack of principle. . . . The principle of nondiscrimination is for all and should apply to everyone equally. . . . There is a feeling in the black community that the greatest beneficiaries of affirmative action have been

---

*In September 1997 Graglia became the focus of a controversy after he said that black and Mexican American students were "not academically competitive" with white students. "They have a culture that seems not to encourage achievement," he said.

affluent white women at the expense of blacks. . . . Indeed it is often said by blacks that white women have hijacked affirmative action. To exclude gender preferences from the initiative would only reenforce this conviction creating the belief that the initiative is in fact a racist measure."[62]

Wood's three-page memo, which included nine points, reflected some of Custred's concerns but focused more on his belief that white males were getting a bad deal. "Sexual discrimination against males is pervasive. The available evidence indicates, in fact, that white males need protection against discrimination on the basis of their sex even more than they need protection on the basis of their race. . . . Omitting gender from the initiative would suggest that CCRI's proponents believe that there is a difference when in fact there is none. This would play right into the hands of the gender feminists and radical feminists, who would take this as an indirect endorsement of their agenda. . . . Leaving gender in CCRI is the conservative course. . . . Anyone who presses for dropping gender from CCRI should first do some survey research to find out how the American public would respond to that question, because that is what opponents would make the central issue in the campaign against it."[63]

Volokh, who had clerked for Supreme Court Justice Sandra Day O'Connor, helped to clarify the gender discrimination paragraph. Two years later, feminists would read the initiative's language on sex discrimination and see red. But in those early days, Wood felt that the academics and Reed and Davidson's legal team were making their initiative broad enough to escape charges of racism—by including gender— and tight enough to withstand court challenges.

State Republicans Discover the Political Possibilities of Affirmative Action

As Custred and Wood conferred with their legal and academic advisors, state Republicans discovered the issue of affirmative action on their own. In the fall of 1993, some 170 miles north of the Bay Area, Manuel Esteban, the new president of California State University, Chico, and his new vice provost, Michael Biechler, proposed a faculty diversity program that would set aside a certain number of positions for women and applicants of color. Five years earlier such a program would have passed with little notice—as it had at Hayward—but the ensuing canon wars on U.S. campuses, a tightened budget, and the anti-PC movement had politicized many conservative professors, some of whom were at Chico State. When Biechler announced the set-asides, the white faculty "flipped out," said Charles Geshekter, a professor since 1968.[64] The debate became front-page news in Chico. "When I came in, it seemed that a faculty diversity program would be well received, but in retrospect that seems awfully naive," Biechler recalled. "I think it was timing. There was an enormous backlash building."[65]

One Chico resident who read about the battle was Republican assemblyman Bernie Richter, a former high school civics teacher who was elected to the assembly in 1992. Richter felt the set-asides were wrong, and he wanted to take up the issue in the assembly. It looked to Custred and Wood like a good time to press their initiative. In October 1993, they filed the initiative with the state attorney general. A month later, William Rusher, the publisher of the conservative *National Review* and a distinguished fellow at the Claremont Institute, a conservative think tank in Southern California, wrote a piece headlined "Can California Voters Reverse the Unintended Consequences of the 1964 Civil Rights Act?" Rusher liked the initiative's political possibilities. "The dilemma into which this will plunge the whole national liberal establishment is obvious," he wrote. "It is a battle the liberals will be compelled to fight and are doomed to lose."[66] Rusher urged his readers to support the initiative for the November 1994 ballot.

Patrick Buchanan, the presidential candidate who later proved to have a sharp ear for issues that would appeal to white voters, also picked up on CCRI early. Even in February 1994, he felt that the groundswell against affirmative action could help return Republicans to the White House. "To win back California, the party must win back the Perot vote, that vast middle-class constituency, alienated and populist, that felt itself abandoned by the Beltway," he wrote in his syndicated column. "To the point: If the GOP is casting about for a populist issue to reunite its old coalition and to slice Bill Clinton's new coalition asunder, that issue is at hand. The California Civil Rights Initiative."[67]

Meanwhile, in the state assembly, Richter proposed Assembly Bill 47, which reflected CCRI and barred the state from taking race or gender into account in employment, contracting, and education. On August 10, 1994, the Assembly's judiciary committee held hearings on it. Conservatives mark the hearings as the occasion when Republican officeholders began to understand the scope of the potential sentiment against affirmative action. "On that day the issue moved from the ivory tower and became a political issue," said Wayne Johnson, a conservative political consultant based in Sacramento.[68] "It became very clear that there were deep divisions in the Democratic caucus on the issue and when you see one party split down the middle on an issue you see a new paradigm."

The hearings were important for another reason. For the first time, Custred and Wood heard Ward Connerly and experienced the effect this black businessman, who had recently been named a regent of the University of California, could have on an audience. Dressed nattily in a dark suit and white shirt, Connerly spoke eloquently against racial preferences. Custred and Wood were mesmerized by what they heard. "He was incredibly articulate," said Wood. "He stole the show." [69]

Affirmative Action for U.C. Regents and Students

Wardell Anthony Connerly was born on June 15, 1939, in Leesville, Louisiana, into an African American family with a mixture of Indian, Irish, and French Creole blood. "Nobody ever gave me any race or sex preferences when I came into the cold fifty-six years ago,"[70] Connerly recalled. Although that changed later in his life, it was true in his early years. Connerly's maternal grandmother, Mary Soniea, owned a small restaurant in Leesville, but Grace, her daughter, never did as well. When Connerly was two, his parents divorced. Soon after, Grace Connerly met William Parker, an enlisted man from New York. They married on the day before Valentine's Day 1943, but by the end of the year, Grace was dead from injuries that she had sustained in a car accident.[71]

Connerly was left to his grandmother, but not without a fight. His father, Roy, was still around, and he filed a custody suit. The charges made back and forth between Roy and Mary Soniea were not pleasant.[72] Roy Connerly accused his child's grandmother of mistreating the child, and his mother-in-law shot back with charges that her son-in-law was a drunk and abusive. Roy's interest in his child, Mary Soniea charged in papers filed by her lawyers, came from the $30 a month his stepfather was sending the child and the fact that Parker had named the young Ward as a beneficiary on his $10,000 life insurance policy. The truth of any of this was never cleared up by the courts, but most important to the young Connerly was the court's decision to give custody to his grandmother.

When Mary Soniea won, she sent Ward to live with her sister Bertha and Bertha's husband, John Lewis. They lived first in Washington, and then later they moved to Sacramento. Along the way, Connerly took to his uncle. "My uncle didn't have more than a second-grade education, but his work ethic was unbelievable," said Connerly. "He'd pile lumber up in the saw mills in California, he dug ditches. He always said you could know the mark of a person by his car, his shoes, and his lawn. Every weekend we'd mow the lawn, wash the car, and shine our shoes."[73] When Ward was nine years old, his grandmother sold her restaurant and moved to California. She had saved enough money to build her own house on the

corner of Grant and Branch Streets in the working-class
Sacramento neighborhood of Del Paso Heights. Ward went
from living with a model of the work ethic to the home of a
woman who believed that a young man needed only two
things to succeed—the Bible and his schoolbooks. She
drummed home the importance of both. "She had a saying for
everything," Connerly said. "It used to drive me crazy."[74]

Through 1995 and 1996, Connerly retold stories of his up-
bringing to reporters who walked away with the distinct impression that it had been a difficult one—he talked about having nothing to eat but sweet potatoes, having to work before
his teens, and going to school with holes in his shoes. But in
May 1997, A. Lin Neumann, a freelance writer for *San
Francisco Focus Magazine,* discovered that Connerly's extended
family based in Sacramento disagreed about just how poor it
had been.[75] Elizabeth Stansberry, Connerly's cousin and also a
Republican, and Connerly's seventy-six-year-old uncle, Arthur
Soniea, didn't so much disagree that Connerly had been raised
modestly—it was a matter of degrees. Most of his relatives
were homeowners, they said, and they made sure Mary Soniea
had the money to raise Connerly. "Our family took care of one
another," Stansberry said. "All the cousins including Ward had
Schwinn bikes and we all had our own plate of food at the
table."[76] Connerly's uncle Arthur added, "I don't dislike the guy
but I dislike what he's said about having nothing to eat. They're
all lies." When told a story that Connerly had repeated about
not having a car, Arthur Soniea was disgusted. "My wife and I
co-signed a loan for him to have a car when he graduated from
high school."[77] Soniea said the whole press ordeal had not
been pleasant for the family. His sister, Bertha, who backed
some of Connerly's stories, was no longer talking to him.

Elizabeth Stansberry had answers as to why the successful
Sacramento businessman was so confused about his upbring-
ing. "Wardell hates being black, and his grandmother 'toler-
ated' black people," she told Neumann. "She thought she was
better than black people." Once this news broke, it was not

long before Connerly's psyche became material for a long profile in the *New York Times,* and by the fall of 1997, *60 Minutes*
was working on a Connerly program. Connerly's answer to the
relatives who disagreed with his version of his early life in
Sacramento was to call them liars. Elizabeth Stansberry had
another take on Connerly's revisions: "My cousin is narcissis-
tically disordered," she said. "Ward has lied so much that I
think he believes his own lies. Ward always disliked being a
child of color. He thinks he's white."[78] Indeed, Connerly
seemed confused about his own heritage. He would tell some
reporters that his grandmother was a full-blooded Choctaw
Indian, others that she was a mixture of Creole and French,
and still others that he was actually more Irish than anything
else. Although Connerly may have viewed himself as multi-
ethnic, the world around him and those who enlisted his help
to combat affirmative action looked at him and saw a black
man—smart, capable, and black.

Connerly finished high school with the grades to get into
the University of California. But that was a world too far away
from Del Paso. He first went to the American River Junior
College and later transferred to Sacramento State. The young
student worked full time selling clothes, studied political theory, became student body president, and graduated in 1962.
The Monday following graduation, Connerly, a registered
Democrat, began work at the California Redevelopment
Agency. Three years later he went to work at the Department
of Housing and Community Development. Connerly never
considered the private sector. "Back in the sixties if you were
black and you graduated from college, you felt the option
available was the government," Connerly said.[79] As it turned
out, he was in exactly the right place in Sacramento: the
young orphan from Del Paso was about to meet the man who
would become his friend and mentor—though he was almost
Connerly's polar image in terms of background.

Whereas Connerly felt obliged to become a civil servant,
Pete Wilson, who was six years older than Connerly and

considerably more privileged, had options. Born in Lake
Forest, Illinois, on August 23, 1933, Wilson was in grade
school when his family moved to St. Louis, where his father
worked as an advertising executive and his mother, a former
model, stayed home. Wilson attended the all-boys St. Louis
Country Day School, and then went to Yale on an ROTC
scholarship. After doing his time in the Marine Corps as a
commissioned infantry officer, Wilson headed west and entered the University of California's Boalt Hall School of Law.
It was an era when competition to get into Boalt was mini-
mal for men from good schools. Wilson was an indifferent
student, but it hardly mattered to his career that it took him
four times to pass the state bar exam. The young man was
more interested in politics than the law. He worked on
Richard Nixon's failed gubernatorial bid in 1962. And then,
on the advice of his law school roommate, John Davies,
Wilson settled in San Diego and practiced law while assessing his own prospects.

In 1965, the same year Connerly went to the Department of
Housing, Wilson decided to campaign for a seat in the assembly,
and he won. Two years later, the thirty-four-year-old assemblyman was appointed head of the new Assembly Committee on
Urban Affairs and Housing. He heard from others in the public
housing sector that the twenty-eight-year-old Connerly was an
up-and-comer, and he wanted him to work for the committee as
its chief consultant. Twice Connerly turned down Wilson's offer.
Although Wilson later denied it, Connerly felt then that part of
Wilson's motive in pursuing him had to do with his skin color.
"The governor says no, but I have my own view, I think it
weighed into the equation," Connerly said in 1995.[80] Connerly
played hard-to-get. Only when Wilson finally raised the salary
did Connerly accept. It wasn't the money—that raise had to be
cleared by another committee—but Wilson's talk of Connerly's
chance to affect policy that did the trick, according to Connerly.[81]

While others had underestimated Connerly, Wilson didn't.
Early in their relationship Wilson asked Connerly what he

wanted to do after working on the committee. Connerly didn't hesitate to respond. He wanted to go back to the Department of Housing and work his way up to division manager. "How can you be so limiting?" Wilson asked. "I was kind of taken aback by that," said Connerly. "I never thought about it. I guess government is sort of a safe haven for blacks. We guess we are going to get an equal shot at government jobs and I didn't have that same level of faith in the private sector."[82] Wilson told him he should consider going into business for himself. Connerly thought, What is he smoking?[83] The conversation was a turning point in Connerly's life. Connerly liked Wilson enough to declare himself a Republican in 1969,[84] and the Yalie and the Sac State graduate became bound by a friendship made more powerful by the promise each held. The friendship had an emotional overlay, as well. Wilson never had children of his own and Connerly had been fatherless from an early age. Although his uncle John Lewis had been a powerful role model, Lewis lacked the sophistication to counsel Connerly in his professional aspirations. Wilson fulfilled these needs. "All these things played a role in our friendship," Connerly later acknowledged.[85]

When Wilson left Sacramento to run for mayor of San Diego, he asked his friend to follow him. Connerly declined and returned to the Housing Department. His time in the legislature, however, had been well spent. He had made valuable contacts. Furthermore, a Wilson-authored 1967 bill that amended the laws that govern local planning gave Connerly an idea for a new business.[86] The law required local government entities—counties and cities—to include an affordable housing blueprint in their long-range plans.[87] Connerly left government and started Connerly and Associates, which consulted for local governments that needed to fulfill the change in the planning laws. The business thrived, and as Wilson moved from the mayor's office to the U.S. Senate and then to the governor's mansion, Connerly returned Wilson's early faith with generous campaign contributions.

It wasn't, however, only the $108,000 in campaign contri-butions from Connerly and Associates that brought Connerly's name to the fore when the governor was ready to make appointments to the Board of Regents.[88] Connerly's skin color also played a role, according to Connerly and others. A year earlier, the governor had appointed John Davies, his law school roommate and longtime friend, to the Board of Regents. The twenty-six regents—eighteen of whom are ap-pointed by the governor—oversee one of the world's premier public university systems. Although the regent's post pays nothing, it is considered one of the plums in the governor's bag of political patronage.

Liberal assemblymen didn't much like the Davies appoint-ment when it was made, and as the time approached to con-firm the wealthy San Diego lawyer, they came to like it even less. In the year Davies had been sitting on the board, the re-gents had made some decisions that left critics wondering whether the board's members were too far removed from the lives of students and faculty. Of most concern was a decision supported by a majority of the board, including Davies, to award former U.C. president David Gardner a generous sever-ance package at the same time that budget constraints had pushed the regents to raise student fees. State legislators, Common Cause, the Latino Issues Forum, and the National Organization for Women promised a revolt over the Davies confirmation. The appointment of another white male mil-lionaire, they argued, would not broaden the board's outlook.

Wilson wanted Davies, but he also understood the need to appease his critics. He had little choice. A 1974 revision of the state constitution required the Board of Regents to reflect California's "economic, cultural, and social diversity . . . in-cluding minorities and women."[89] As of 1993, the board's eigh-teen appointees included twelve white men, one Asian American, two Latinos, four women, and one black.[90] With pressure building on the Senate Rules Committee, which con-firms appointments, Wilson cut a deal. If the committee approved Davies, Wilson would fill further vacancies with women and minorities.[91] One of the governor's first diversity appointees was Connerly. In a sense, the Connerly appointment reflected Supreme Court Justice Powell's recommendations on affirmative action in the *Bakke* case. Connerly was entirely qualified—he had proven himself a capable businessman—but race was among the many factors that Wilson considered. "The external pressure to make the board more diverse caused the governor to focus on me," Connerly acknowledged, while adding that it is an appointment that he could have asked for and received at any time. "The external pressure caused Wilson to say I am going to have to lean on Ward to take this, and he did kind of lean on me," Connerly recalled.[92] If the critics of the Davies appointment weren't completely happy, they could hardly object. Even though Connerly was another Wilson crony, he was one who had been raised in a different world. With one member absent, the Senate Rules Committee approved Connerly's appointment four to zero in February 1994, and the full Senate followed with a thirty-seven to zero vote of approval. Little did they know that Connerly would prove to be Wilson's Trojan horse.

Connerly's early actions on the board quickly indicated that he would become an outspoken ally of U.C.'s 162,000 students and faculty.[93] He voted against fee hikes, closely questioned all financial decisions, and in January 1994, he wrote an open letter sharply criticizing his fellow regents for being too anxious to please U.C. administrators and approve every measure presented by U.C. President Peltason. "If we subscribe to this view, there is no reason for us to meet," he wrote. The board, Connerly argued, failed to give faculty and students enough time and consideration. Connerly's opinions at meetings were just as strong. He dared to question matters that had been considered off-limits: one of them was affirmative action. It was Connerly's interest in this issue and his willingness to work extra hours on university business that led Chairman Clair Burgener to suggest in August 1994 that the new regent meet with Jerry Cook, a statistician and lecturer at the private University of San Diego, and his wife, Ellen, an accounting professor. "It was an admissions problem," Burgener said as he recalled his role in the meeting, adding that he believed Connerly would be helpful in explaining to Cook why his son had been rejected. "I thought that it would be constructive. I knew that Connerly had an interest. He's a minority. I never had any idea of how far he intended to go."[94]

Burgener and those who testified on Connerly's behalf during the hearings on his appointment as a regent might well have known if they had bothered to read the *Sacramento Bee* closely. Soon after Wilson was elected governor in 1990, the *Sacramento Bee* focused on some of the conservative African American businessmen who had supported Wilson. By this time, Connerly had been named to a few committees, represented several construction associations, and had developed an unusual position toward minority contracting. Although his own business had registered as a minority firm to take advantage of minority contracts—a step Connerly said he was forced into taking to protect business he already had—he disliked the preferences. "I'm opposed to it [affirmative action]," Connerly told the *Bee* in 1991. "For me it's the ultimate insult. I don't need any brownie points from anybody. I don't want any from anybody. And to my knowledge we have never taken advantage of it."[95]

In the same year that Connerly was publicly speaking against affirmative action in contracting, Cook's son James, a sixteen-year-old graduate of U.C. San Diego, applied to five University of California medical schools. When young Cook was rejected by all five schools, his father decided to find out why. The average age of those admitted was twenty-five and a half,[96] and while his son's age was an obvious stumbling block, his father saw it differently. As he put it: "I walked across the street where they keep the records of people who apply to medical school. I bring the records home and it takes me five minutes to conclude that it wasn't about my son."[97] Cook found that Latinos with lower grade point averages and test scores were three and a half times more likely than whites and Asians to gain acceptance at Davis. Blacks with similarly low numbers were over two and a half times more likely to be admitted. The University of California's medical school admissions, Cook concluded, violated the Supreme Court's 1978 *Bakke* decision on affirmative action. That decision said the university could consider race as a factor in deciding whether to admit a student—as long as it was not the only or the primary factor. Even though the university's lawyers saw it differently, Cook decided that in the medical schools' admissions policies, race had become the ultimate deciding factor and he wasted no time in going to the authorities. By July 1994 the University of California's lawyers issued their report: in it they argued that the medical schools had complied with *Bakke*— that all of the applicants had been considered by one committee and that no slots had been set aside for underrepresented minorities. Cook was unsatisfied. "It was a pure slap in the face," he said. "I called this guy Burgener and said this is all garbage, and he said, 'What did you expect them to say?' He said, 'You should meet Regent Connerly.'"[98]

Cook and his wife flew up to Sacramento and were ushered into the white clapboard Victorian on Twenty-first Street where Connerly and his wife, Ilene, have their consulting business. "We sit down in this room and this black man walks in and I look up and think, 'Oh God,'" Cook said later.[99] He had been unaware that Connerly was black. "He sits down and I pull out the data. I was afraid that he was going to pick me up and beat the crap out of me," recalled Cook. Instead, Connerly proved to be as disturbed by the data as Cook himself.

Connerly didn't like what he heard, and he spoke privately that summer with Wilson, U.C. President Jack Peltason, and other regents. Although Wilson had been a longtime supporter of affirmative action, his discussions with Connerly began to have an impact. In the summer of 1994, though, the governor was too busy with his reelection campaign to pay much attention to affirmative action.

Connerly, however, had plenty of time, and he was way ahead of the governor in thinking about the university's use of race as a criterion in its admissions decisions. He'd already made up his mind when Wood and Custred attended the State Assembly's Judiciary Committee meeting on August 10, 1994, to hear testimony on Assemblyman Bernie Richter's proposed bill to ban affirmative action. "There was a time when affirmative action had a value," Connerly told the standing-room-only audience that included Custred and Wood. "There was discrimination in all sectors of California and we needed some sort of shock treatment. The time has come to take off the training wheels."

Richter's bill failed to make it out of the committee, and despite support from conservative commentators like William Rusher and Patrick Buchanan, Custred and Wood could not attract the money they needed to run their initiative campaign. Instead, they began to talk to Connerly, and they watched as Proposition 187 began to gather momentum. Ultimately, it became the defining issue of the 1994 elections and cut the electoral path for CCRI.

CCRI's Political Precursor

The social and political environment that pushed Proposition 187 to the fore had been planted even before Custred and Wood met. When Pete Wilson was elected governor of California in 1990 and gave his first state-of-the-state address, the Democrats who had opposed him were elated. He sounded like one of them—calling for better health care and more social services for the poor. But Wilson's moderate rhetoric was to change quickly. By 1993 only 15 percent of the voters wanted to give the ex-Marine a second chance as governor.[100] It was no wonder—his first term had been a series of disasters, although most weren't of his making. Wilson took office in 1990 just as California's recession-proof economy lost its lift. The housing market fell, Washington closed military bases, and defense contractors laid off employees. In some Southern California towns, For Sale signs were as ubiquitous as mailboxes. Wilson's finance department warned him in 1991 that events were moving beyond his control. Professionals who paid taxes were selling their high-priced homes and moving out, and poorer residents who used tax-based services were moving in. "California's major tax receiver groups—students, welfare recipients, prisoners and Medi-Cal eligible—are growing more quickly than its taxpayer group," his finance department stated flatly in its 1991 report. "Much of this growth is based on increases in the number of school age children, resulting from immigration and a recent surge in the birth rate."[101] The California dream was turning sour.

Hard times bring out the best—and the worst—in people. Californians are no different. When the economy went into a tailspin in 1900, whites chased Chinese laborers off the farms. In the 1920s the Orange County Farm Bureau passed a law excluding the Japanese from owning property and warning, "A nonwhite majority is envisioned if today's immigration continues." And during the Great Depression, the state rounded up Mexicans, many of them legal residents, and dumped them over the border. It was to this tradition that Wilson turned for political salvation. In a 1991 interview with *Time* magazine, Wilson seemed to throw up his hands. Since 1985, Wilson told *Time,* the state's population increased by 18 percent, school enrollments by 23 percent, welfare by 31.5 percent, and Medicaid by 49 percent. "We will have to minimize the magnetic effect of the generosity of this state," he said. "There is a limit to what we can absorb."[102]

When his critics jumped on these remarks, Wilson retreated. Nonetheless, through his first term, he continued to insist that Washington reimburse the state for the cost of serving illegal immigrants. Wilson was not alone in linking the state's budget problems to increases in illegal immigration. U.S. Senator Dianne Feinstein, former San Francisco mayor and a Democrat who had narrowly lost the 1990 governor's race to Wilson, began to pressure Washington in early 1993 to increase the number of agents patrolling the border. With Democrats like Feinstein and California's other U.S. Senator, Barbara Boxer, taking up the issue, Wilson renewed his attack. In August 1993 he declared that California was "under siege" from illegal immigration and made a series of proposals. The two most dramatic: deny citizenship to children born on U.S. soil to illegal immigrants, and cut off health and education benefits to anyone in the state illegally.

If liberals, Catholic leaders, and even some Republicans, such as former Housing and Urban Development Secretary Jack Kemp and former Education Secretary William Bennett, criticized Wilson for scapegoating, the governor's attack against illegal immigrants resonated with many ordinary voters. In the years since World War II, the strong pull of California's flush economy and a 1986 amnesty program had significantly changed the color of Los Angeles, Santa Ana, Oakland, and other major California cities. More than one out of four Californians was Latino.[103] The changes scared longtime residents. Instead of blaming bad, overcrowded public schools on funding cuts, voters blamed the decline in schools and city services on the presence of too many immigrants with too many language problems. "We are becoming a third world state," Robert Lacy, a computer executive, told a reporter in 1994.[104]

Still, the numbers were on Lacy's side: the electorate was white. Whites represented only 52.8 percent of the population but accounted for 88 percent of all registered voters; in contrast, the nonwhite registered voters were 11 percent Latino, 6 percent black, and 5 percent Asian.[105] Latinos were the fastest-growing segment of the population, but the voting power of their 31 percent population share would take years to emerge—the majority were too young to vote and many of those who were old enough failed to file for citizenship. Instead of representing the growing power of ethnic minorities, the state's demographics exaggerated the power of white voters.[106] If whites had a gripe with the new immigrants, they could register their complaints in the voting booth. And in 1994 that is exactly what they did.

Wilson's talk of rescuing California from a deluge of illegal immigrants never led to action. His own proposals to end health care and education for illegal immigrants never made headway in the legislature. But the concerns about illegal immigration that came from Wilson and the state's two Democratic senators, Feinstein and Boxer, had stirred up white Californians. Once riled, they didn't need an elected official to change California's laws. Under the state initiative process citizens can propose new laws or changes to the state constitution by collecting enough signatures to put an initiative on the ballot. Proposition 187, an initiative to ban state services to undocumented workers, was drafted by Ron Prince, an accountant living in Orange County; Harold Ezell, an outspoken former regional director of the INS; and Alan C. Nelson, director of the INS during the Reagan Administration. The initiative caught on like an October brushfire. At last, people had someone to blame for lost jobs, lousy schools, and limited prospects. And Wilson, already on record as opposed to educating the children of illegal immigrants, became Proposition 187's point man. So dedicated to the issue did he become that he spent $2 million in television commercials that featured Proposition 187. One of his campaign commercials showed night vision video clips of immigrants sneaking across the border. "They just keep coming," the tag line read. Wilson promised to turn them away from schools and hospitals. He would reserve those services—which cost $2.5 billion in tax dollars—for California's legal residents.

By September 1994 a governor whose future had nearly fallen through the political cracks over the economy now found that few residents talked about the downturn anymore. Instead, they talked about illegal immigration. Wilson made the front pages of the *New York Times* and *Washington Post* and the cover of *Time*. No matter that most legal analysts argued that the courts would declare the initiative invalid, most voters felt that

Proposition 187 would send a message to Washington. Although the measure provided no mechanism to force Washington to pay up, Wilson too said it would pressure Washington to reimburse the state for the cost of providing health and education services to illegal immigrants.[107] On the morning of November 9, the governor's political instincts proved on target. He won almost as resoundingly as Proposition 187—Wilson won with 55.2 percent of the vote and Proposition 187 won with 58.9 percent of the vote.[108] The *Los Angeles Times* described Wilson's landslide victory as "one of the most dramatic comebacks in California political history." And the paper noted its consequences. The victory thrust Wilson "firmly into the ranks of possible Republican contenders for the White House in 1996."[109]

2

Hitting a Nerve

The Angry White Males of 1994

The web of American communications, influence and politics is so sensitive that when touched in the right way by men who know how, it clangs with instant response.

THEODORE H. WHITE
The Making of the President, 1960

He was only running for governor in 1994, but Pete Wilson's stance on immigration transformed him into a national figure with presidential prospects. More important, Wilson had demonstrated with Proposition 187 that California was fertile political ground for racial wedge issues—issues that could split white males away from the Democrats and send them to the Republican Party. White men voted 63 to 37 percent in favor of Proposition 187—in nearly the same proportions in which they voted for Wilson.[1]

With a presidential campaign less than two years away, political analysts looked at the Proposition 187 vote and saw the beginning of a new backlash building. "Whites are confronting futures that look increasingly limited even as women, minorities and others get the lion's share of the establishment's attention as worthy subjects of concern," wrote Peter Schrag, a *Sacramento Bee* columnist and editorial page editor, one week after the 1994 elections. "Never has the disaffection been so strong and never before has it had as big a megaphone as it has developed in the (largely male) talk shows."[2] No matter that income for black men had declined at nearly twice the rate of income for white men since 1978.[3] "The truth is people are really facing declines in their wages," said Stanford economist Martin Carnoy. "When the guy can't get a job and he sees a minority person get it, he thinks: 'Affirmative action.'"

Custred and Wood mark December 27, 1994, as the turning point in CCRI's life—the day it went from being "their" initiative to becoming the lure for all those angry white males who had voted in November. Up until then the post-election analysis of the Republican sweep mentioned affirmative action as a likely target, but few reporters called Custred and Wood's office on Martin Luther King Jr. Way in Berkeley. On December 27, however, Washington officeholders and journalists opened the *Washington Post* to read: "California voters gave the nation a jolt from the right last month when they passed Proposition 187, which would deny nonemergency medical care and education to illegal immigrants. Now the state could be on the verge of doing it again. Conservatives hope to place the anti–affirmative action measure on the 1996 presidential primary ballot."[4] Wood told the reporter, "The tide has turned; there is an anti–affirmative action issue coming down the pike in California that is going to make 187 look like kindergarten."[5]

Suddenly, the media bombarded Custred and Wood. "It was like the phone was levitating," said Wood.[6] Soon CCRI became a buzzword for the end of affirmative action. Scott Reed, who worked for the Republican National Committee and would later become Senator Bob Dole's campaign manager, sent a note to Scott Taylor, the Republican National Committee's field person in California: "This looks like something to watch."[7]

Custred and Wood could not handle all the press calls, much less the questions about strategy and timing. They desperately needed a political campaign team, and waiting in the wings was a group of conservative Republican men—libertarians all—whom they had met during the previous year. On a rainy December day at the Radisson Summit Hotel in West Los Angeles, the new team gathered to split up the responsibilities.

Larry Arnn, the forty-two-year-old president of the Claremont Institute, became chairman. Arnn, a personable man more interested in talking about British history and the American Revolution than about current events, founded the conservative think tank with three other graduate students in 1979. In the mid-1980s it opened an office in Sacramento and began funneling policy papers to conservative legislators, many of them concerning Arnn's thinking about returning the country to core values. One of the institute's distinguished fellows was William Rusher, the publisher and founder of the *National Review* and one of CCRI's early supporters. Arnn first ran into Custred and Wood at a 1994 *National Review* conference in San Diego. Arnn had long been a foe of affirmative action. Although he believed it went against the basic American principle of equality under the law, he explained, "It had never occurred to me to make it a public issue, but the minute I heard the idea, it resonated with me."[8]

Joe Gelman, Mayor Richard Riordan's appointee to the Los Angeles Board of Civil Service Commissioners and a Republican Party activist, signed on to run the Los Angeles office. Gelman, an Indianapolis native who had grown up in Israel, became friendly with Arnn because of a mutual interest in Winston Churchill. The two, along with a group of other Churchill buffs, had been meeting at Arnn's home to smoke cigars and share their favorite stories of the British leader.[9] Gelman had the zeal of a true believer and the energy of a twelve-year-old.

Arnold Steinberg, a Los Angeles–based pollster for Republicans, had contacted Custred and Wood after reading Rusher's 1993 *National Review* article about CCRI's promise. "Most of the time it's just business," Steinberg, a slim man with sandy red hair, later recalled.[10] "But I feel in synch with this issue. I really believe government classifications by race are wrong. It pits tribe against tribe." Moreover, his own experience with affirmative action had not been a positive one. In his 1976 work, *The Political Campaign Handbook*, he wrote: "Some broadcast reporters may attend a news conference without any prior research or preparation, their questions are often sophomoric, and they may even be unable to define the story's lead. These problems have been aggravated by the FCC's 'affirmative action' emphasis to encourage or *force* television and radio stations to hire reporters on the basis of racial, ethnic, or sexual quotas."[11]

Steinberg, who lived and worked out of a mansion he built on a hilltop in Calabasas, just north of Malibu, had developed a reputation as a wunderkind in Republican political circles. In his work for CCRI, he would fret over the most minute detail, writing memos and considering every aspect of the campaign's strategy. "He's considered a kind of hermit genius," said Shawn Steel, the treasurer of the California Republican Party. He was also connected. Steinberg played chess with Republican Mayor Riordan and was good friends with Democratic presidential advisor Bill Wardlaw. From his hilltop mansion, he kept in touch with a number of influential congressmen in Washington and, in his efforts on behalf of CCRI, Steinberg used all of these connections.

When the new CCRI team met in December, they decided Wood and Custred would participate in strategy sessions and speak on behalf of CCRI in public forums. Arnn, Steinberg, and Gelman would run the day-to-day operations. In early January, Arnn drafted a "Confidential Overview" of CCRI that provides insight into their libertarian—get the government out of everything—thinking. The section titled "Introduction" stated, in a tone that sometimes sounded like a manifesto written by teenage zealots, "CCRI has begun in the past few months, to generate intense publicity without the use of professional help—indeed, without the making of any coordinated effort. It has done this because it appeals to the basic belief of the public inequality and fairness, and because it promises to strike a heavy blow at the heart of the bureaucratic regulatory state. It destroys the legitimacy of that state. It divides the party that has fostered and maintained that state. Its effects upon the state and local elections of 1996 are therefore likely to be profound, possibly decisive."[12]

The next section, "Opportunity and Danger," stated, "The opportunity is dual: first to make history by making affirmative action quota contracting illegal for California state and local governments (thereby profoundly affecting the private sector); second, consequently, to divide the Democratic Party."[13] Under sections titled "Strategy" and "Timing" the document referred to the campaign's need to be inclusive. "The campaign must be open to all—Democrats and Republicans, whites and non-whites, men and women—who support the measure. The presumed conservative Republican constituency greatly understates the base for this issue, especially if an inclusive approach is aggressively pursued."

The memo explained why reaching out to Democrats was not at odds with the damage the initiative could do to Democrats. "A March campaign would suggest that the measure's supporters, in statesmanlike fashion, are trying to avoid a 'wedge' issue for November," the overview stated referring to the campaign's intentions to attempt to put the measure on the March 1996 primary ballot. Even if this were to occur, however, Republicans still won. "In fact," the overview continued, "this issue is inherently divisive for Democrats and its effects would be cataclysmic nationally throughout 1996. Clearly, a March election would have spin-offs in other states for the balance of 1996. . . . Given the importance of this issue to our country, it would be derelict not to consider March/1996 as a way of involving Democrats in our effort."[14]

Over the next ten months the campaign team made a lot of noise and occasionally scored a touchdown, but it spent much of its time running down the clock. Arnn, for example, liked his role as chairman because it offered him continued

political visibility—his first attempt at politics, a 1994 run for
the Republican spot in the Forty-third Congressional District's
race, had failed. But he wasn't cut out for the fund-raising his
new position demanded. "I had never done fund-raising for a
cause like this," he said. "It often happens that there is some
interest group that has a lot at stake, but there isn't a natural
interest group for this one. In the end, people give because
they believe in it, and they have to feel that it is urgent."[15]

With affirmative action quickly becoming part of the national debate, few donors felt it was urgent to support a state
measure that might duplicate federal efforts or be overtaken
by the decisions of an increasingly conservative Supreme
Court. Corporate sponsors, another likely source of initiative
money, shied away from CCRI because a stand either way was
likely to set them in opposition to at least some of their employees and customers. The absence of ready funding sources
meant Arnn had to be all the more aggressive in pursuing the
big donors he did know. But his reticence was apparent in his
attitude toward Henry Salvatori, an Italian immigrant and oil
magnate who had given generously to Claremont. "He's
ninety-four, and I for one wasn't going to try and impose
something new on him," he said. "I'm not a political fund-
raiser to the extent that it is done by people who put pressure
on people."[16]

The other team members lacked the connections even to
try raising money. Gelman, even with all his energy, was too
low in the state Republican Party hierarchy to get anyone's
attention. He did, however, manage to keep the initiative in
the news. Every affirmative action issue with an iota of controversy that came before the county civil service board
Gelman blew up into a news story. Between January and
June 1995, CCRI and affirmative action were mentioned
dozens of times in the Los Angeles media. "We got little fires
burning all over the city," Gelman recalled gleefully. "It was
fairly well calculated to keep things going. Ultimately we created this aura of invincibility, that we had a lot of money and

a lot of supporters. Nothing could have been further from the truth."[17]

No one regretted the lack of funds more than Steinberg, who was anxious to make his first statewide initiative campaign a success. Steinberg drew up plan after plan to begin direct-mail and media campaigns, but instead of following through on any plan, he found the team moving from crisis to crisis. As the months wore on, he became increasingly frustrated and anxious about failing. "We never had any seed money in place," Steinberg said later.[18] "I wanted mailings to go out early, to do test mailings, but ready money was never there. Dollars spent properly early on can make a real difference later, but we didn't have it."

The Republican National Committee kept abreast of the initiative's progress but provided no immediate financial support. The committee's field man, Scott Taylor, dropped by CCRI's small office in Berkeley in early 1995 to look at a poll Steinberg did. Taylor was impressed. "CCRI was popular with every subsection in their study," said Taylor, who at thirty-four had already logged more than a decade in politics. "I hadn't seen anything like the intensity of support since Proposition 13," he said, referring to the 1978 California antitax initiative. "I wasn't around for that, but from what I hear, this is as strong and there was no gender gap as far as we could see."[19]

A couple of weeks later, Taylor visited Washington. He was standing around the Republican National Committee's headquarters when one of House Speaker Newt Gingrich's aides approached him and asked if he would brief the Speaker on California. Taylor was ecstatic. He ended up meeting with Gingrich in a limousine—the Speaker was on his way from the Republican National Committee near Union Station to a fund-raiser at the Hay-Adams Hotel, near the White House. Taylor found him already "well-versed on the issue."[20] According to Taylor, Gingrich promised to do anything he could to help. The Speaker was slow, however, to publicly support CCRI.

Back in California, money was trickling in. Gelman said the team's lack of credibility with big California donors was apparent early on. In January 1995 at Pasadena's Ritz Carlton Hotel, the team pitched their case to Howard Ahmanson, the son of the founder of Home Savings of America; Ed Atsinger, the owner of more than a dozen Christian radio stations; and Ron Unz, the Silicon Valley businessman who won 34 percent of the vote in the 1994 Republican primary against Pete Wilson. Some of the donors had formed the Allied Business PAC, which spent $2.3 million—more than any other PAC—to support conservative candidates in California's 1994 legislative races. Ahmanson, a converted fundamentalist Christian, had been the PAC's largest contributor and a supporter of the Claremont Institute.

CCRI had hoped to raise $300,000 from the meeting, with a promise for $300,000 more,[21] but Gelman sensed that the group wasn't going to bite. "They said they didn't have confidence in the organization," Gelman said.[22] Although the PAC members were familiar with Arnn—some had contributed to his 1994 campaign—they declined to support CCRI as a PAC. But because Ahmanson liked the issue, he wrote a check for $50,000—sufficient for CCRI to begin the painstaking process of building a donor list.

Unz chipped in, too. When he ran against Governor Wilson in 1994, one of his most effective mailings had discussed the problems of affirmative action. Although Unz opposed Proposition 187, he felt that attempts to classify Californians by race were impossible in a state where interracial and interethnic marriages were increasingly common. "The entire anti-immigrant backlash in America, which extends far beyond illegal immigration, draws heavily from whites' fears of having their rights trampled by ever-increasing numbers of ethnic minorities," Unz wrote. "Either California's multiethnic society re-establishes the principle of equality of opportunity for all—whites included—or grim days lie ahead."[23]

Unz dropped by CCRI's Los Angeles office in mid-February 1995 and found it lacking in the most basic equipment. He took Gelman to Office Depot, and they loaded up their carts with nearly $4,000 in supplies. The Silicon Valley businessman left another $3,000 behind and said he wanted to stay in touch. But after giving another $16,000 in April, he lost interest. Ultimately, Steinberg said, Unz wanted more control than the CCRI team was willing to give. A few other big donors came through that spring—$10,000 from Theodore J. Forstman, an influential Republican fund-raiser from New York; $25,000 from Patricia Hume, the wife of conservative San Francisco businessman Jerry Hume; and $5,000 from the Lincoln Club, one of the largest PACs. These contributions helped keep CCRI afloat, but much of the money was going to salaries and legal and consulting fees, and CCRI still seemed like a long shot.

March Madness

Although the CCRI team itself may not have been ready for prime time in early 1995, affirmative action as an issue was. The state and national poll numbers clearly showed that voters wanted to ban "preferential treatment." Although some of the same polls showed voters actually favored "affirmative action," the public's disdain for "preferences" was overwhelming, and neither the Democratic Party leaders nor mainstream Republicans who had supported affirmative action bothered to make the nuanced distinction or to understand that if the battle could be waged on affirmative action, it might be won.[24]

They went with the rhetoric, and it indicated that the thirty-year-old legacy of the civil rights era could divide white, working-class voters from the Democratic Party as neatly as abortion, gun control, and immigration had in earlier elections. The strategists predicted that a Republican presidential candidate opposed to affirmative action would divide President Bill Clinton from the white, working-class voters he needed to return to the White House. This scenario was particularly threatening in

California, where angry white voters had recently been responsible for Wilson's reelection and Proposition 187's approval.

One politician who began to change his mind about affirmative action was the governor of California. As a state legislator, mayor of San Diego, and U.S. senator, Wilson had consistently supported affirmative action. As recently as
September 1994, he had signed legislation to make it easier
for minority-owned companies to qualify for state assistance.
In addition to his longtime support of affirmative action, however, he had a record of occasionally exploiting it for political
advantage. Early in the 1990 governor's race, the popular
Dianne Feinstein pledged to appoint women and minorities in
proportion to "their parity of the population." In a public exchange of faxes, Wilson urged Feinstein to recant her support
of "quotas." Feinstein shot back that her program was not a
fixed quota, but a goal that would be reached over time.
Despite this explanation and Feinstein's record against fixed
quotas, Wilson ran a commercial that played on voters' worst
fears about affirmative action. "Dianne Feinstein promised as
governor to fill state jobs on the basis of strict numerical quotas," a narrator charged. "Not experience. Not qualifications.
But quotas. It's unfair, it's extreme, and it's wrong." Two weeks
later, Wilson's lead jumped from two to eleven percentage
points.[25]

Voters hated quotas, but would a stand against affirmative
action provoke the same bile? By early January, Wilson was
ready to find out. He gave a copy of his state-of-the-state address to George Gorton, the governor's key political strategist.
The draft contained a passage that questioned the fairness of
considering race as a criterion in admissions or employment.
Gorton objected. "I didn't think he'd had enough time to
think it through and I argued him out of it. I was opposed to
doing anything on affirmative action," Gorton recalled.[26] In
his view, affirmative action still had too many supporters.
Moreover, to him, the words continued to prompt a positive
response. As of January, he was unconvinced that it would be

wise for the governor to strike out directly against such an established notion. The governor left it out of his January 8 address and, instead of testing the waters himself, he carefully watched the public's reaction to Ward Connerly's moves on the University of California's Board of Regents.

During the summer of 1994, Wilson and Connerly discussed the Cook case, and, according to Connerly, Wilson promised to support the regent's decision to question U.C. administrators on their affirmative action programs.[27] At the mid-January Board of Regents meeting, Connerly went even further and asked his fellow regents to consider the possibility that the affirmative action policies pursued by U.C. administrators might be unfair. "I tell you with every fiber of my being that what we're doing is inequitable to certain people," Connerly told the regents. "I want something in place that's fair."[28] The impact of a successful black man publicly questioning affirmative action in the name of fairness was powerful. This was a regent who talked about the humiliation of drinking from a fountain labeled "Colored Only." The predominantly white board listened with rapt attention. Just as he had mesmerized the audience at the Richter hearings that summer, Connerly now captivated the regents. The policy of affirmative action was decades old, and few boards like to upset the status quo, but if a black regent had lost faith in affirmative action, how could others keep the faith? "You can't underestimate Ward's impact," said Ralph Carmona, a regent in favor of affirmative action. "He's a black man, he's articulate, and people became caught up in the polls and in what he was saying."[29]

Governor Wilson was no exception. He was looking at the polls and his aide, Gorton, was also meeting with the CCRI team. Gelman recalled that Gorton was enthusiastic about the initiative, but, according to an internal memo, Gorton was also concerned that the anti-Wilson activity would focus around the governor's position on CCRI.[30] By the time the state Republican Party held its semiannual convention at the end of February, Wilson had been reassured, and he was ready to abandon his previous support for affirmative action. As the television cameras rolled, he endorsed CCRI and asked all Californians "to once again send East from California a message about fairness. . . . I ask you to join me in changing the law to restore fairness, to make real again that American dream."[31] Getting the party to endorse a resolution in support of CCRI was no problem at all—the governor was on board and Gelman was chair of the resolution's committee.

Events in California, a must-win state for Clinton in 1996, and developments in Washington, where the Republicans now controlled Congress, began to shape the political beliefs of a number of other politically prominent men. President Clinton, for one, refrained from unequivocally supporting affirmative action and instead in February called for a review of all federal affirmative action programs. "In March of 1995 we thought that this was going to be the issue that was going to race through America," George Stephanopoulos recalled in October 1996 at a Beverly Hills fund-raiser. And in the spring of 1995 the Administration was unclear how to stop the issue from becoming critical to the president's reelection. Even if CCRI didn't sweep the country, holding its own in California could be enough to do Clinton in. "At the very beginning was I concerned about it?" asked Bill Wardlaw, who was responsible for Clinton's California campaign in 1992 and continued to be an advisor. "You bet." Wardlaw was keeping abreast of the initiative's progress through his friend Steinberg.

Meanwhile, Clinton was talking to different advisors, including legislators like the Democratic senator Joseph Lieberman from Connecticut. Lieberman chaired the Democratic Leadership Conference, which middle-of-the-road national Democrats like Clinton founded in 1985 to redefine the party's liberal agenda. The DLC had addressed the issue of affirmative action in its 1990 New Orleans Declaration, and it was less than enthusiastic about supporting it. Clinton, who was then chairman of the DLC and governor of Arkansas, signed that document, which outlined the DLC's agenda for the nineties: "We endorse

[Andrew] Jackson's credo of equal opportunity for all and special privileges for none. . . . We believe the promise of America is equal opportunity, not equal outcomes."[32] By 1995 Lieberman and others in the DLC wanted changes in affirmative action.

Republican Majority Leader Bob Dole, Clinton's likely Republican challenger in 1996, was also having his ear bent on affirmative action. Dole and other Republican congressional leaders were meeting in early 1995 with a group of conservatives interested in writing legislation to end affirmative action. Among them was Clint Bolick, the vice president of the Institute for Justice, a libertarian public interest law firm, and the author of the 1993 *Wall Street Journal* op-ed that dubbed Lani Guinier the "quota queen." Also present was Linda Chavez, a member of the Equal Employment Opportunity Commission under Bush and the president of her own lobbying group, the Center for Equal Opportunity. "Dole listened but we could never tell where he stood," recalled Chavez.[33]

That spring, even Clinton appeared ready to cast off old beliefs. In early March, President Clinton, not yet finished with his review of affirmative action, held a forty-five-minute press conference and suggested that it might make sense to base affirmative action on economic need rather than race.[34] This was a historic moment. For the first time in three decades, a Democratic president was suggesting that taking race and gender into account in hiring and employment was outdated. An outcry from women, blacks, and the Reverend Jesse Jackson put an end to Clinton's suggestion, but Dole could see just how vulnerable a political spot the president was in: influential moderates were advising Clinton to make substantial changes in affirmative action, while the liberal base of the Democrats threatened mutiny if he did.

If Clinton would not placate the Reagan Democrats, Dole would. Ten years earlier, Dole had fought to retain goals and timetables in federal affirmative action programs. But by mid-March of 1995, in a sharply worded speech on the Senate floor, he announced, "Race-preferential policies, no matter how well-intentioned, demean individual accomplishment. They ignore individual character. And they are absolutely poisonous to race relations in our great country."[35] In the same week that Dole made his announcement, the Glass Ceiling Commission issued its report. A bipartisan group created at Dole's suggestion as part of the Civil Rights Act of 1991, the commission ended its three-year study and issued the following statement: "Before one can even look at the glass ceiling, one must get through the front door and into the building. The fact is large numbers of minorities and women of all races and ethnicities are nowhere near the front door of Corporate America."[36] No matter; affirmative action was on the block.

From the vantage point of California, it looked as if the president and his chief challenger were running away from affirmative action as fast as they could. Wilson, too, was unable to resist the logic that said affirmative action might be his ticket to the White House. On March 23—five months after promising California voters that he would remain in California if reelected governor—Wilson announced he had "not just an opportunity, but a duty" to explore the possibility of running for president. From the outset, it was evident that affirmative action would be central to his campaign strategy. "Some things are right and some plainly are wrong," he said. "It is wrong to reward illegal immigrants for violating our borders. . . . It is wrong to engage in reverse discrimination, giving preferences . . . not on the basis of merit but because of race and gender."[37]

Custred and Wood, still pressed for money to run an expensive initiative campaign, were delighted by Wilson's support and Clinton's obvious unease with the issue. It looked to them like they might now have a bipartisan issue that would win big. In April, Wood met with the Democratic Leadership Conference's officials Al From and Will Marshall. "From seemed quite cynical about the Democrats' position on affirmative action," Wood wrote to his colleagues.[38] "We could probably get an endorsement from him. The whole interview however was monopolized by Will Marshall, who insists on the admissibility of racial and gender preferences in outreach in making up for past discrimination. Marshall is hopeless but From is ideologically already on our side."

When the CCRI team called the California DLC president, Bill Podlich, the reception was also friendly. "We really thought they might go with us," Wood recalled.[39] In fact, even the mainstream state Democratic Party appeared to be wavering. Duane Garrett, the Democratic strategist who ran Senator Dianne Feinstein's campaign,[40] surfaced to support the drive to end affirmative action and called CCRI "a very moderate proposal."[41]

State Democratic Party leaders were curious enough about the initiative to invite the CCRI team to Palm Springs in early February 1995 for the party's executive committee meeting. Wood and Errol Smith, a black business executive from Southern California and a conservative former radio talk show host, represented CCRI in a debate on Saturday afternoon. They felt the response was cool. Wood recalled it as "civil."[42] Nevertheless, he stayed overnight, and the following morning he had breakfast with Bill Press, the chair of the state Democratic Party. "I had the feeling he was checking me out," Wood said.[43]

Custred, Wood, and Arnn began to suspect that even though the state Democratic Party might not endorse the initiative outright, it would support a strategy to avoid a confrontation in November 1996, when the state's fifty-four electoral votes were up for grabs. Accordingly, they sought the party's support for legislation to put the initiative on the March ballot. The appeal for CCRI's team was clear: the legislature also had the power to put initiatives on the ballot. It could pass a bill to amend the state's constitution and residents would vote on that bill in March. This development would save CCRI the expense of raising the $1 million it would take to collect the nearly 700,000 signatures they needed to put CCRI on the ballot.[44]

Wood met in late March 1995 with state Senate President pro Tempore Bill Lockyer, a Democrat from Hayward. "It was Wood's contention that they really wanted it to be a nonpartisan and bipartisan effort," said Lockyer.[45] "They were getting these offers of help from Republicans who saw some partisan advantage of putting it on the November ballot, and Wood preferred the March ballot because it meant they were less dependent on Republican donors." Lockyer and his colleagues were ambivalent. "I told him I would be happy to discuss it with members of my caucus," Lockyer said. "But there was a lack of sufficient consensus to do anything."[46]

Nevertheless, Lockyer enlisted the aid of political independent Quentin L. Kopp to draft a Senate bill to put the initiative on the March ballot. While Wood worked with Kopp to refine the initiative's language even further, Custred and Steinberg visited Assembly Speaker Willie Brown. Generally a political pragmatist, Brown had indicated in January 1995 that he might be willing to support a bill to put the initiative on the March 1996 primary ballot. That would mean that legislators up for reelection would not have to run against the measure. But by the time Custred and Steinberg dropped by that spring, Brown had changed his mind. "He looked me right in the eye and said you shouldn't abandon the core principles of affirmative action," Custred recalled later, shaking his head at Brown's formidable charm.[47] "Then he launched into a tale about his childhood in Texas. When the meeting ended, he took my hand and said, 'I wish you all the ill luck in the world.'" Kopp's measure was killed at the end of March by a five-to-four vote along party lines in the Senate Governmental Organization Committee.

After Kopp's bill failed, CCRI's only option was to raise the money to collect the signatures. Their start was a slow one. Two modest direct-mail efforts in the spring netted only 6,000 small donors. Frustrated, the CCRI team met in Los Angeles in early June with the Republican National Committee's Taylor and with representatives from the state Republican Party and Wilson's campaign. "They kept promising help," said Gelman. "We wanted them to come through with it."[48] Taylor had a different point of view. "They were out of money because they weren't raising any," he said. "They were more concerned with getting their names in the newspaper. They were like a welfare case."[49] Taylor and the others promised to come through with help by the end of the summer, but they warned CCRI to file the initiative with the state attorney general, fund-raise, and start collecting signatures.

CCRI did get one boost in early summer. The U.S. Supreme Court weighed in on affirmative action on June 12 calling "all racial classifications" by federal agencies "inherently suspect and presumptively invalid." The five-to-four decision in the case of *Adarand Constructors v. Peña* involved a federal highway program that awarded a road repair contract to a Latino firm in Colorado that had submitted a slightly higher bid than a white contractor. Justice Sandra Day O'Connor, writing for the court, said that as a last resort a limited program of preferences could be justified to remedy a clear pattern of "prior discrimination" against minorities.[50] "Any person, of whatever race, has the right to demand that any governmental actor subject to the Constitution justify any racial classification subjecting that person to unequal treatment under the strictest judicial scrutiny. The Fifth and 14th Amendments to the Constitution protect persons, not groups. It follows from that principle that all governmental action based on race . . . should be subjected to detailed judicial inquiry to ensure that the personal right to protection of the laws has not been infringed."[51]

Wood, however, cautioned his colleagues against thinking that their work had been done. The *Adarand* decision applied the strict scrutiny test to federal affirmative action programs that the court had previously applied to state and local governments in *Richmond v. J.A. Croson Co.* In a July memo,

Wood warned: "Many (perhaps a majority) of preferential policies at the state and local level have survived *Croson.* We need to walk a thin line here between claiming that *Adarand* was a major ideological setback for the preferences lobby (which it was), while recognizing that much more needs to be done. Only two justices—Scalia and Thomas—went the whole distance of denying the legitimacy of any racial preferences, even to make up for past discrimination (against others). So only these two justices supported the position of CCRI."[52]

Meanwhile, the CCRI team kept pursuing Wilson and other Republican presidential hopefuls to sign fund-raising letters. Two Steinberg memos to Arnn referred to these efforts. "For Gramm," Steinberg wrote, referring to Phil Gramm, "I've received no word back despite repeated efforts. . . . For Dole, you and I must discuss how to proceed . . . with Gramm, Dole and with others. Rusher (William) is weary of pushing more with Dole at this point. We want at least Gramm, Dole and Wilson involved and to make them compete with each other for involvement."[53] Later that month he updated his progress. "I am still trying Dole contacts. . . . Wilson has agreed to do a fundraising package for CCRI, and he is first in the mail due to the inaction of the Gramm and Dole people. However, they still have time to at least get parity on the issue here in California."[54] In July, however, it appeared that Wilson would prove the most useful.

Political Theater

Just as Wilson had shown California that he was prepared to withhold benefits from illegal immigrants, he was now ready to show the country he could stand up to the blacks and Hispanics who benefited from affirmative action. George Gorton, who was now running Wilson's presidential campaign, still felt that affirmative action was a questionable target, but when the governor decided to make it an issue, it became a central part of his campaign. "You can't hide from it,"

Gorton said. "It's a big red flag and you can't put it behind you, so you might as well maximize it."[55] That was exactly what Wilson did.

From spring 1995 on, Wilson and U.C. Regent Connerly played the issue of affirmative action like a political relay team, keeping it on the front page of every California newspaper. First, Wilson would announce an end to a state affirmative action committee or position. Then, Connerly would grasp the baton and press the regents for more details of the university's admissions policies. Even when Wilson was sidelined for two months while he recovered from throat surgery, Connerly kept affirmative action in the news. "It's one of those things you could get a lot of publicity on," said Dick Dresner, Wilson's pollster. "It wasn't in the same category as illegal immigration, but it was strong."[56]

But not strong enough to overcome Wilson's other problems and push the governor ahead of the Republican pack. By June, Wilson was floundering in the polls. Aides blamed the candidate's failure to emerge as a front-runner on a combination of factors. They had overestimated the willingness of California voters to ignore Wilson's broken campaign promise to stay in the governor's office for a full term, and they had underestimated the impact that a poor showing in California polls would have on support elsewhere. Wilson's throat surgery and subsequent inability to talk for two months—to voters or contributors—broke his already modest momentum and created a sense that the presidential candidate was going nowhere.

Searching for effective issues, the Wilson campaign team decided that affirmative action was still Wilson's best bet. Other candidates could claim to oppose affirmative action in principle, but Wilson's position as governor and president of the Board of Regents meant that he could actually do something about ending it. In June, Connerly and Wilson conferred on the phone almost daily. In the first week of July, Connerly informed board chairman Burgener that at the July 20 meeting, he would ask the regents to consider ending the use of race, religion, sex, color, or ethnicity in admissions and hiring. Connerly, who in January 1994 had chastised his colleagues for failing to listen to students and faculty, now paradoxically warned Burgener against being held hostage by students and advised him that it was unnecessary to consult with the faculty before making a decision on this sensitive issue.

The proposal to overturn the University of California's affirmative action policy was serious business. It was also a media sensation. No important newspaper or network could afford to miss the story, and in the weeks before the meeting was held, it became clear that the complicated and emotional policy questions that centered around affirmative action would be subsumed by a well-orchestrated political drama. No matter how sincere Connerly's opposition to affirmative action was, his proposal to end the program at the University of California in the midst of Wilson's run for the Republican presidential nomination turned the debate on affirmative action into a political spectacle.

Civil rights leader Jesse Jackson—threatening to enter the primaries against Clinton if the president failed to support affirmative action—announced he would appear at the meeting to challenge Wilson and Connerly's proposal. Wilson, who had not attended a regent meeting since 1992, when he voted for a 24 percent hike in student fees, promptly announced that he would be there as well. The showdown promised to be big news, and, within days, 250 to 300 reporters had booked rooms in San Francisco. Wilson's campaign staff was ecstatic. "These kinds of things are defining opportunities for Pete Wilson, which will get attention not just in the state, but across the country," said Craig Fuller, chairman of the governor's presidential campaign and George Bush's former chief of staff. "You don't get too many of those in campaigns."[57]

The warm-up act began immediately. Still in Chicago, Jackson threatened to disrupt the meeting and Wilson took up his challenge. "If he seeks to disrupt the meeting . . . then I think he will succeed in being detained," Wilson responded obligingly in an interview on the Sunday morning CBS news program *Face the Nation*. When Jackson arrived in town, Wilson's greeting was on the front page of the local newspaper. "We must not allow our country to be infected with the deadly virus of tribalism," the governor warned. Support for affirmative action, Wilson implied, would put the nation's health at peril. The Rev. Jesse Jackson fumed. What the governor planned to do, Jackson said on arriving in San Francisco, was "illegal." Wilson would have hell to pay. Jackson gathered his troops of black ministers, civil rights lawyers, and students. "Jesse, Jesse, Jesse," chanted more than a thousand protesters jammed into the pews of the Third Baptist Church on the evening before the regent meeting. "We plan to make a moral appeal, a rational appeal," Jackson began, and then made it clear that if these didn't work, he was ready to go further. "We are willing to offer our bodies and offer our lives to save our children." The crowd roared. Emotions were raw. Extra security was called in for the next day's meeting.

For Wilson, a candidate who wanted to identify himself with the interests of white voters, Jackson was an ideal opponent. Republican candidates had long tainted challengers by linking them with Jackson, an icon of black, radical liberalism. In 1988 George Bush's campaign manager, Lee Atwater, boosted Dukakis's negative ratings by sending prospective voters literature that included photographs of George Bush standing next to Ronald Reagan and one of Jackson next to Michael Dukakis. "If Dukakis is elected to the White House, Jesse Jackson is sure to be swept into power on his coattails," the literature read.[58]

Democrats running for national office considered it wise to maintain distance from Jackson. Clinton had managed to do that in 1992 by publicly attacking Sister Souljah, a black rap singer, at a rally of Jackson's National Rainbow Coalition. Clinton could now have made a further separation by supporting the abolishment of affirmative action. Instead, two days before the regents met, Clinton concluded his five-month review and endorsed the civil rights program. The country needed to "mend it," he said, not "end it." When Jackson arrived in San Francisco, he told reporters that Clinton's speech was a step in the right direction. To others, it looked like Clinton's "mend-it-don't-end-it" vernacular pandered to Jackson, making the candidate and the black reverend soul mates. Now it was Wilson, the moderate, pro-choice governor of California, and the black, moderate Connerly against Clinton and the radical Jackson.

From the moment Wilson's sedan rolled through the iron gates to the University of California's Laurel Heights campus in San Francisco on July 20, it was clear that the governor would control the day. Wilson entered the building without a hitch. No one was there to jeer, throw eggs, or block the driveway. The reverend was trapped in a recording studio, and his student troops had yet to materialize in any significant numbers. The extra guards relaxed.

The chancellors of all nine U.C. campuses opposed Connerly's proposals, and in memos, statements, and press releases, they tried to explain why. The regents had been reminded that the university's enrollment still fell far short of reflecting the numbers of Hispanics and blacks who graduated from California high schools. Affirmative action ensured at least a modicum of diversity. "If we are going to continue preparing leaders for California's increasingly diverse society, we must be able to take race, ethnicity, and in some circumstances gender into account as one factor among many in our programs," Jack W. Peltason, president of the university, told the regents.

The university's affirmative action program, fine-tuned over nearly two decades, met the demands of the state's 1960 Master Plan for Higher Education and the 1978 *Bakke* decision. The plan directs the nine campuses to draw their freshmen from the top 12.5 percent of the state's high school graduating seniors. All but 5 percent of U.C.'s students in the mid-1990s came from this group, and any student who made the cutoff would be admitted to one of the system's eight campuses with undergraduate programs. Some, however, failed to get their first-choice campus, and one of the reasons was the university's goal of greater diversity.[59]

Since many more whites and Asians graduate in the top 12.5 percent—and in the upper percentile of the cutoff—an admissions system pegged solely to test scores and grades would mean that top campuses like Berkeley and UCLA would be predominantly white and Asian. To ensure diversity, university officials argued, blacks and Hispanics in the top 12.5 percent had to be distributed among the campuses.

To do this, each campus admitted 40 to 60 percent of its entering freshmen by test scores and grades alone. For the remaining group (still from the top 12.5 percent), the university took into account a number of factors, including race, geography, and family income. This meant that a black or Latino student with lower grades was often admitted to his or her first-choice campus ahead of an Asian or white student with higher grades. Even with race being a factor, the freshman class still represented a rarefied group of students—the mean grade point average on a 4-point scale was 3.4 for blacks, 3.7 for Hispanics, 3.8 for whites, and 3.9 for Asians.[60] The university reached below the top 12.5 percent of graduating seniors for only 5 percent of its freshman class. For these students, the university took into account such factors as special athletic talent, music ability, and race. In 1994, 1,374 students were so-called special admits; 19 percent of these admits were black, 39 percent were Latino, 11 percent were Asian, and 28 percent were white.[61]

The arguments for considering race remained similar to those made in 1975, when the regents first approved affirmative action. The decision to consider race as a factor in admissions recognized that the quality of public schools varied dramatically. The children of wealthier parents lived in the better school districts, and, even in 1994, income disparities fell along racial lines: the mean parental income of Latino and black applicants in 1994 was half that of the white and Asian applicants. The regents decided in 1975 to try leveling the playing field in two ways: through admissions and through special tutoring programs aimed at preparing black and Latino students better. The tutoring programs worked, but reached only 9 percent of all black and Latino high school students.[62]

The complications of graduation rates, eligibility rates, and income disparities were ignored by Wilson at the July regents meeting. Doing so might have been a political decision, but it had been made easier by the very administrators who opposed him. Those officials had lost some credibility. Since March, the regents had been demanding information about the admissions process, and U.C. administrators had divulged it slowly. Less than two weeks before the meeting, for example, U.C. President Peltason wrote the regents a letter informing them that he would be making a few changes in the admissions policies at Berkeley, UCLA, Davis, and Irvine. He had found that at Berkeley and UCLA, admissions officers reviewed all the applications but some more than others. All white and Asian applicants with comparatively low academic records and no other distinguishing features were rejected without further review. In contrast all nonwhite applicants were reviewed very closely. Moreover, Peltason said, Davis and Irvine automatically admitted all academically eligible minority applicants. These practices, he promised, would be stopped, but that they had been going on at all failed to help his case. In fact, they demonstrated to many that Connerly had been right—that to some, the University of California was technically in violation of the Supreme Court's 1978 *Bakke* decision. That decision said that race could be a plus, but not the only factor in admissions.[63]

Peltason's statements made it easier for Wilson to turn the conference room where the regents met into a stage for presidential politics. On such a stage, Wilson didn't need to argue the fine points of affirmative action. He needed to sear a new image into the voter's mind, an image of himself as a white governor who wanted to "reward and honor people who work hard, pay their taxes and obey the law."[64] The photos would tell voters that Wilson stood in opposition to Jackson, a black man, dressed in black, who defined his constituency as "the damned, the disinherited, the disrespected, and the despised."[65]

Wilson defined the debate in racial terms—the programs that helped blacks and Hispanics were unfair to whites and Asians. "We cannot tolerate university policies or practices that violate fundamental fairness, trampling individual rights to create and give preference to group rights," the governor told the regents. "The people who work hard to pay those taxes and who play by the rules deserve a guarantee that their children will get an equal opportunity to compete for admission to this university—regardless of their race or gender."

Regent Roy Brophy, a Sacramento real estate developer who had known and supported the governor for years, could see that the regents were not going to have time for a real debate on affirmative action. He wanted to buy U.C. administrators and the regents some time. The board, he believed, would never recover from the unspoken awareness that the governor was pushing so hard that a few members would feel compelled to vote against their true feelings. Brophy thought he could save the board from this fate. With every U.C. chancellor in opposition to Wilson, many regents wanted a compromise that would let everyone win. Brophy tried to devise one.

While the regents listened to testimony from a list of speakers, Brophy met privately with the governor. A stocky man who studied law but ended up making millions in construction, Brophy made his case slowly. He had been a regent since 1986. He liked Wilson—he had worked on the governor's first campaign—but he did not want to see Wilson use the board to play politics. Brophy argued that the regents should support Connerly's proposals to ban affirmative action, but give the

administrators a year to study affirmative action and then re-
visit Connerly's proposals a few months before they went into
effect. By that time, he argued, the regents would know if
CCRI had succeeded. The regents would also have a better
idea of whether it would be feasible to create a diverse university without regard to race.

Wilson listened to Brophy for thirty minutes and then, according to Brophy, said flatly: "I don't want a compromise."[66]
"That was it," said Brophy. He would get no help from the governor. "It was a hot political issue so it had to be done right
away," Brophy noted.[67] "Normally you'd have several meetings, some rhetorical arm wrestling, but this was a completely
uncompromised proposal."

Brophy and Wilson returned to the meeting room and
waited through the list of more than forty speakers. Reverend
Jackson's name was called near the end, and it was clear that
his was the name everyone had been waiting for. The regents
pulled their seats forward. Reporters who had been chatting
in the overflow room turned to their laptop computers to take
notes. Wilson looked at Connerly as Jackson walked to the
podium.

"Let us stand together and join hands and have prayer," the
reverend said. The appeal caught the regents off guard. Some
shifted in their seats. Few wanted to rise and pray, but no one
wanted to be disrespectful to Jackson publicly. "Let us stand
and have prayer," the reverend continued, as everyone looked
at the person seated nearby for direction. The governor remained seated. "Let us stand together and have prayer if you
will," the reverend demanded for the third time. Slowly, everyone stood. Everyone except Wilson.

"Our Father and our God," Jackson began. Wilson allowed
Jackson to go on for forty-five minutes—thirty minutes longer
than any other speaker. When Jackson finished his speech—a
mixture of prayer, politics, and parable—he strode over to
Wilson to shake his hand. The handshake appeared the following day on the front pages of newspapers across the coun-

try. But as soon as the photo was snapped, Wilson was ready for a vote.

He was not alone. The sheer length of the meeting was beginning to wear on people. The television lights had made the room unbearably hot, and the regents were getting testy. "This is becoming hell," muttered Frank Clark, the only remaining regent who had been appointed by former governor Jerry Brown. Then, providentially, someone called in a bomb threat and the building had to be cleared. Outdoors, Wilson and Connerly continued lobbying other regents, making sure that no one had changed their mind. Hoping to win Clark to his side, Connerly scribbled an amendment on a piece of paper that restated the regents' commitment to diversity.

When they returned, the regents voted fifteen to ten to end affirmative action in hiring and promotion. Brophy was one of only two white men appointed to the board who voted against the resolution. The other was William Bagley, a San Francisco attorney and a former Republican state assemblyman. The other "no" votes from appointees came from Ed Gomez, a Latino student regent; Alice Gonzales, a Latina and former state employee; and Tom Sayles, a black executive appointed by Wilson in 1994. The remaining "no" votes came from U.C. President Jack Peltason and the four Democrats who held their seats on the board by virtue of their elected positions. Next, the regents would vote on ending affirmative action in admissions.

As Brophy offered his compromise on admissions, the affirmative action supporters in the audience looked frantically to Jackson for leadership. Jackson just stared at the regents. Then a young man in the audience got up and stood on his chair. Others followed. Unsure at first how to respond, Jackson finally joined the protesters. Wilson and the regents rose and left the room as security officers formed a line between the protesters and the empty table. The protesters were left to sing to themselves.

A contingency room had been set up for precisely this kind of eventuality and the regents now took their seats in the new room. Reverend Jackson followed and pleaded with the governor and regents to return to the main room. Wilson doubted the room could be secured. "Governor Wilson, can we go downstairs and make an appeal for order?" the reverend pleaded. "No," said Wilson, "we need to get on with business." Even when the security officer assured the regents that it was safe to return, the governor refused. "Let me point out it's not simply a question of security," Wilson explained. "I don't think people here are concerned particularly with their security. What we are tired of is being unable to complete the business of a duly noticed meeting."

In the contingency room, the regents barely listened to a final appeal by UCLA Chancellor Charles E. Young. They wanted to get on with the vote. Regent Judith Willick Levin, the president of the Alumni Association, was stunned. "I'd like to make a statement, although I don't think it matters," she said, clearly baffled and frustrated by the day's events. "I'm still terribly concerned about the fact that for a long time we have heard from the chancellors, the administration, the office of the president, the academic senates, and the students that this policy is a policy that works well. I don't know why we are sitting here and saying, 'It's not working. Let's change it completely.'"

By now, however, the meeting was more about power and presidential politics than affirmative action. The governor, a presidential candidate, wanted to be the man to end affirmative action and most of the regents were there to support him. "The chancellors?" one regent observed much later, when asked why the opposition of the nine chancellors had failed to sway any of the regents.[68] "Who knows what a chancellor is? We were appointed by a governor and everyone knows who the governor is." The vote proceeded and when Wilson concluded the roll call with a raspy "Aye," the University of California became the first major university to reject the Supreme Court's guidelines on affirmative action. Henceforth, the university was ordered to ban the consideration of race as a factor in admitting students. The vote had been fourteen to ten.[69]

Fifteen Minutes of Fame and a Fifteen-Month-Long Shadow

Suddenly, Wilson's ratings, which had been lagging in the national polls, went up five points and he enjoyed his biggest fund-raiser yet—a $1,000-a-plate dinner in Orange County that nearly four hundred people attended. On the same day that Wilson banked nearly $400,000, Senator Bob Dole stopped dragging his feet and introduced path-breaking legislation in the Senate to end affirmative action. Dole called the affirmative action programs he had supported for more than two decades a "Band-Aid" that failed to help minorities and women and "a corruption of the principles of individual liberty and equal opportunity upon which our country was founded."[70]

The flurry of activity in August made it seem as if the March madness that had even President Clinton questioning the value of race-based affirmative action had not been a fluke; mainstream politicians now viewed affirmative action as outdated and unfair. Custred and Wood felt redeemed. Fresh financing was within their reach, so, for the second time since they met in 1991, they filed CCRI with the state attorney general. This time around, however, Gelman was careful to meet with Chief Deputy Attorney General David Stirling to ensure that no mistakes were made. The CCRI campaign considered Custred and Wood's first filing in 1993 problematic because the attorney general's office returned a title and summary that said the impact on state and local government would be the "elimination of affirmative action programs . . . elimination of voluntary school desegregation programs."[71] CCRI's campaign team wanted the words *affirmative action* excluded from the title and summary because some polls showed that voters supported affirmative action by a slim margin.

Despite an earlier meeting between CCRI supporters and Attorney General Dan Lungren at the Republican state coven-tion and Lungren's support of the initiative, Steinberg dis-trusted the attorney general's office to get the title and sum-mary right. He advised Gelman in May to talk to Stirling. "Please allow enough time in Sacramento to see David Stirling. . . . We seek no special treatment. . . . We want to maintain a cordial relationship with the AG's office, but we are conscious of (1) the error made in title-summary on the school choice (changed by the AG from 'parental choice' to the pejorative 'voucher'); the error made in title and summary on the last Wood-Custred submission; (3) that Stirling did not even know the AG had previously titled CCRI."[72] Gelman fol-lowed Steinberg's advice. "We wanted to make sure that they didn't screw up," Gelman recalled, adding that they didn't want the term *affirmative action* "highlighted" and they didn't want "politically stupid things that would come back and bite us in the butt."[73]

Meanwhile, the Republican National Committee's field man in California, Scott Taylor, had finally been able to get Haley Barbour, the chairman of the Republican Party, to lean on a few donors. One was Darrell E. Issa, the founder and presi-dent of Directed Electronics, Inc., which manufactures and markets a top-selling car alarm and is based in California. He wrote a check for $50,000. House Speaker Newt Gingrich, who had made critical statements about the anti–affirmative action efforts in late March, appeared ready to send out a fund-raising letter.

By the end of August, New Hampshire voters were watching television commercials boasting that Pete Wilson was "the first to outlaw affirmative action quotas in state hiring and end preferences for college admissions. . . . The Power of Ideas . . . The Courage to Make Them Happen." Wilson's pollster Dick Dresner tested the commer-cials in six markets including Maine, South Carolina, and Arizona. In every market, Wilson's ratings jumped from the single digits into the teens or low twenties, according to Dresner.[74]

Alas, for Wilson, all of this excitement about CCRI and affirmative action as a powerful presidential issue was short-lived. Too many of the governor's financial backers wanted him in California. He had promised them as much when they filled his reelection coffers in 1994, and now they refused to ante up more for a presidential race. By the end of September, Wilson dropped out of the race. CCRI's popularity held steady in the polls, but no one wrote about it much. Instead, reporters had become interested in General Colin Powell. He was to prove Custred and Wood's worst nightmare: Powell was black, a war hero, and as popular as a rock star. What's more, he favored affirmative action.

Powellmania was more than any potential candidate or campaign manager could have been prepared for.[75] No one even knew in the summer of 1995 if the retired general, the first black chairman of the Joint Chiefs of Staff, was a Republican or a Democrat; they knew only that they wanted him to run for president. With polls showing him more popular than Dole and even with Clinton, Powell embarked in September on a nationwide book tour.[76] Although the public knew little about his stand on the issues, the general soon made clear his attitude toward affirmative action—it was a civil rights program from which he had directly benefited. "Let's not deceive ourselves into thinking the playing field is equal," he said. "We should not deceive ourselves that we are a color-blind society."[77] When asked about preferences, he replied that the United States "is a nation full of preferences."[78] People in Washington, he added, "who scream about quotas and preferences go right back on Capitol Hill to vote preferences which give corporations some things in the way of specific benefits that they don't deserve. And it's paid for by the middle class."

In the same month that Powell began his tour—flanked by fans and reporters wherever he went—the state attorney general

returned CCRI's registration as a ballot initiative.[79] Gelman's
work with the attorney general's office had paid off. The title and
summary mentioned neither affirmative action nor any impact
on voluntary desegregation programs. By state law, however, the
clock began running. CCRI had 150 days—until February 21,
1996—to collect 693,230 signatures.[80] If CCRI succeeded, the
initiative would appear on the November 1996 ballot and, for
the first time in history, Americans would vote on a major civil
rights program.

Money to collect those signatures was still a problem. The
prospect of a Powell candidacy had dampened the enthusiasm
of many of CCRI's potential donors. Steinberg had been un-
successful in persuading Powell to support the measure. He
wrote the general in August and reminded him of their talk
about CCRI at a reception at the Library of Congress. "The
issue need not be unduly politicized if people of good will can
work together," Steinberg wrote and included a text and short
explanation of CCRI.[81] Powell wrote back a short handwritten
note: "Thanks for the note. I understand the CRI [sic], but I
still believe there are broader issues involved."[82] He signed the
note, "best of luck." By mid-October, Wood was concerned
about a Powell candidacy. "Would it pay one of us to call
Kristol (William) and sound him out about Republican thinking about Powell. . . . How much support could we expect
from the RNC or even the CRP with Powell as the standard-
bearer for the party? My guess is: absolutely none," Wood
wrote in a memo to Steinberg.[83]

The drive to get signatures had problems other than Powell.
The initiative process had started as a populist ideal decades
ealier, but by the 1970s signatures were collected not by volunteers but by paid signature gatherers.[84] A volunteer-driven
campaign to collect these signatures would have been particularly difficult in CCRI's case. Polls showed that as many as 70
percent of the voters favored the initiative, but they weren't organized. Unlike the anti-immigration initiative, Proposition
187, which had drawn on a network of organizations that had

long been working to curb immigration, few groups had been working against affirmative action. Ironically, the California Association of Scholars, Wood's employer and the one organization explicitly opposed to affirmative action in education, had decided against supporting the measure because it went beyond the scope of education. "CAS is an academically oriented institution, and there is enough on our plate to concern ourselves with," said John Bunzel, the former president of San Jose State University and a senior fellow at Stanford's Hoover Institution. "This was not a moral issue, but a political issue and I felt it was inappropriate to get involved with something on the ballot."[85] In the end, the board's debate became so acrimonious that Bunzel and others resigned. Without CAS or any national organization to provide a base of volunteers, CCRI had to start building one from scratch. And Wood and Custred were not pound-the-pavement types.

At the fall San Francisco Gun Show, CCRI did manage to set up a booth. It looked, however, like a wallflower lost among twenty-five tables selling everything from Ruger Mini-14 rifles to beef jerky and Nazi paraphernalia. The CCRI booth, staffed by volunteers such as San Francisco firefighter Patrick Skain, had two small folding tables, no overhead banner, and no pizazz. "We're still looking for the right way to present the initiative to people," reported Skain despondently. "With 187 we could stop people by saying, 'Do you want to put a stop to welfare benefits for illegal aliens?' People connected with that immediately, but we haven't found the poetry to use with affirmative action." In addition, many ordinary citizen volunteers were nonplussed by the CCRI organization. "They're a bunch of intellectuals," Skain said.

Even the paid petition drive was having trouble. Although the initiative's campaign team staged a dramatic kickoff to their campaign in Los Angeles, the signature campaign was anything but robust. "It was all smoke and mirrors," said Gelman. The $50,000 Issa check enabled them to give Mike Arno's American Petition Consultants a $45,000 deposit to help generate signatures, but Arno needed more—much more. He subcontracted his work out to a handful of smaller companies that hire the men and women who stand with petitions in front of grocery stores and outside sporting events. Their enthusiasm—the willingness to get out of bed on a rainy day or stay in front of a market for several hours to solicit support—depends on how much they earn per signature. "More money," said Arno, "is always the elixir for more petitions."[86] In the early months of the campaign, Arno's contract paid him 70 cents per signature; subcontractors were paying as little as 35 cents a signature on the street. At that price, the least bit of discomfort—weather or harassment—sends petition gatherers home. There were other deterrents, too. The workers who collect signatures usually come from the ranks of the unemployed, many of whom are black or Latino. "We usually do well in Los Angeles, but we're finding women and ethnic minorities who refuse to work," Arno said early in the campaign, referring to the unwillingness of women and minorities to collect signatures for a measure that ran against their own interests. "And then there's a group that could take it or leave it, and they'll leave it if they get hassled."[87]

By the end of October, however, Arno's drive had built from collecting 15,000 signatures a week to a respectable 54,000 a week. At that rate, he would comfortably reach his goal of collecting nearly 700,000 valid signatures by the February 21 deadline. Then, a couple of days before Halloween, Steinberg called with some news: "He said they didn't have any more money and they didn't know where they were going to get it," Arno recalled.[88] Arno immediately called the petitioners off the street. Gelman went public with the news that CCRI was broke and said that if it was to be saved, the people who "talked the talk would also have to walk the walk." The state Republican Party's offices started getting hundreds of phone calls. So did Governor Wilson.

Republicans to the Rescue

At this point, CCRI could have died. But because Wilson had staked his reputation on a promise to end affirmative action, even though his presidential hopes for 1996 had been dashed, neither he nor the Republican Party dared let such a potent political issue go by the boards. Within days, the campaign got a powerful second wind—and financial support. "If people thought it was political [his newfound position on affirmative action], he would have to prove to them that it was not," George Gorton, his campaign manager, said later in trying to explain why Wilson chose to save the CCRI campaign.[89]

Others came through, as well. After months of being pursued, Gingrich finally endorsed CCRI. His letter—to a small mailing list controlled by the Speaker's staff—went out at the end of October. Arnn, well aware that the campaign needed a leader with more financial clout than himself, had been talking to Connerly. Wood had approached the black regent in early 1995 about heading the campaign, but at that time Connerly was busy ending affirmative action at the University of California. "I could tell that he was tempted," Wood said of Connerly, recalling their initial meeting, "but he said he had a responsibility as a regent. He didn't say 'no' and we stayed in touch."[90] After the meeting in July 1995 at which the regents voted to end affirmative action at the University of California, Wood said, they "started a full-court press" to get Connerly.

The U.C. regent would later tell reporters that he decided to chair the initiative campaign because he feared the regents' decision would be rescinded. This is exactly the argument Wood had used with Connerly in an October 22 memo. "I enclose an article from the *San Francisco Chronicle* by Edward Epstein about the U.C. Academic Senate, which voted 124 to 2 on Tuesday to call on the regents to rescind their votes to abolish race and gender preferences at U.C. This action has provided me with some additional reasons why both you and the Governor should get heavily involved—even in a highly

public and visible way—with the initiative. . . . Right now the
opposition has two things to attack, but without CCRI loom-
ing ahead of them, you and the regents would face the full
brunt of their wrath. Consequently, you and the others who
voted for your resolutions have, I am afraid, much to fear if
the vote on July 20 is not ratified by the voters in November
1996. A clear victory for CCRI at the polls is the only thing that
will silence the opposition."[91]

At the end of October 1995, Wood reported to the campaign
his telephone conversation with Connerly. "Ward just returned my phone call. He did not say whether he would take
an official position with CCRI and I did not raise the question
myself. Since he will not take the Chairmanship without assurances from Wilson that the initiative will succeed, his acceptance would have clinched our success. However, I am
pretty much convinced that the fact that he did not decline is
good news. . . . He has spoken to the Governor within the last
couple of days. He told him that "they" (the Wilson crowd)
would have to fish or cut bait or the initiative will fail.
According to Connerly, this message has gotten through loud
and clear."[92] By the end of November, Connerly was on board.

In Connerly, the campaign not only got a close friend of the
governor—one who they believed wouldn't have taken the job
without assurances from Wilson that money to fund the campaign would be forthcoming—but a successful African
American. "To be blunt the fact that he was black was very important," said Gelman.[93] "It's like using affirmative action to
defeat affirmative action. It's slightly unprincipled, but the fact
was he brought some positive things like the full weight of the
governor's office."

Connerly's arrival represented the ascendence of the politicians over the intellectuals at CCRI. Gelman, who was considered too unpredictable, was asked to leave. Wood and
Custred, who had already been sidelined by Gelman and
Arnn, were even more out of the loop. Neither complained as
they watched Connerly in action. Earlier CCRI had difficulty

getting to Wilson—Connerly now could speed-dial the governor's office. Wilson offered his mailing list of small donors, asked state legislators to have their staffs collect signatures, and even called on donors himself. "I'll give him things I had been trying to do forever, and they're done in a day," said Steinberg referring to Connerly.[94]

For the first time, money was not a problem for CCRI's organizers. Less than a month after Connerly took over, Wilson raised more than $500,000, including $464,859 from the state Republican Party.[95] The going rate for signatures mushroomed to more than $1 a signature. Suddenly, paid workers were happy to stay out longer. CCRI's speaker's bureau, which had been dormant through the summer and fall, became a one-man show. Connerly spoke on dozens of radio programs between December 1 and the February 21 deadline. Every time he spoke, the telephone lines in the Los Angeles CCRI office lit up, and more volunteers signed on.

By the time the Republicans met at their state convention in mid-February in Burlingame, few doubted CCRI would be on the ballot and some believed that it would be a big Republican issue in the November elections. Wood and Custred, dressed in light-colored suits, sat in the Hyatt Regency's atrium like two middle-aged men on a park bench enjoying their triumph but left out of the parade. Their earlier dream of making the initiative nonpartisan no longer held any promise for them. Custred remained an independent, but he acknowledged the Republicans' claim to the issue and sounded just slightly regretful that he and Wood had little to do that weekend. Had he met with Connerly? "Oh yeah, yeah, I saw Connerly. We had a brief meeting in the hall," Custred later said without a trace of bitterness.[96]

Connerly was too busy for much more than a handshake. Reporters shadowed the new CCRI chairman's every move; party leaders squired him as if he were visiting royalty. He was one of only a handful of blacks among eight hundred convention-goers and the only black to address the gathering.

"We're going to do this in California so the people of this state can say once and for all, 'We favor equal opportunity for all and preferences for none,'" he said to applause. He asked for his listeners' help with the confidence of a man who didn't need it.

At the big Saturday night dinner, more than a dozen of California's political leaders were introduced as they took their seats at the head table. Connerly was the only one to receive a standing ovation. Some wondered what would happen when Jack Kemp, the keynote speaker, began to talk. Earlier that year, he had irritated other Republicans when he said he wouldn't participate in the 1996 campaign if race were an issue. Furthermore, Kemp appeared to support affirmative action and said flatly in July 1995, "I think race is a legitimate factor to take into consideration."[97] Why, some California Republicans wondered, had Kemp been invited to give a keynote speech with Ward Connerly at the head table? They got their answer less than ten minutes into his speech. The popular Republican politician talked about what a great country, what a great state, and what a great party Republicans shared. Then he paused and turned toward the head table and toward the businessman from Sacramento. Mr. Connerly, he said, was "destined to be a hero in his own time."

In the end, more than a million signatures were collected by the February 21 deadline. Connerly worked hard, but it didn't hurt him to have friends in high places. If his enthusiasm inspired others, it didn't ignite a groundswell of volunteer signature gatherers. Ultimately, Wilson and the state Republican Party could take the credit for putting CCRI on the ballot. It was they who pumped nearly $500,000 into the campaign and paid the signature gatherers to stay on the street.

3

The Opposition

The Split between Northern
and Southern California

This could become Armageddon.

BILL PRESS
*chair of the California
Democratic Party*

For California's civil rights activists, 1994 wasn't the worst of
years, but it came close. It had begun hopefully with the candidacy of Kathleen Brown, Jerry Brown's younger sister, for
the governor's seat—an effort by the Democrats to recapture
the office that Republicans had held for twelve years. She was
popular and she was on the right side: their side. She sent out
a call to defend immigrant rights against the draconian provisions of Proposition 187. The measure promised to cut off
health and education benefits for undocumented workers and
their families, and, despite advice to soften her stand, she held
firm.[1] Activists got excited. It felt as though an energy from the
1970s had returned. Progressives were ready to rise and reclaim their place in California politics.

They were terribly wrong. Brown's defense of undocumented workers turned out to be political suicide. Most voters
wanted to send them back to Mexico, not fight for immigrant
rights to free schooling and medical care. That November the
Republican revolution swept through California, picking off

state offices almost as cleanly as migrant workers clearing a field of lettuce.[2] And when the new conservatives claimed victory on November 8, they didn't stop to savor their triumph. They wanted more. They were ready to take on affirmative action. Their motives were varied but not terribly complicated: Some believed affirmative action represented a morass of government regulation and intervention that needed to be cut away; some believed it was unfair to white males and too generous to undeserving blacks, Latinos, and women; and some believed it was just plain unfair.

The task of coming up with a strategy to defeat the California Civil Rights Initiative fell to the clusters of men and women in San Francisco and Los Angeles who had dedicated much of their professional and personal lives to civil rights causes. And they were feeling vulnerable. Their failure even to come close to defeating Proposition 187 revealed their weakness. They were unable to turn out the vote. In fact, they couldn't even keep their own constituents together. It wasn't for lack of brain power. The state's civil rights activists represented some of the best and brightest of their communities. It would soon become clear, however, that they were not the astute politicians or political magicians needed to beat the popular initiative. Nevertheless, they were the only people willing to try.

In San Francisco, there was Eva Jefferson Paterson, the executive director of the Lawyers' Committee for Civil Rights. Paterson, a black woman who described herself unabashedly as a beneficiary of affirmative action, had degrees from Northwestern University and the Boalt Hall School of Law, University of California, Berkeley. A large, dramatic woman with the oratorical skills of an ordained minister, Paterson provided legal services to the poor, became a skilled civil rights litigator, and cofounded a shelter for battered women.

David Oppenheimer, a law professor at Golden Gate University, had followed the antiwar movement from New York to Berkeley; when that battle was over, he applied to forty-six law schools. The only one impressed with his degree from the Bay Area's alternative University Without Walls was Harvard. Upon graduation, he clerked for California Chief Justice Rose Bird and set up a legal clinic at the Boalt Hall School of Law. At forty-five, he taught, wrote extensively on civil rights issues, and always returned calls when someone in the civil rights community needed an extra hand.

Jan Adams, a forty-eight-year-old native of Buffalo, New York, worked as an organizer for the United Farmworkers, Central American solidarity groups, the African National Congress, and gay and lesbian causes. She was still willing to put in fifteen-hour days—even going door-to-door in communities generally ignored by others. There were dozens of women and men like Paterson, Oppenheimer, and Adams in San Francisco who rallied to the cause.

The Los Angeles civil rights community was equally impressive. Constance Rice, the daughter of a black Air Force colonel, graduated from Radcliffe College and then the New York University Law School. She was the Western Regional Legal Counsel for the NAACP Legal Defense and Education Fund.[3] Rice could size up an adversary in seconds, and she recalled facts with computerlike speed. She could be devastating in debate and compelling from the pulpit.

Her colleague and fellow Radcliffe alumna Molly Munger, a white Presbyterian from Pasadena and Harvard Law School graduate, had given up a six-figure salary as a partner in Fried, Frank, Harris, Shriver, and Jacobson to join the NAACP Legal Defense and Education Fund. Tall, open, and warm, Munger was as comfortable and adept at talking to corporate executives as she was sitting around her kitchen table in Pasadena chatting with black friends.

Anthony Thigpen, a former Black Panther, self-effacing and committed, still lived in the South Los Angeles neighborhood where he grew up. Like Adams in San Francisco, he believed—against all the wisdom of prior elections—that untapped power lay in those communities and he wanted nothing more than to show that, with time and organizing, their votes could make a difference. Then there were the legions of lawyers at the Asian Pacific Legal Center and the Mexican American Legal Defense and Education Fund, or MALDEF.

All these men and women agreed on one thing: Their efforts to defeat Proposition 187 had been a textbook case of how not to run a campaign against a popular initiative. They had waited until too late to organize. They had failed to offer voters who were confused and angry about immigration a reason to support illegal immigrants. And then there were major public relations fiascos, including a massive march in Los Angeles against Proposition 187 that further provoked Californians upset by immigration: the marchers, many of them young, defiant Latinos, waved Mexican—not American—flags.

The activists promised to do things differently for the campaign against CCRI. This time, they got started early. Paterson talked to her colleagues about a statewide campaign even before the ballots for the 1994 election had been counted. She brought together dozens of interested Bay Area individuals and nonprofits under the Northern California Coalition to Defend Affirmative Action.[4] It became an umbrella for committees and provided strategy, fund-raising, and speakers. Paterson, Munger, Rice, and other volunteers debated Wood, Custred, and their allies—and they debated well.

But debating well wasn't enough—the problem of beating CCRI in a fast-paced campaign was more difficult than winning a debate. On the face of it, affirmative action had some support—even CCRI's poll showed that.[5] But the initiative didn't actually mention affirmative action. CCRI's language stole the high ground. When voters walked into the booth in November 1996, they wouldn't be asked to dump affirmative action. They would be asked to support an initiative that prohibited the state from "discriminating against, or granting preferential treatment to, any individual or group" on the basis of race or gender. Who could disagree with such an exalted principle? The proposal sounded as if it had been written by Martin Luther King, Jr., himself. Early on, it became apparent that voters loved it. Polls showed support at anywhere from 59 to 77 percent.

How could civil rights leaders explain in a thirty-second sound bite that affirmative action, which is carried out through an assortment of programs, was the basic enforcement mechanism to ensure the intent of Congress's 1964 legislation? It was fine for Custred and Wood to decide that affirmative action violated the Civil Rights Act of 1964, but the initiative process turned personal opinions into law. It took complex policy issues—ones like abortion, gay rights, and civil rights that the courts and legislatures had tussled with for years—and put them into the political arena where money and sound bites counted most. Opponents knew that this arena favored any issue that could be used as a racial wedge. The experience of politicians from George Wallace to Pete Wilson had proven as much. It's unlikely that even the Civil Rights Act of 1964 would have survived a popular vote in California.[6] The same year it was approved by Congress, Californians approved Proposition 14—an initiative that showed they thought little of civil rights legislation and effectively nullified the Rumford Fair Housing Act. Later, the state and U.S. Supreme courts ruled that Proposition 14 was unconstitutional, but its popularity offered an indication of how reluctant Americans were to embrace civil rights legislation. In 1994 Americans—especially those in California—weren't feeling any more magnanimous.[7]

And even if they were, CCRI's opponents would have difficulty reducing their argument to sound bites. The measure's very name—the California Civil Rights Initiative—appropriated the ideals of Martin Luther King, Jr., so opponents first had to explain the confusion. Next, they had to take a listener through some legislative and legal history of how the courts had interpreted the Civil Rights Act of 1964. Toss in a few numbers and the argument for affirmative action became an hour-long debate. On the other side, CCRI's supporters could ignore legislative and judicial history and read the Civil Rights Act literally. It forbids discrimination. Any government program that helps one American, they argued, necessarily discriminates against another. Period. Opponents listened to Wood and Custred's sound bites, read the polls, and concluded that they could lose everything on November 5, 1996. It scared them.

It scared the state Democratic Party, too. Its strength lay in the number of its elected officials, and it had lost dozens by standing against Proposition 187. As Bill Press, chairman of the state party, and Steve Smith, his political analyst, assessed the damage, both wondered if the party had made a terrible error in coming out so decisively against such a popular initiative. They weren't about to let the same thing happen with affirmative action. "It has opened a lot of doors of opportunity for people who could not get through the door," Press told reporters.[8] "At the same time, if it's broke, we've got to fix it." This was the party that in 1992 had handed California's fifty-four electoral votes to a Democratic presidential candidate for the first time in forty-four years. But the promise of that victory was ruined two years later by Proposition 187. "A train wreck with no survivors," campaign advisor Bob Mulholland said, referring to the 1994 election results.[9]

Largely on the popularity of Proposition 187, the state Democratic Party lost enough races in 1994 to eventually give the Republican Party working control of the assembly for the first time in twenty-four years. Democratic gubernatorial candidate Kathleen Brown, ahead fifteen points a year earlier, lost with only 40 percent of the vote. Democrat Dianne Feinstein, who also opposed Proposition 187, barely won reelection to the U.S. Senate. She might have failed if, in the last two weeks of the race, Republican challenger Michael Huffington had not been forced to admit that he employed an illegal Latina nanny, a revelation that made his support of Proposition 187 seem hypocritical. And it was an initiative that voters took seriously, particularly suburban white voters.

The Democratic Party feared that if it took a strong stand against CCRI, the anti–affirmative action initiative would prove just as destructive to the party. After all, whites were the

Californians who voted. The Democratic Party needed them in order to win elections, and so it should have surprised no one that though the civil rights community felt that the attack on affirmative action put thirty years of social progress at risk, the state and national Democratic Party wondered if it was worth saving. Bill Wardlaw, the Clinton advisor some credited with winning California for the president in 1992, explained the logic of party politics: "When you looked at the poll information available in 1995 when all this started and when you looked at the impact of 187, why would you expect the Democratic Party organizations whose job it is to elect individuals to office to divert its energies, efforts and treasuries to other fights particularly when they could have a negative impact on the party? Logic tells me you would not do that."

Only one constituency in California relished a confrontation with Custred and Wood's initiative—the state's women's rights groups. Women had stayed home in 1994, and women's rights leaders escaped the Proposition 187 battle fatigue that plagued Democratic Party and civil rights circles. Nevertheless, the 1992 election had already proven that women could be marshalled to vote as a bloc. Angry about the way in which a U.S. Senate panel had treated Anita Hill, a law professor who testified at confirmation hearings that she had been sexually harassed by Supreme Court nominee Clarence Thomas, women—supported by other women—had picked up a record number of offices in 1992.

The National Organization for Women and the Feminist Majority, founded by former NOW president Eleanor Smeal in 1987, knew they could turn out the vote if women felt threatened. All they needed was a catalyst, and an attack on affirmative action looked to them like the perfect stimulus. Women had benefited the most from affirmative action, but they were far from entrenched in the higher levels of elected office or corporate boardrooms. They had a lot left to win and a lot they could lose. Leaders of NOW, the Feminist Majority, and other women's groups believed affirmative action was as powerful an issue as abortion rights. If the Republican and

Democratic Parties viewed affirmative action as a racial wedge issue that would split white male voters away from the Democratic Party, the women's organizations had a different take on it. They saw affirmative action as a wedge issue with the potential to split white women away from the Republican Party. To make that happen would take lots of work. Early polls showed that women favored CCRI. To beat the initiative, women's rights groups would have to turn them against it.

Katherine Spillar, the Feminist Majority's national director based in Los Angeles, was particularly ambitious. She had cut her professional teeth in the pro-choice movement. Early on, she and Smeal, her boss in Washington, saw CCRI as a direct threat to all women. With an anti–affirmative action initiative on the ballot, they could test one of the Feminist Majority's founding principles—that women had the clout to swing elections in their direction. At thirty-nine, Spillar was younger than many of the civil rights organizers in Los Angeles, but she was cocky. Unlike others, Spillar had mentors with experience and money.

Smeal had been the president of NOW for two terms, and she was a veteran of countless initiative battles to ensure a woman's right to an abortion. She believed deeply that certain issues had strong gender gaps and the women's movement could use those to its advantage. Smeal's first experience with the gender gap was during her undergraduate years at Duke University in the early 1960s. At that time, the women and men had separate campuses and Smeal was active in moving to racially integrate the private university. The measure to do so lost a campuswide popular vote, but the women had approved it by a substantial margin. "I'll never forget that," Smeal recalled later.[10] Working beside someone with this kind of experience gave Spillar depth. And there was an added benefit to working for Smeal—Peg Yorkin.

Smeal cofounded the Fund for the Feminist Majority with $250,000 in seed money from Yorkin. At the time, the sixty-four-year-old native New Yorker had just ended a thirty-year marriage to Bud Yorkin, a television producer who co-owned Tandem Productions with Norman Lear. She came away with some $40 million, and in 1991 increased the endowment to the Fund and the Feminist Majority Foundation, a sister organization, by $10 million. For Spillar, Smeal was only a phone call away, and Yorkin was down the hallway in her own production offices. The three women worked together, and they understood that when Yorkin said they didn't need the state Democratic Party, she meant it.[11]

By early 1995 the opposition to CCRI amounted to three loosely organized groups: civil rights leaders casting about for a strategy to save affirmative action, the Democratic Party looking for a way to win the next election, and women's rights leaders fixed on testing the gender gap's political power. One element complicated this scene: geography. Civil rights leaders in San Francisco and Los Angeles had the same goal, but they lived 381 miles apart and in distinctly different social and political climates. San Francisco had been one of the few cities to defeat Proposition 187, and voters there were generally more progressive. In fact, by the end of 1995, the city would elect Willie Brown, the liberal state assembly Speaker, as its mayor. Los Angeles, however, had the businessman Richard Riordan at the helm. Moreover, the 1992 Los Angeles riots had revealed how deep the racial divides between whites, blacks, Latinos, and Asians still were. The O. J. Simpson trial had only widened them. San Francisco may have felt like a melting pot, but Los Angeles had boiled over.

A Weekend in Palm Springs

Civil rights activists in Los Angeles were on guard about being sold out by elected officials, and their early contact with the state Democratic Party didn't do much to reassure them. It began with a phone call. The state Democratic Party called the ACLU's Ramona Ripston, a sixty-nine-year-old native New Yorker with a laid-back charm and the looks of a movie star.

The party was inviting Wood and one of his key supporters, black businessman Errol Smith, to a meeting that weekend of the party's executive committee in Palm Springs in early 1995; they needed a white woman to fill out the team that would debate Wood and Smith. Ripston begged off, but called Molly Munger, a white lawyer at the NAACP Legal Defense Fund.

It was already late in the day and Munger was getting ready to leave the office. She didn't know whether to be amused or insulted by the invitation. Wasn't asking the men who wanted to set back the civil rights agenda to the Democratic Party's weekend retreat a little like the Christian Coalition ushering pro-choice leaders into their smoke-filled room? Why was the Democratic Party scrambling to find someone to debate the CCRI team at the last minute? And why were they so insistent on having a white woman? She wondered if she should accept, but she wanted to know what the Democratic Party was up to and the debate invitation was a chance to find out. She hung up and walked down the hall to Connie Rice's office. "Listen to this," she said, explaining the invitation to her black colleague. "I think you ought to come with me."[12]

Munger picked up Rice early on Saturday morning and they set off together along Interstate 10. Their route cut through West Covina, Ontario, and Banning—cities in the shadow of the San Bernardino Mountains that offered a glimpse of why affirmative action would be so difficult to defend. In the Thirty-fourth Congressional District, which runs from Montebello to La Puente and from Whittier to Santa Fe Springs, the Democrat Esteban Torres had held onto his office since 1982. Sixty-one percent of the voters were registered Democrats and Latinos were the largest ethnic minority. But even with these numbers, the voters in the Thirty-fourth District had barely defeated Proposition 187. Further east along Interstate 10 in the Forty-first and Forty-second Congressional Districts, where manufacturing layoffs had been steady, Proposition 187 had been approved by 65 percent of the voters. These were the men and women—white, working-class victims of downsizing—who were most likely to support CCRI.[13]

Munger and Rice had left Los Angeles early that day because they wanted to arrive in Palm Springs with enough time to scout out the situation before the late afternoon debate. After they pulled up along the palm-lined drive of the Riviera Resort and Racquet Club, they got their opportunity. The executive committee, a group of two hundred party leaders, was assembled in the dining room for a luncheon. All the heavyweights were there: Don Fowler, the national cochairman of the Democratic Party; Lieutenant Governor Gray Davis; Bill Press, the chairman of the state Democratic Party; and an assortment of legislators, contributors, and political consultants. "The message they all delivered in one way or another was we need to be very cautious about affirmative action," Munger later remembered.[14] "They said essentially that our main goal is to get Bill Clinton elected and let's not all get diverted on side issues. It was almost a finger wagging in advance."

The arguments that party leaders made at lunch weren't much different from the ones Bill Press outlined in an article that appeared on the front page of that morning's *Washington Post.* "This could become Armageddon," Press said, referring to the anti–affirmative action initiative. "It's potentially worse than Proposition 187, much more divisive really. It will turn neighbor against neighbor and brother against brother. Not only is this an area where there's a possibility of compromise, we have to be aggressive in seeking a compromise in order to avoid a bloodbath in 1996. I say that as a longtime supporter of affirmative action. But like a lot of good programs, it can be abused by people with the best intentions. There are cases where people can point to where it's been discriminatory. If it's broke, I think we've got to fix it."[15]

As Rice listened to the speakers, she fumed. "This is a meeting where you are supposed to pull your troops together and you invite these two clowns," she said referring to Wood and

Smith. "It showed me how incompetent the Democratic Party is. They operate out of fear and they don't understand the issues."[16]

What they understood were the numbers. "The Democrats have spoken for have-nots, but have-nots don't vote," Darry Sragow, a political consultant for the party, later explained.[17] "If we move to the center to win elections, you risk spinning off some other candidate or party from the left, someone like Jesse Jackson, but if we stay to the left and placate this group, then we lose elections. So when it comes to affirmative action and elections, the Democratic Party has a serious problem. It's my distinct understanding that the Democratic Party leadership saw this problem, and it's a terrible problem and, understandably, they sort of hoped it would just go away."

Sragow, however, also appreciated the state's demographics, and he cautioned the executive committee about playing it lukewarm on affirmative action. "I can do the numbers as well as anyone else," Sragow recalled telling the group. "But the demographics are that 70 percent of the voters in California are either women or people of color and if the Democratic Party doesn't want to represent them, then someone else will."[18]

By the time the luncheon ended, Rice was livid. She wasted no time in telling Press that his views were unacceptable. Munger tried to soothe her. "There wasn't that much we could do about the situation right then. I was just hoping we could survive the afternoon," Munger recalled.[19] Harry Pachon, the president of the Tomás Rivera Research Center, was scheduled to join Munger on the dais, but Barbara Lee, the black assemblywoman from Oakland, had failed to show up. All the arrangements had been so lax," Munger said.[20] They began to wonder if Munger had been set up to fail. Was it possible the Democratic Party actually wanted to find a way to support CCRI?

At 4:30 P.M., Munger, Pachon, Wood, and Smith faced a standing room–only audience for the debate. Munger's fears

quickly abated. The audience was with her. "It was an enthusiastic crowd," Munger recalled. "As a trial lawyer, you generally
don't get applause, so I remembered the applause."[21] Steve
Smith, the party's political director, watched from the audience. He had been concerned about inviting CCRI to Palm
Springs. He knew it would look like the party was waffling on
affirmative action and he feared the press would run with the
story. But as he watched the audience react enthusiastically to
Munger and Pachon, he decided he had been wrong.[22]

From Smith's point of view, the debate mobilized the party.
But these were activists and the votes of two hundred party
activists would not win any election. Moreover, a certain faction liked what it heard about CCRI. In the week after the debate, Smith began getting calls from members of the state
Democratic Leadership Council. They wanted to know what
the party's reaction would be if they came out in support of
the initiative. "I told them that they were out of their minds,"
Smith said.[23]

In the end, neither Munger nor Rice left reassured by Press
and Smith. They returned to Los Angeles to share their experience with Spillar, Yorkin, and Ripston. The women were not
happy.

Dinner at Prego

After Palm Springs, Munger and Rice mistrusted the party,
but they also felt it was still important to keep trying to convince state leaders to stand with their constituents. It was one
thing to have a reticent party, but women and minorities could
never win a battle over affirmative action if the Democrats
abandoned it. They asked for a small meeting with Press and
Smith. Instead, in March, Munger got another late invitation.
This time, it was to a dinner at Prego in Beverly Hills. Rice
was in San Francisco and Munger called to discuss what they
wanted out of the meeting. Rice had a wish list. The
Democratic Party's state convention was coming up in April,

and Rice wanted the party to know that African Americans were upset about the attacks on affirmative action. She also wanted access to the convention floor, access to all the workshops, and a private meeting with President Clinton.

When Munger walked into the private room at Prego, she could see that it would not be easy to deliver on Rice's list. This was not the intimate gathering she had requested. Press, a blocky build with a thick head of prematurely grey hair, presided over a long table, where about twenty state Democratic Party higher-ups had gathered to discuss affirmative action. They included Ira Yellin, a developer and major contributor who was also founder of the Public Counsel, which is one of the largest pro bono legal offices; Gil Ray, a black partner in O'Melveny & Myers, Secretary of State Warren Christopher's old law firm; Percy Pinkney, an aide to Senator Dianne Feinstein; Yorkin from the Feminist Fund; and Steve Smith, the party's political director. Still, Munger liked the crowd. Yorkin was a friend, Yellin was a hero of hers, and Pinkney and Ray were sharp. If she didn't know the others very well, at least they were Democrats.

Munger reminded those at the table that African Americans were an important constituency, and she wanted to know if the party was going to be with them on affirmative action. Yellin cut her off. "I was stunned to be interrupted by Ira who was really quite short and annoyed with me," she recalled.[24]

"Ira says, 'I hate this issue' and he didn't want the Democratic Party to get involved in it," Munger said.[25] One by one, they went around the table. Most of those who spoke were not keen on affirmative action. In fact, most seemed to challenge it. Like it or not, declared one of the guests, affirmative action was perceived as a black issue, and it was not popular.

The room began to feel more like a summit of political enemies than a dinner among comrades. The guests played with their food. Where was Press leading this discussion? Finally, Ray, a measured, tactful lawyer, tried to change the evening's direction. "I'm here to tell you that if an associate at my firm handled an issue this way, he would be fired."[26]

Munger tried to pick up on Ray's remarks. "I have to say I agree with Gil. It's not just that we're prejudging an issue. It's that there's no communication. It's a bad sign that we can't have a conversation about this."[27]

Press exploded, "Well, if you think I am doing such a bad job, just who is the salvation of the Democratic Party?"[28]

Munger saw her chance for reconciliation: "Bill, we all are. If we all just work together."[29]

The evening never got much better. "It was a shouting match," recalled Yorkin. "Molly and I got very angry, but the Democrats didn't want to take any position. They wanted to reelect Clinton and they didn't want anyone to muck up that effort. They thought we would just go away."[30]

When the dinner broke up, Munger tried again to mend the relationship with Press. She approached him, touching his shoulder. "I understand that you're doing your job and I was just trying to do mine," she said apologetically. Press, according to Munger, looked impatient, but Munger went on. "We have this Democratic convention coming up and we should talk about things that we need to do so that it goes smoothly."[31]

Press looked at her with disdain. "You are nobody," Munger recalled his saying. "You are not an elected official or a major contributor. You are nobody I have to listen to." He walked away.

Munger was stunned. She was the representative of the NAACP Legal Defense and Education Fund, and the head of the state Democratic Party had just told her that she was nobody. "I wonder how I would have felt if I was black," she said later.[32]

A Convention in Sacramento

If Rice, Munger, and Yorkin suspected after Palm Springs that they could not depend on the Democratic Party's leadership to defend affirmative action at its April 1995 convention, they were convinced of it after dinner at Prego. The women's groups and members of the civil rights community began laying plans to take their case to the April convention. The convention was particularly important because it would set the stage for the 1996 presidential elections. It was a time to rally the troops around President Clinton, who would speak to the delegates, and it was a time to consider any major election issues. With the prospect of CCRI on the ballot, the civil rights community wanted the party on record opposing it. They also wanted to let Clinton know that he risked losing their allegiance if he wavered in his support of affirmative action. For their part, the party leadership wanted to demonstrate to Clinton that they had the power to deliver the state's fifty-four electoral votes.

In the weeks before the convention, NOW's California president, Elizabeth Toledo, received a copy of the resolution on affirmative action that Press and other state party leaders wanted to introduce. "It would be kind to say that it was a modest proposal to endorse affirmative action," Toledo said.[33] "They wanted to marginalize the issue and us." The women decided to organize their assault on the convention around getting a stronger resolution introduced from the floor. This meant they would have to lobby the caucuses, collect signatures, and create a sense of overwhelming support for their resolution. "We'd learned how to do this working with NOW to fight platform language at other conventions," said Spillar.[34] "Once you understand the process of how conventions work, it's easy to get what you want."

The conference room at the Sacramento public interest building, so-called because of all the nonprofit organizations housed there, became their war room. NOW, the NAACP Legal Defense Fund, MALDEF, the Feminist Majority, and a long list of other organizations were on board. Spillar, Yorkin, Rice, and a dozen or so other activists flew up from Los Angeles. Key to their success was Jan Adams, a longtime activist who had done grassroots organizing to oppose Proposition 187. Adams, built like a lumberjack and as organized as an efficiency expert, got on the phone. Within days, she had found volunteers in San Francisco, armed them with signs, buttons, and banners, and loaded them on a bus for the state capital. The Young Democrats, Adams knew, would be inside as delegates and she contacted them to be ready to help.

When the party's leadership got wind of the organizing, they were not pleased. In the week before the four thousand delegates converged on Sacramento, several leaders called Toledo to see if they could avoid a showdown. "They wanted us to stay away," Toledo said. "They kept asking why we wanted to do this. My answer was, we wanted the party to defend affirmative action, period. There was no possibility of a deal to keep us from going."

If the party couldn't block their arrival, Press could ignore them—or at least try to. "If I had one goal, it's for these 4,000 Democrats to leave Sacramento as missionaries and go out there and preach the Clinton gospel for the next eighteen months," Press said, the day before the convention opened.[35] But that was not to be. The women's and civil rights organizations flooded the Sacramento Convention Center. Adams's volunteers stood at the entryway with "No retreat on AA" stickers, posters, and banners. Delegates couldn't register without getting a sticker for their lapel. "Most people thought we were official staff and they put on their stickers," Toledo said.[36] Delegates who slipped through without a button wanted to know why it wasn't in their material from the party.

Inside the convention center, volunteers carried signs, hung banners, and collected signatures. Spillar, Toledo, and Yorkin watched the door; when they sighted a powerful delegate, one of them pulled him or her aside for a briefing on affirmative action. Instead of turning out to be a revival meeting for Clinton, the convention became a pep rally for affirmative action. In one particularly surreal scene, Toledo later recalled, Press stood among the signs promoting affirmative action and the delegates with "No retreat" stickers on their lapels and insisted to a television crew, "This convention is not about affirmative action. It's about Bill Clinton."

"It was almost sad," said Toledo, not at all sadly.[37] "The only thing that anyone was talking about was affirmative action." It was also the only topic reporters covering the convention were writing about. Steve Smith, the party's political director, said later that party officials never expected to be able to control the convention. The women, he added, had lobbied hard but they worked in a room full of activists who were anxious to support affirmative action.

As the meetings wore on, Topic A was how Senator Barbara Boxer and President Clinton would handle the issue on Saturday morning. Two months before, Clinton had called for a review of all federal affirmative action programs; he was still waiting for the results. Keenly aware of the political tides, some of his advisors cautioned against a blanket endorsement of affirmative action. California was a must-win state; Clinton's advisors didn't want him to go down with affirmative action as Kathleen Brown had with Proposition 187.

Word leaked out that neither Boxer nor Clinton wanted to talk about the issue. No matter. The affirmative action activists considered the information more of a challenge than a fact. Senator Boxer spoke first. When she failed at first to mention affirmative action, delegates and others chanted from the floor, "No retreat, no retreat." Boxer paused in the middle of her speech and gave the activists a sign of support. The delegates went wild with a standing ovation. Boxer, an astute politician, followed the crowd and defended affirmative action. Clinton made the crowd wait until the end of an hour-long speech. As he began to broach the issue, activists demanded, "No retreat, no retreat." The president pleaded, "Don't scream. Let's talk. They win the screaming matches. We win the conversations."[38]

Clinton expressed support for affirmative action, but he was mindful of the electoral strength white males had shown in the midterm elections. Affirmative action, he explained to the audience of party activists, needed to be defended, but in a way that recognized that this is a "psychologically difficult time for a lot of white males."

"Imagine what it's like for them, just for a moment. . . . They go home to dinner and they look across the table at their families and they think they've let them down somehow," he said. "You may be aggrieved, somebody may have been discriminatory against you. But that doesn't make their feelings any less real either." It probably marked the first time a Democratic president stood in front of party activists—many of them women and minorities—and asked them to feel the pain of white males. If activists viewed this as pandering to white males, it was also consistent with Clinton's strategy to reach out to a broad spectrum of voters. It is a strategy he followed in 1992 when he campaigned on the same day in the black urban neighborhoods of Detroit and the nearby white suburbs. And it is one that he would adhere to in 1996. The civil rights and women's rights groups were an important constituency to the Democratic Party, but they weren't the only one the president's advisors had to worry about and that became clear in Sacramento.

Rice failed to get her meeting with Clinton, but she, Toledo, Spillar, and Yorkin did sit down with his advisor. George Stephanopoulos heard the women out and then got right to the point of the party's problem: The women's groups had professional women with them on affirmative action, but he wondered about the other women who would go to the polls in November 1996. A March field poll showed that women supported CCRI in the same numbers as men. Stephanopoulos looked at those numbers and saw trouble. Spillar and Toledo looked at them and saw a dormant voting bloc ready to be goaded into action. If the opposition to CCRI could make women realize how much they would lose if affirmative action were shelved—if it could frame the debate around women, who voted more regularly than men—the opposition believed that the field poll numbers would change.

Democratic party leaders and consultants disagreed. They knew that women favored President Clinton, but the same women who favored the Democratic president, they believed, would vote for CCRI. Ron Gray, a Democratic political consultant, told the *Sacramento Bee* that affirmative action "is going to be a tough sell to voters, even to Democratic voters. I don't think there's going to be too many statewide office holders who will be jumping at the opportunity to oppose this initiative. Nobody should mistake what happens here this weekend as marching orders for Democratic candidates."[39]

Although the women failed to convince Stephanopoulos and others, they felt energized by their impact on the convention. On the final day of the convention, delegates voted overwhelmingly to oppose CCRI as one of several "misguided attempts to repeal affirmative action progress in this nation."[40] Moreover, Assembly Speaker Willie Brown, one of the few elected officials with the potential to rise to national prominence, had come out firmly on their side. After Clinton spoke, Brown told delegates that he didn't believe in a halfhearted defense of affirmative action. "I am not interested at all in having people tell me there's some way we can modify (affirmative action) to make it more palatable," he thundered. "What we need to do is come face to face with it. There is no place to shade, there is no place to dance, there is no place to fake it."[41] This was a change of tactics from January, when Brown had told reporters that he was considering the politically pragmatic step of helping to put CCRI on the March ballot. When reporters asked how he could change his mind so quickly, he answered by paraphrasing Ralph Waldo Emerson: "Consistency is the conduct of small-minded people."

The women and civil rights leaders scored one other victory that weekend. Press finally realized that the issue of affirmative action was not going to disappear. If he wanted to avoid an Armageddon, he better have a plan. He appointed a task force.

Reading the Polls

The task force had representatives from the party; civil rights organizations; the Democratic National Committee and other state movers, such as Aleita Huguenin, manager of governmental affairs for the California Teachers Association (CTA); and Dean Tipps, her counterpart at the Service Employees International Union (SEIU). CTA and SEIU were important players in Democratic Party politics. They represented hundreds of thousands of voters, and, unlike the party, they had money to burn. The group also included Eva Paterson from the Lawyers' Committee on Civil Rights in San Francisco and Lorraine Sheinberg, who ranked thirty-fifth among Hollywood political contributors—thirty slots below her husband, Sidney Sheinberg, a former MCA chairman. Sheinberg was particularly interested in the issue because her father was married to an African American woman; some of her nieces and nephews were Korean; and despite her privileged position, the inequities in Los Angeles had not escaped her notice.

Press didn't want the women's rights organizations out there on their own, sniping at Clinton. He wanted them in the fold, according to Steve Smith, the party's political director. Press knew Spillar was key and he put her on the committee. If only he had visited Spillar's offices, he might have chosen someone else. A *Thelma and Louise* movie poster dominated the entryway. "You get what you settle for," it proclaimed.

The first thing Press's group wanted was more information. Huguenin, a busy woman who downs Slim Fast for lunch and describes herself as being "in the business of winning elections," looked at all the polls on CCRI and didn't understand why voters felt so strongly about it. Using their research budgets, she and Tipps ordered up a poll and focus groups that included a broad sector of the state's voters—women executives;

professional women; white, male professionals and blue-collar workers; Latinos; and blacks. The results were sobering. "Racism is popular," Huguenin said, recalling her first reaction to the polls.[42] The focus groups showed that even when someone explained what voters would be losing if CCRI were approved it failed to change many minds. Instead of identifying with the gains they had made under affirmative action, white women feared that it prevented their husbands and sons from finding jobs. It became clear to Huguenin that affirmative action could lose, that "we could wake up the day after the election and there would be nothing."[43]

In the spring, Huguenin made the rounds with her polling data. "Some people just didn't want to hear the news," she said.[44] "Within more liberal civil rights circles there was denial. This couldn't be the case, they would say. 'We can beat this thing.'" To Huguenin and the state Democratic Party, the polling data confirmed their belief that they would have to offer voters an alternative to CCRI. The alternative would satisfy the sense among voters that affirmative action was flawed and needed to be fixed. Civil and women's rights leaders in the north and south of California reacted differently to this conclusion.

The South and the Alternative Initiative Strategy

Many in the south thought this idea was dead wrong. Spillar, Yorkin, Munger, and Rice hadn't been impressed by Press or Smith and they weren't about to be led by the state Democratic Party—although the task force had been useful to Spillar in hooking her up with Sheinberg. "You get what you settle for" was more than a movie poster's warning. It was a mantra and they lived by it. They knew the state Democratic Party's agenda: The party wanted either to ignore affirmative action or put an alternative initiative on the ballot that would let Democratic candidates offer voters a way to reform it.[45] Others in the south—MALDEF and the ACLU—suspected they were right. But Joe Duff, president of the NAACP in Los Angeles, disagreed. "We have a tradition in the progressive community of just saying no to things, and all the aggressiveness has been on the other side to take things away," Duff said.[46] "In this area we know enough about it that we should be guiding the changes instead of trying to unite around saying no." Duff's influence on other Los Angeles civil rights leaders, however, was marginal. "The NAACP is in disarray and we're not really big players," Duff acknowledged.

Spillar's confidence in disregarding an alternative initiative came from two sources. First, no one she spoke with in the women's groups in Washington disagreed with her. In March 1995, Eleanor Smeal, the president of the Feminist Majority; Patricia Ireland, the president of NOW; and leaders of a handful of other groups rallied for affirmative action and held a ninety-minute meeting with Clinton's senior advisors. The president, they warned, risked a backlash if he failed to fully support affirmative action.

Second, Spillar had a poll taken that indicated her strategy had wheels. The Louis Harris poll, ordered by the Feminist Fund and conducted in the last week of March and the beginning of April 1995, showed—as other polls had shown—that when voters were asked directly whether they favored or opposed CCRI's ban on "preferential treatment," more than 78 percent said they supported it. "Every major group in the state at first glance supports the initiative: sizeable majorities of women, liberals, blacks, Latinos, feminists, and supporters of affirmative action," Harris reported.[47] The problem was that most people reading the language of the initiative had no idea that it would result in wiping out most current affirmative action programs. When voters were asked if they would still support the measure if they knew it would outlaw all affirmative action and end programs to help minorities and women, support for CCRI dropped to 31 percent. Spillar and others in the south viewed the results of the Harris poll as proof that CCRI could still be defeated.

This view was shared by Anthony Thigpen, an organizer in south Los Angeles who worked closely with Mark Ridley-Thomas, a city councilman. Thigpen and Ridley-Thomas had watched the assault on affirmative action with deep concern. What bothered them most was the lack of outrage. They knew residents in south Los Angeles were angry—about the lack of jobs, the proliferation of liquor stores, and the disrespect they endured from just about everyone—but they appeared resigned to losing affirmative action. Thigpen and others wanted to get the community's attention—to make the community believe in something. He could not inspire residents by telling them to fight for an alternative initiative that mended the wrongs in affirmative action. To rally these neighborhoods, he needed to tell residents that Martin Luther King's life's work was at risk.[48] Rice, an admirer of Thigpen, introduced him to Spillar. They agreed to work together.

The North and the Alternative Initiative Strategy

The civil rights community in the north disagreed. They wanted to win in November, and they believed CCRI was unbeatable. They believed the only way to avoid defeat was to offer an initiative that fixed what voters perceived was wrong with affirmative action. If the civil and women's rights community in the south mistrusted the labor unions tied to the Democratic Party and the state party, those in the north felt otherwise. No one from the north had been to the debate with CCRI in Palm Springs or to the dinner at Prego. They had worked longer hours with Huguenin and Tipps, and they felt comfortable with the labor leaders. Steve Smith, the party's political director, they believed, was serious about wanting to defeat CCRI. And unlike those in the south, the Northern California Coalition didn't find cause for optimism in the Harris poll. It was fine, they felt, to discover that voters might reject CCRI once they understood that it would end affirmative action, but the ballot that voters read in November would not inform them of these repercussions; it would merely ask them to vote on an initiative that ended discrimination and preferential treatment. To many groups in the north, the south's refusal to consider an alternative initiative was a typical knee-jerk response. It reminded them of the south's assurance in 1994 that Proposition 187 could be beaten. Moreover, the leadership in the north figured, the election was a year and a half away; from their point of view, it was too soon to rule out any strategy that might beat CCRI.

The Split between the North and the South

The clash between north and south came to a head at a May 1995 meeting. At the Marriott Hotel near Los Angeles International Airport, the Southern California civil rights and women's rights groups gathered to hear the arguments for pursuing an alternative initiative strategy. Diane Feldman, who had conducted the CTA's poll and had just presented its results to a meeting of the Democratic Caucus in Sacramento, went to the airport with Steve Smith. They planned to attend the meeting in Los Angeles together, but, when they arrived at the airport, there was only one seat left on the plane. "Feldman took it," said Smith.[49] "And I don't think she'll ever forgive me for that one."

More than fifty people attended the meeting. It was already under way when Feldman arrived and discovered that she and her associate, Ron Lester, had been allotted five minutes to speak. "It was hostile from the start," said Feldman. "There had already been an effort to turn the audience, and we could feel it."

Feldman spoke for about fifteen minutes before Spillar broke in. She wanted to know if Feldman had done gender-matched calling, which means using women to poll women and men to poll men. She hadn't, but it didn't matter. The question, Feldman said, was intended to bait rather than provoke a discussion. Spillar acknowledged later that the meeting

was "a disaster."[50] The basic problem, she said, was the clash
between different strategies and personalities. Spillar wanted
a "No on CCRI" campaign and Feldman and others wanted an
alternative initiative. Spillar refused to compromise and she
had some wealthy backers. Moreover, many activists from the
south viewed Feldman as a pollster tied to the Democratic
Party and the unions, and thus tainted and untrustworthy.
Press, they believed, was only trying to devise a strategy that
permitted the party to duck the issue of affirmative action.
Why take a defensive position on affirmative action if the
Harris poll suggested CCRI could be beaten?

The North Decides to Go It Alone

The northern coalition returned to San Francisco, confused
by the south's position. "We had worked with these people for
many years and they thought we were terribly wrong," said
David Oppenheimer, a civil rights lawyer and law professor
who had been meeting with the northern coalition.[51] "We had
to consider what they said, but in the end our political and
legal analysis told us that it was a good idea to go with an alternative initiative." With the southern groups openly hostile
to the party, Smith worked hard to keep the northern coalition
engaged. The south questioned the issue of the party's loyalty
to affirmative action. Would the Democrats be there at election time, and would they have the full financial support of the
unions? "It took a lot of conversations to convince the north
that we would not walk away from the fight and that we were
just trying to figure out the best way possible to defeat CCRI,"
Smith recalled.[52]

Throughout the summer of 1995 a special committee of
lawyers from the Northern California Coalition worked on an
alternative initiative. They needed language that the civil
rights community and the Democratic Party would tolerate.
The initiative had to preserve affirmative action but offer voters a sense that it also answered some of their concerns about

fairness. The group included Oppenheimer; Ted Wang from the Lawyers' Committee; Philip Monrad from Remcho, Johansen, and Purcell, a law firm that the Democratic Party used; Judy Kurtz from the Equal Rights Advocates; Martha Jiménez, the lead lawyer from MALDEF's San Francisco office; Mary Hughes, a political consultant; and Jim Moore, a pollster from Sacramento. Duff, from the NAACP's Los Angeles office, was the only link to the south.

The lawyers started with a brainstorming session. "We thought of six different counterinitiatives that ranged from mandating affirmative action, which would be the most militant, to the most pragmatic, which was to prohibit anything that permitted quotas," said Monrad.[53] "We wanted something that would preserve the good elements of affirmative action and we wanted to be practical and beat CCRI," added Wong.[54] "We worked with those two fundamental assumptions and we were guided by what appealed to people."

The group was also guided by the strong reception that Clinton's July "mend-it-don't-end-it" speech received. In the speech, he strongly defended affirmative action, but he also recognized that others had the right to question it. He didn't damn them as racist, but he acknowledged their concerns. "There are people who honestly believe that affirmative action always amounts to group preferences over individual merit, that affirmative action always leads to reverse discrimination, that ultimately, therefore, it demeans those who benefit from it and discriminates against those who are not helped by it," he said.[55] "I just have to tell you that all of you have to decide how you feel about that, and all of our fellow countrymen and women have to decide as well. But I believe if there are no quotas, if we give no opportunities to unqualified people, if we have no reverse discrimination, and if, when the problem ends—the program ends, that criticism is wrong."

The opposition's polling data indicated that Clinton was onto something. Voters didn't want to abolish affirmative action. They wanted to reform it. The opposition believed that rather than making real changes in affirmative action, they needed to confront and change the public's perception of affirmative action. Like it or not, their polls showed that most people equated affirmative action with quotas and the hiring of unqualified applicants. Although quotas had been consequences of early affirmative action programs, they had since been outlawed by Supreme Court decisions. Voters didn't believe that. They appeared convinced by the arguments of CCRI's supporters that goals and timetables were essentially the same as quotas.

As the lawyers committee worked on the alternative initiative, they tested different concepts through polling that cost thousands of dollars and was paid for by the unions and civil rights groups. In an August poll for the Equal Rights Advocates, the Sacramento pollster Jim Moore interviewed 650 likely voters and found that 41 percent favored affirmative action, and 45 percent opposed it. When pollsters read the language of CCRI to voters, they found that 77 percent would vote for it compared to 17 percent against it. "The language of CCRI is so attractive even a majority (52 percent) of the base affirmative action supporters respond favorably to it," Moore concluded in a memo.[56] Everything Moore found underscored the difficulty of defeating CCRI on a straight up and down vote. "Exposing the underlying implications of the CCRI will be extremely difficult because the measure is so appealing and simply stated," Moore wrote. The only solution, he concluded, was to offer an alternative to "mend" affirmative action.

The memo continued, "If an alternative measure that contains some significant affirmative action reforms were placed on the ballot at the same time as CCRI, the public opinion debate would be framed as a choice between two measures—one that reforms AA and the other that eliminates it. Without an alternative reform measure on the ballot, the issue cannot be framed as a choice between two ideas—mending it or ending it. . . . In summary, I see three tasks that need to be addressed immediately. 1. Formulate a 'reform AA' concept that addresses the real and perceived weaknesses of AA; 2. Gather evidence that convincingly makes the case that CCRI will 'eliminate' AA. 3. Refine our arguments further through focus groups."[57]

As the months wore on, the group refined the alternative initiative's language. It would be called the *equal opportunity initiative,* and it would outlaw quotas and the hiring of unqualified applicants. In a sense, the initiative would make the U.S. Supreme Court's decisions and refinements of affirmative action part of the state constitution. The lawyers wanted to make sure the alternative initiative reflected the strength of the Supreme Court's decisions. The political consultants wanted an initiative that voters could understand. "Simplify, simplify, simplify," the consultants warned.[58]

The lawyers committee produced hundreds of drafts over nearly five months. The language was distilled so that the initiative—Equal Opportunity Without Quotas—was the same length as CCRI.[59] "The state shall ensure equal opportunity," it began, "and shall prevent discrimination based on race, sex, age, color, ethnicity, or national origin." In fewer than a dozen clear sentences, it amended the state constitution to prohibit quotas, the hiring of unqualified applicants, and it threatened fines for anyone who fraudulently benefited from a state affirmative action program.

"We sent it everywhere for review," said Huguenin.[60] "Two to three former judges saw it. It's been all over the East Coast and the White House. We had conference calls with twenty to thirty people, and still there are some people who said they hated it." Since most of those people were in Southern California, the Northern California Coalition made one final attempt to convince their counterparts in the south that their alternative initiative strategy made sense.

This time, the meeting went on for a whole day. Instead of being lined up in folding chairs facing presenters, participants sat around a long table and spoke their minds. Pollsters Diane Feldman and Jim Moore and Jerome Karabel, a U.C. sociology professor who had been analyzing all the polling data, made the north's presentation. Paterson, from the lawyers committee, chaired the meeting. As the pollsters outlined the data, Spillar cut them off. "This is taking too much time," she said, according to several people who attended the meeting. "Let's get to the discussion." Paterson intervened and the presentation went on. When they finished, Spillar made it clear what she thought. "We hired the best that there is," Spillar said referring to Louis Harris. "And you hired all these other people." Participants looked around. Feldman passed Paterson a note: Is she saying we are not qualified or that we're not the best qualified? Paterson put her finger to her lips and the meeting went on.

"It was an emotional meeting," Moore recalled.[61] "The people in the south felt like they were being betrayed and they weren't going to compromise. Spillar is very bright, very intelligent, but she had a plan and she didn't want anyone to get in the way." The south remained united. Thigpen, who had been organizing in south Los Angeles, felt like it would be impossibly confusing and demoralizing to ask residents to work and vote for the lesser of two evils. "They had the best of intentions," he said of the Northern California alternative initiative's authors. "But it was worse than CCRI. It gave into the premises and the assumptions of the right wing."[62] Moreover, he felt that the organizing he was doing in the south and that Adams's work in the north were starting to pay off. "I've done a lot of this and generally it's like pulling teeth, but this time I began to feel like I couldn't keep up with all the people who wanted to help," he said.

Others, like Rice and Munger, felt it was dangerous to mix political strategy with constitutional law. "We looked at the alternative strategy at the very beginning," said Rice.[63] "All the political consultants will tell you that it's the cheapest way to defeat another initiative, but we're trying to fiddle with the Constitution through politically motivated tricks." Did it make sense, she asked, to trick voters into approving a ban on elements of affirmative action that had already been outlawed by the Supreme Court? Along with others in the south, she argued that once the initiative was adopted and the Constitution had been changed, the conservative judges on the state Supreme Court could reinterpret the legality of a whole slew of voluntary affirmative action programs.

The lawyers from the north were aware of the risks involved, but they viewed the alternative initiative strategy as one that would at least preserve most elements of affirmative action. "The polls showed that we just weren't going to win if we tried to defeat CCRI without an alternative," said Kurtz.[64] "People's initial reaction to CCRI was much stronger than it was to Proposition 187. I'm not comfortable with putting any programs at risk, but if CCRI passes, it's going to be the end of public sector affirmative action in California and that would be a disaster. It would take a long time to recover and get back to where we are now. We don't have the option of being politically pure. It might make you feel better, but the stakes are too great."

When the October 1995 meeting in Los Angeles broke up, everyone had spoken, but no one's mind had changed. In fact, the southern California groups had already started to organize their own "No on CCRI" campaign, although they had agreed to hold off on opposing the alternative. Karabel, Paterson, Moore, and Feldman returned to San Francisco and huddled with the Northern California Coalition. They were upset that the opposition in the south questioned their strategy, but they still felt that the alternative initiative offered the best hope. Late that month, organizers in the north decided to file the initiative. Oppenheimer hoped that if the state attorney general and the legislative analyst returned positive reports on the impact of their initiative, they could—with the help of the White House—convince the south to unite behind the mend-it-don't-end-it alternative strategy. The alternative initiative felt like a winner. It responded to what voters liked—equal opportunity—and did away with what voters hated—quotas. The last polls the Northern California Coalition commissioned showed that it beat CCRI.

But then, in the time it takes a fax machine to etch out a one-page letter, more than nine months of work were suddenly wiped out. On December 8, 1995, Steve Smith was working at home and watched the legislative analyst's report fall into his In basket. "I took one look at that letter and I knew we would not be able to do this," Smith said. The letter was from Elizabeth Hill, the legislative analyst in charge of assessing the impact of proposed initiatives. The first part of her analysis on the opposition's alternative initiative looked good. It concluded that there would be no impact on the measure's prohibition of quotas in public employment and contracting because, "We have been unable to identify current programs or activities in these areas where quotas are used." She chose, however, to interpret state affirmative action programs in education as programs that did have quotas, because they were set up specifically for minority students. The measure, she concluded, could save the state $38 million by eliminating "magnet school and racially isolated minority school programs."

The donors who support civil rights causes would not write checks for an initiative that wiped out programs that benefited minority students. It didn't matter if those who wrote the alternative initiative believed that Hill's interpretation would not stand up in court. The alternative initiative strategy was dead. The Northern California Coalition to Defend Affirmative Action was back to square one. If they had no strategy to defeat CCRI, the women in the south did.

4

The Republican Party and Affirmative Action

How a Wedge Issue Cuts Many Ways

> The Republican leadership has been spinning around like a weather vane in a hurricane on this issue.
>
> REPRESENTATIVE CHARLES CANADY
> (R-Florida) in an interview at the
> Republican National Convention

Through the years, Ward Connerly had run his consulting business with a tight grip. And in the beginning, he was able to do the same as the chairman of the California Civil Rights Initiative. "I was a dictator," he said almost wistfully in May 1996 as he recalled the days before Pat Buchanan, Colin Powell, Bob Dole, and Jack Kemp insinuated themselves into his campaign.[1] By May, Connerly had discovered that few men dictate in American politics. He could, with the governor's help and the state GOP's money, get CCRI on the ballot, but his belief that he could control the campaign, that he could determine how others would use the issue of affirmative action, met reality as the presidential primary season got underway.

Affirmative action is a national issue mixed up in how Americans feel about race, the civil rights movement, and themselves. Although Connerly hoped for a civilized debate, affirmative action focused squarely on race and inclusion—emotional issues with a political history. That history wasn't pretty, and it was likely to reemerge in any debate over a ballot measure that promised to end affirmative action in the country's most populous state.

Politicians have long used racial wedge issues to attract white voters. "Attacks based on race survive," wrote Kathleen Hall Jamieson, dean of the Annenberg School for Communication at the University of Pennsylvania and author of several books on the media and presidential politics. The racial appeals of the late 1980s and early 1990s, she argued, "were forecast in earlier years in such coded words and phrases such as 'the tyranny of the courts,' 'law and order,' 'Your home is your castle,' 'neighborhood schools,' 'forced busing,' 'individual rights,' and 'quotas.'"[2] It didn't take long before this brand of racial politics began to affect the debate in California. Connerly was prominent and capable, but he could not control the debate. In May 1996 he shook his head at the wonder of it all: "When I started this at the university in July 1994, the construct was pretty well defined, but this is totally different. You're totally unable to define it."[3]

The Republican Primaries and Race Baiting

Specifically, affirmative action became enmeshed in Republican Party politics, and in the winter and spring of 1996, that domain defied definition. On the surface, all of the major candidates held the same position: They were against affirmative action. But beneath the appearance of unity, sharp differences existed between the new religious and social conservatives and the old-line suburban Republicans.

First there was the problem of Pat Buchanan. The conservative commentator and presidential candidate had been one of the first politicians to recognize the beauty of CCRI as a vote-getter. "To win back California, the party must win back the Perot vote, that vast middle-class constituency, alienated and populist, that felt itself abandoned by the Beltway," he wrote in his syndicated column in February 1994. "To the point: If the GOP is casting about for a populist issue to re-unite its old coalition and to slice Bill Clinton's new coalition asunder, that issue is at hand. The California Civil Rights Initiative. . . ." [4]

For Buchanan, CCRI wasn't merely a matter of convenience. He was genuinely opposed to affirmative action. Buchanan's rivals didn't feel the same ideological commitment. But by the time the Republican primaries rolled around, they had all taken the pledge to end affirmative action. Buchanan showed them early on how to use the issue to win votes. It was in Louisiana, far from California, where affirmative action would actually be on the ballot, that Buchanan demonstrated how the issue can appeal to white voters. Texas Senator Phil Gramm had been working Louisiana for months and was widely expected to win handily and have the momentum going into the Iowa caucuses and the New Hampshire primary.[5] Buchanan, however, knew that despite Gramm's strong lead he still had a chance. As Wayne Parent, a political science professor at Louisiana State University, put it, "there's a black-white thing going on here."[6] Buchanan was unafraid to exploit it.

Before the Civil Rights Act of 1964, the south's "black-white thing" was explicit in the Jim Crow laws of segregation; afterward, it became implicit in white opposition to federal civil rights programs such as busing and affirmative action. Campaigning against busing or affirmative action—directly or using the code of states' rights—secured the white vote. The strategy gave former Alabama Governor George Wallace some success in 1968 and 1972, and it provided the modus operandi of President Nixon's southern strategy in 1972.

By 1990 Republican politicians had found that attacks on affirmative action offered a particularly effective bridge to white voters. North Carolina senator Jesse Helms proved this in his 1990 race against Harvey Gantt, the popular black mayor of Charlotte. Trailing with two weeks to go, Helms aired an ad that zoomed in on the hands of a white man crumbling a rejection letter. "You need that job," the voice-over said in an ad created by Alex Castellanos, a political media consultant. "And you were the best qualified. But they had to give it to a minority because of a racial quota. Is that really fair? Harvey Gantt says it is. . . ."

That same year, Louisiana state representative and former Ku Klux Klansman David Duke made the runoff in the governor's race by campaigning against affirmative action.[7] In 1995 Duke was still playing the race card. "We have got to make a choice if we want this state to look like Haiti or have it be like it was planned by the forefathers of Louisiana,"[8] he said in one early debate for potential gubernatorial candidates. When Duke declined to run, he backed Mike Foster, a white state legislator whom few had expected to capture the Republican nomination. Running on an anti–affirmative action platform, Foster not only clinched the nomination, but also won handily in a runoff against the black congressman Cleo Fields. No sooner had he been sworn in than Foster issued an executive order barring state affirmative action programs. The order was gratuitous—Louisiana had only a handful of such programs—but the fact that it was issued at all made it clear whom Foster wanted as allies. "Most of his vote was remnants of the Duke vote and he did it to appease a constituency," said Parent.[9]

When critics called the new governor mean-spirited, Buchanan rushed to the Bayou state to stand "squarely behind Mike Foster and his decision to end set-asides."[10] Then, just in case his message had been overlooked, Buchanan drove it home by hiring Foster's campaign manager, Ray Fletcher, to run his campaign in Louisiana, and airing commercials that emphasized the connection. "Mike Foster is right," Buchanan told Louisiana voters in a thirty-second spot in which he promised to end affirmative action nationwide.[11]

Although Gramm also vowed an end to affirmative action, he failed to understand how much Louisiana voters wanted to hear this promise over and over again. In contrast, Buchanan's reiterated opposition to affirmative action and abortion, and his alliance with Foster—the only governor in the nation to endorse him—defined him as the kind of conservative many Louisiana Republicans like—and those were just the voters who actually went to the polls.[12] "Race was the main concern here," said James Llorens, chairman of the political science department at Southern University in Baton Rouge. "That's exactly what it came down to."[13]

Buchanan's upset victory in Louisiana effectively took Gramm out of the running. Suddenly, Buchanan was the conservative challenger to front-runner Dole. Shifting his emphasis to economic populism, Buchanan ran a close second in Iowa, then came in first in New Hampshire. Mainstream GOP leaders were aghast. All winter, Clinton had successfully used the budget battles with Congress to cast the Republicans as extremists. Now, Buchanan was proving how extreme the party could be.

Senator Bob Dole and Affirmative Action

In California, where the citizens believe they are far too sophisticated for Louisiana-style race baiting, Connerly watched the Buchanan juggernaut with horror. Although the conservative commentator had been one of the first to endorse CCRI, Connerly didn't want him anywhere near the CCRI campaign. The black U.C. regent had nothing in common with Buchanan. True, they both supported CCRI, but the press was reporting speculation that Buchanan was anti-Semitic and racist,[14] while Paul Gigot of the *Wall Street Journal* described Connerly as "daring" and CCRI as "the most important election of 1996, the presidency included."[15] Buchanan was threatening to crash Connerly's party. Connerly was determined to keep him out. In no uncertain terms, Connerly rejected Buchanan's backing. "Will I go to a press conference where Pat Buchanan is endorsing CCRI?" Connerly asked rhetorically. "Absolutely not."[16]

Instead, Connerly and Wilson prevailed on Dole to endorse CCRI. The state's March primary would be the perfect moment. Dole's primary victory was a foregone conclusion, and his endorsement would tie CCRI to the moderate winner.

Up until the winter of 1994, Dole, like many Republicans, had long supported affirmative action. He hadn't abandoned that position when the Reagan administration tried to repeal Executive Order 11246—the 1965 order signed by President Lyndon B. Johnson that calls for the government to "provide equal opportunity in federal employment for all qualified persons." Attorney General Edwin Meese III had argued that the executive order imposed quotas and resulted in reverse discrimination. Ralph Neas, executive director of the Leadership Conference on Civil Rights, had participated in the negotiations and said that Dole was one of twenty-three Republican senators who asked President Reagan not to change the executive order. They argued that goals and timetables had been an effective measure in countering discrimination. In 1991 Dole played a key role in persuading President George Bush to sign a civil rights bill that retained goals and timetables.

The senator's views changed abruptly, however, after November 1994. At that time, Republicans led by Georgia Representative Newt Gingrich and a bevy of new conservatives, known as "the freshmen," took control of Congress. For a few frantic months, House Speaker Gingrich's Contract with America became Washington's legislative blueprint. Although the plan didn't include affirmative action, there were plenty of conservatives eager to correct that omission. Early in 1995 Dole began attending the meetings with conservatives Clint Bolick from the Institute for Justice and Linda Chavez, president of the Center for Equal Opportunity, a Washington-based think tank. Another important voice at these meetings was Dennis Shea, a senior Dole aide. A graduate of Harvard Law School, Shea had taken a leave of absence as Dole's counsel in 1992 to run for Congress in New York's middle-class, Seventh Congressional District, in Queens. Shea's contribution to the race was to test the issue of affirmative action. He accused the incumbent, Queens Democratic Party chief Tom Manton, of "making skin color more important than merit and qualifications." Although Shea lost, he and others in the GOP felt that he was on to something. "Republicans have an opportunity to stake out principled positions in the areas of affirmative action and immigration policy," he wrote in a February 1993 op-ed piece in the *Washington Post.*[17] "For Reagan Democrats, unfettered affirmative action means fewer jobs and reverse discrimination; unfettered immigration means more welfare and more chaos. With his so-called diversity pledge, Clinton appears to have swallowed whole the ideology of affirmative action, giving Republicans the rhetorical opportunity to promote the principle of race-blind merit."[18] When he returned to Dole's office, Shea began testing the idea on his boss.

Whereas the meetings with Dole were dominated by libertarians and the conservative wing of the Republican Party, the campaign against affirmative action was moving rapidly into the mainstream. With Bill Clinton, the most prominent advocate of civil rights, calling for a review of all affirmative action programs, it was only a matter of time until Dole fell into step. That happened on March 15, 1995. "After nearly thirty years of government-sanctioned quotas, timetables, set-asides and other racial preferences, the American people sense all too clearly that the race-counting game has gone too far," Dole announced on the Senate floor.[19] Despite his conclusion that discrimination continued to be "an undeniable part of American life," Dole had soured on affirmative action as a remedy he had so long defended. "Race-preferential policies, no matter how well-intentioned, demean individual accomplishment," he told his Senate colleagues.

At the end of the speech he asked his fellow senator from Kansas, Nancy Kassebaum, to request hearings on Johnson's Executive Order 11246.[20] Kassebaum, then chair of the Labor and Human Resources Committee, was less than enthusiastic. "I think we have to be careful not to throw the baby out with the bathwater," she told a reporter.[21] First she wanted to hold hearings on the Equal Employment Opportunity Commission and its backlog of 100,000 discrimination complaints.[22]

Dole promised in early 1995 to introduce legislation in the Senate to end federal affirmative action programs. But as spring progressed, he hesitated. "His heart wasn't in it," said Bolick. Dole's interest in the issue might have died altogether if it hadn't been for events in the West. There, one of Dole's challengers for the presidential nomination was making headlines with the issue of affirmative action. Governor Pete Wilson successfully engineered an end to affirmative action at the University of California at the July meeting of the U.C. regents. His reward: national coverage and a five-point jump in the polls. Watching these developments from Washington, Dole lost his timidity. Seven days after the California regents' meeting, Dole introduced the Equal Opportunity Act of 1995. Representative Charles Canady of Florida followed suit in the House. The Dole-Canady bill promised to end affirmative action in the awarding of federal contracts and the employment of federal workers. Still, conservatives questioned whether it was politics or passion that had moved Dole. "I watched his speech on CNN and even then you could see he was not into it," said Bolick. "He never looked up from the podium. He didn't feel comfortable with the issue."

No matter. Dole had committed himself to legislation that would end affirmative action and if he wasn't impassioned, he appeared increasingly at ease with the issue. In November 1995, in an op-ed piece in the *Los Angeles Times,* Dole endorsed CCRI. The article, which Shea helped to write, argued that CCRI was a direct descendant of the Civil Rights Act of 1964. "Both measures stand for the simple proposition that Americans should be judged as individuals on the basis of their own unique talents and abilities and not on the basis of skin color or gender," it read.[23]

Connerly was delighted to have Dole join his party and excited when the senator agreed to endorse CCRI publicly before the state's March primary. On a campaign swing designed by Governor Wilson, the presumptive nominee would use immigrant California as a backdrop. On Sunday, March 23, Dole would endorse CCRI and make a major policy address on affirmative action in the heart of Republican Orange County's Vietnamese community. Two thousand people—most of them Vietnamese, many of whom spoke only broken English—gathered early in the atrium of the Little Saigon Shopping Mall on Westminster Avenue. It was a small, two-story shopping mall packed with shops and a food court offering everything from egg noodles to jade bracelets. The banner behind the speaker's podium read "Bob Dole and CCRI."

It might as well have been in Greek. No one of more than two dozen people interviewed knew what *CCRI* stood for and what it would do. Only a few recognized it when the acronym was spelled out. Many of those who did recognize it believed CCRI was a civil rights initiative, that it extended opportunities for racial minorities.

Dole's speech failed to elucidate. In fact, the segment on CCRI was over so quickly that some in the audience missed it altogether. Backed by Governor Wilson, Ward Connerly, and Korean, Vietnamese, and Irish dancers who had warmed up the crowd, Dole gave his long-awaited major policy address on affirmative action: "So, Ward, I will thank you for your commitment and courage and I believe too that the governor is right, we should support and I have supported the California Civil Rights Initiative," the senator said quickly, barely looking at the audience. "We ought to do away with preferences. It ought to be based on merit. This is America and it ought to be based on merit." That was it. The candidate moved on to foreign policy.

Back in Sacramento, Connerly offered an explanation for the brevity of Dole's endorsement: "He's still getting comfortable with the issue. It takes a while. It's difficult for a lot of people to grasp." Aides told reporters that the segment of Dole's policy speech on affirmative action was jettisoned at the last minute because his notes kept slipping off the podium.

The Senator Pursues the General

Even if Dole's failure to deliver a major policy address on affirmative action could be blamed on the tilt of the podium, he was less than eager to reschedule. As soon as he had wrapped up the nomination in California, affirmative action appeared only briefly in his California stump speeches. Nor was he pushing the Equal Opportunity Act in Congress. The reasons for Dole's inertia went beyond any personal discomfort with his newfound position. The truth was that affirmative action had yet to electrify any voters except the most conservative Louisianans. True, CCRI was popular in California, but polls showed that many voters failed to understand that in voting for CCRI they would be ending affirmative action. And when voters were polled on what concerned them, affirmative action ranked near the bottom of the list. In other primary states, affirmative action registered as a concern with less than one percent of the electorate. "The term *welfare* will empty the room," said William Schneider, a political scientist with the American Enterprise Institute and CNN's leading on-air elections analyst.[24] "Illegal immigration will empty the room. But the term *affirmative action* does not empty the room. In southern states, there is an anti–affirmative action backlash, and there are voters who will vote on that issue, but to most voters it is not an intense concern."

Moreover, the powerful wedge issue that political analysts predicted a year earlier turned out to be trickier than expected. Not only had it failed to excite voters; it was just the kind of issue that threatened to push the button of two types of voters with whom Dole was already weak: women and moderate swing voters. Republican women were deserting Dole in droves. By spring, Dole's gender gap vis-à-vis Clinton's registered between seventeen and twenty points. If affirmative action was not at the top of a woman voter's list of reasons for this, the national women's movement was trying to put it there. This scared Dole. "It makes him extremely nervous," said Linda Chavez, who had attended the early 1995 meetings with Dole.[25] "He has terrible gender gap issues, and CCRI doesn't help."

Swing voters—Republicans who voted for Clinton in 1992, Democrats who voted for Bush, independents, and Perot voters—also favored Clinton. One of the principal reasons was that Clinton succeeded during the winter budget deadlocks in casting the Republican-led Congress as extremist in its zeal to cut Medicare and Social Security. A battle on affirmative action, congressional leaders believed, might only reinforce that reputation. "There are very few people who are opposed in principle to what we are going to do," said Bill McGrath, Representative Charles Canady's assistant on affirmative action in the spring of 1996.[26] "But there are those who think that tactically it is a mistake to do it now. It is clearly the case that some members say we got our clocks cleaned on the budget, and we don't need to take on another controversial issue. This will be a bloody fight and we might lose."

Even California's staunch Republicans were starting to backpedal on affirmative action. With California still recovering from the 1992 Rodney King riots and the 1995 O. J. Simpson acquittal, former governor George Deukmejian cautioned that a heightened campaign around CCRI could "create further divisions in the community."[27] "I support the language of CCRI; however, I am concerned about it appearing on the November ballot," Deukmejian wrote, explaining his advice to Dole. "The Los Angeles area has recently felt the impact of the jury decision in the first Rodney King trial, the campaign and passage of Proposition 187, and the reaction of the African American and non–African American communities to the jury decision in the O. J. Simpson case."[28] Militant groups on both sides of the issue, he feared, "will try to exploit this issue, which could create a dangerous atmosphere."[29] Los Angeles mayor Richard Riordan, a Republican businessman, also felt strongly about the initiative's divisiveness—and his inability to get reelected without the backing of minority leaders in Los Angeles whom he would offend if he stayed silent or supported the initiative—and he came out against it.

Connerly, flustered by charges that the initiative was anything less than a bold call for fairness, became entangled in a semantic knot. He wasn't against affirmative action, he told the press. He was against race-based preferences. CCRI, Connerly explained in an April press conference, "is an attack on preferences. It is not an attack on affirmative action. You will not find the words *affirmative action* in it anywhere."[30] Opponents believed this omission was deceitful, and the press could not get Connerly to give them any examples of affirmative action that excluded race and gender criteria. Finally, Connerly tried a new qualifier—CCRI wasn't anti–affirmative action but "anti–race-based affirmative action."

One other factor stopped Dole from carrying the flag to end affirmative action: retired General Colin Powell. By early summer, the only source of enthusiasm for Dole was the very hypothetical possibility of putting Powell on the ticket. The retired general had already said he was unavailable as a running mate, but Dole and the press refused to believe it. In May, Dole began courting the popular general. In a commencement address at Bowie State University in Maryland over Memorial Day weekend, Powell made it clear where he stood on affirmative action and, specifically, on CCRI. "We must resist misguided efforts that seek to shut it all down, efforts such as the California Civil Rights Initiative, which poses as an equal opportunity initiative, but . . . puts the brakes on expanding opportunities for people who are in need."

The impact of Powell's statement was immediate. When Dole met with Powell the first week of June, the candidate complimented the general on his Bowie State speech. When Dole returned to California the following day, affirmative action and CCRI were dropped from his stump speeches. On June 11, Candy Crowley, CNN's congressional correspondent, asked Dole about the differences he had with Powell on affirmative action. Dole responded, "Well, affirmative action I think we can certainly disagree on that. . . . I mean as I told him (Powell) Saturday I've been for affirmative action. I think there are some changes that should be made." Suddenly, Dole's position on affirmative action sounded no different than Clinton's—mend it, don't end it.

Others were having second thoughts as well. House Speaker Newt Gingrich had sent out a fund-raising letter for CCRI in October 1995, and the Republican Party had been responsible for saving the signature drive from bankruptcy. But by the end of June, Gingrich was arguing that CCRI was too important to be a partisan issue. It would be, Gingrich decided, a "strategic mistake" for Dole to become a strong advocate of CCRI.[31] Haley Barbour, the chairman of the Republican National Committee, also advised caution: "I think the people of California . . . don't have to have somebody from outside to make a big issue of it."[32]

Connerly was flustered. "People who run for office, especially for president, should be expected to give their definition of the kind of society we should have," he said. "On an issue this important, they should not only be expected, but required to speak out."[33] The Republican retreat meant that Connerly was left holding the bag. He didn't like it. He wanted the issue to be mainstream and moderate, but by late July, his allies had been reduced to some of the country's least popular politicians—Buchanan and Governor Pete Wilson.

A Matter of Timing or Conviction

Some veteran political observers, however, suspected that Dole had merely put affirmative action on his back burner. At the end of May, Fred Barnes, the executive editor of the *Weekly Standard*, laid out the conservative's scenario: "Now, born again, Dole has one final chance to prove himself nationally. And this time, he has a model: the Bush campaign in 1988.

Bush created his own issues against Democrat Michael
Dukakis—the Pledge of Allegiance, Willie Horton, Dukakis's
ACLU membership—that the media and much of the
Republican establishment loathed."[34] No matter, Scott Reed,
Dole's campaign manager, told Barnes: "That's exactly what
we're going to do. A half-dozen conservative issues have been
chosen: a tax cut, ending affirmative action, opposition to gay
marriage, cutting wasteful spending, real welfare reform, and
crime. That's the package."[35]

Negative issues play best late in a campaign because the
short time frame lessens the risk of backlash. Some strategists
looked on affirmative action's retreat from the forefront of the
campaign, therefore, as pure serendipity. "Issues management
is a tricky thing," said Scott Taylor, the Republican National
Committee's political liaison in California.[36] "We had a major
problem when affirmative action heated up on its own last
year. It was very hard to manage. The issue cooling down now
is a very good thing, because the likelihood that an issue will
stay intense through the whole campaign is not good. We
would like it to come back to the forefront in early fall or late
summer. I would much rather [voters] be aware of CCRI in
mid-October than in mid-June."

But Connerly needed the money in mid-June, and he strug-
gled to get affirmative action back in the news and to bring
along the reluctant GOP. In the same week that Dole told the
CNN reporter that he had been a longtime supporter of affirmative action, Connerly reminded him in the *Los Angeles
Times:* "Whether he likes it or not, this issue is already around
his neck. Whoever is the candidate needs this issue more than
CCRI needs that individual."[37] When it became clear that he
would not be asked to address delegates at the Republican
Party's convention, Connerly became petulant. "I am trying to
avoid coming to the conclusion that they are deserting this,
but I am getting that impression," he said. "All you need is to
say it's divisive and there they go running for the hills. Right
now we're not the ones who are thirty points behind in

California. Dole and the Republicans should recognize that they need us more than we need them."

Instead of hearing Connerly's version of civil rights, they would hear Powell's. Connerly was beside himself and publicly scolded the retired general. "You have not served us well by your contribution to the debate," Connerly wrote in the letter published in the *Weekly Standard* the same week the Republicans held their convention in San Diego. "For General Powell to use this convention to take on an issue supported by eighty percent of Californians is the ultimate insult."

The news that Dole would name former Housing and Urban Development secretary Jack Kemp to be his running mate represented yet another setback to Connerly's hope that his issue would be front and center in the presidential campaign. Although Kemp had called Connerly a "hero in the making" in March 1995, he had conspicuously refused to endorse CCRI. It had been Kemp, after all, who warned Dole and others in 1995 that he would not participate in a campaign that took advantage of racial wedge issues.

"Jack Kemp would endorse this in a heartbeat, but this is what is tearing at him," a frustrated Connerly explained.[38] "He was secretary of HUD and he met a lot of black people, and he became the one guy in the Republican party viewed as a moderate champion of the poor. He gets on the board of Howard University and he's still kind of perceived as moderate. People who he rubs elbows with all the time say, 'You are different.' I think he likes being perceived in that fashion. He likes that persona and that is outweighing his natural instinct."[39]

As soon as Connerly heard that Kemp was likely to go on the ticket, he faxed a long memo to Kemp outlining the arguments against affirmative action. As Dole prepared to announce that Kemp would be his running mate, Connerly had still not heard back. The Sacramento businessman went to San Diego grudgingly. "I want to become a deeply committed Dole soldier," he said. "I want to do that. Thus far, I haven't found a reason to place my energy in him to that extent. He's a decent man and he's very knowledgeable. But he has to make the case. We're not talking about electing a city council member here."[40]

Connerly was not alone in his concern for how the Republican retreat on affirmative action would affect the CCRI campaign. For Arnold Steinberg, CCRI's manager, the summer had been disastrous. Once again, the campaign had money problems. "It's going badly. People are not coming through with what they said they would. Worse, when they say they will do something, then they don't," Steinberg complained on the night Powell would address the convention.[41] "I can't plan, or plans get fouled up, because you make plans based on what money you think you will have. I don't have a paid finance staff or a finance director and I don't have a real donor community. I'm getting worn down." By August, Steinberg could not see where the money would come from to finance a big media campaign. He complained to conservative columnist Robert Novak, "I have never in my life been lied to so much and double crossed so often."[42]

The campaign team for CCRI—now christened Proposition 209 by the Election Commission—had taken on two co-chairwomen—Pamela Lewis, a Democrat and a lawyer from Walnut Creek in the East Bay, and Gail Heriot, a law professor at the University of San Diego. Wood and Custred as well as Lewis and Heriot attended strategy sessions in Sacramento, but most of the decisions were made by Connerly and most of the planning was done by Steinberg. The truth was that plans could be drawn up, but, without money, few decisions had to be made. As long as they had no money of their own, the most important task the CCRI team had in the summer of 1996 was keeping the opposition from getting any. Steinberg didn't feel that large Democratic Party donors were a threat as long as Clinton remained on the sidelines, but California corporate donors might feel local political pressure to enter the fray. To keep them away from the opposition, the campaign needed a heavy hitter and no one was more effective than Governor Wilson.

As his tactics at the U.C. regents July 1995 meeting had demonstrated, Wilson knew how to play hardball. When the chairman of Pacific Gas and Electric Company, Stanley T. Skinner, observed in a press release on August 1 that Proposition 209 would "represent a serious setback," Wilson immediately fired off a letter. "Dear Stan," the governor wrote. "I am more than disappointed by your news release express-ing opposition to Proposition 209."[43]

And when Steinberg, now a member of the California Coastal Commission, where utility executives sometimes had to appear to get permits, ran into one utility executive, Steinberg gave him some advice: "If you think it is so impor-tant for the state to enforce these preference programs, maybe commissioners should investigate the utility practices more closely to see if they are in compliance before giving a license or passing a procedure."[44] When asked if such a threat was a misuse of his position, Steinberg said, "No, because I sort of said it in jest. I was trying to impart to them in a humorous way that there were people other than myself interested in this. These people really respond to a squeaky wheel."[45] It wasn't subtle, but it worked. "They got the message," Steinberg said flatly in mid-August.[46] No corporate sponsors stepped forward to fund the "No on 209" campaign.

Money wasn't the only problem for the CCRI advocates. All of the energy Connerly had spent trying to cast Proposition 209 as a measure that would retain certain types of affirmative action—as an initiative that was *not* anti–affirmative action—had begun to confuse their supporters. This became apparent when he and Steinberg listened to a focus group reacting to the ballot summary. The summary reads: "Generally prohibits discrimination or preferential treatment. . . ." One member of the focus group, hearing that Proposition 209 would "gener-ally" end affirmative action, responded: "Aha, see, we told you." The participant wanted to support an initiative that would end affirmative action, but all of the press around what it would do had begun to make him feel that it might actually extend preference programs. "They saw conspiracy" in the language, Steinberg said.[47] "Three of the participants felt the initiative called for more preferences."

The only bright spot was Steinberg's success in developing the campaign's slogan, and in this he acknowledged the opposition's help. Equal Opportunity Without Quotas had been the title of their alternative initiative strategy, and try as he might to come up with something else, Steinberg kept returning to it. Already poll-tested, it was, Steinberg said, "better than anything I came up with."[48]

The Republican Convention

The Friday before the convention opened in San Diego, Steinberg visited the coastal city to attend a fund-raiser for Proposition 209. House Speaker Newt Gingrich, who had now decided the initiative could help Republican candidates, was there, as were representatives from the Dole campaign. Gingrich appealed to donors to support the initiative, arguing that it was a good one for Republicans running for office in California. Just as Proposition 187 had helped Republicans in 1994, Proposition 209 would help in 1996. Although checks never materialized, Steinberg was optimistic.[49] Other developments in San Diego indicated that support from the GOP and the party's ticket would finally fall into place.

Even before Steinberg arrived in San Diego, the platform committee had endorsed Proposition 209. Although its stance on abortion provoked a fight, its anti–affirmative action message sailed through without debate. "We never even discussed it," said William Gribbin, an aide to Senate Majority Leader Trent Lott and a cochair of the platform committee team responsible for the section on individual rights. Gribbin drafted the section, and his view on civil rights programs favored an uncomplicated approach. It ignored the problems of how to provide equal opportunity in a skewed world and instead simplified a Republican-led government's role. It had only to ensure "equality before the law" and "individual rights." The platform stated, "Because we believe rights inhere in individuals, not in groups, we will attain our nation's goal of equal rights without quotas or other forms of preferential treatment. We endorse the Dole-Canady Equal Opportunity Act to end discrimination by the federal government. We likewise endorse this year's Proposition 209, the California Civil Rights Initiative, to restore to law the original meaning of civil rights."[50]

By mentioning Proposition 209 by name, the committee had given Steinberg more than he had expected. Connerly, too, was comfortable with the platform. "The government has no business making the playing field level," he told wealthy donors later in the week.[51]

The task of getting the Republican presidential ticket to embrace Proposition 209 as unquestioningly as did the platform committee would be more difficult. Or at least it appeared so. Dole's choice for vice president was in step with his summer retreat on affirmative action. Kemp had been one of the Republican leaders who had encouraged retreat, advising that the initiative sent the wrong message. Although Kemp never opposed Proposition 209 specifically, its anti–affirmative action message was at odds with the image of a man who reached out to blacks and Latinos. As early as July 1995, Kemp had warned in an interview with the *Washington Times*, "Our nation needs racial recognition now and healing, not division, and we need to be a party of growth, jobs, and equality of opportunity, not racial division. . . . Theoretically, you could win on a wedge issue like race, but you can't govern" on it.[52]

But a closer look at Kemp's public statements on affirmative action showed that he avoided any attempts to take a clear stand. He reached out to blacks and Latinos, but never so far that he alienated conservatives. His need to please both groups came to the foreground during and after a 1995 summer breakfast hosted by the *Christian Science Monitor*. Kemp attended the breakfast shortly after Dole introduced legislation in the Senate to end federal affirmative action programs.

At the breakfast, Kemp had spoken candidly about his views on affirmative action. The news stories that followed quoted Kemp as having opposed the Republican position on affirmative action. Kemp objected. His remarks, he protested, had been taken out of context. Not so, said Godfrey Sperling, an editor who tape-recorded the conversation at the breakfast.[53] "He clearly was stating his opposition to the GOP position on affirmative action when he told us his party 'would find it hard to govern the country if it runs a campaign that separates people by race and by gender.' And beyond any doubt, he told us he would vote against the position taken by California Governor Pete Wilson when Wilson led the majority of the University of California regents in ending minority preferences in university hiring and admissions."[54]

A month after Sperling's article appeared, Kemp responded in a *Washington Times* op-ed piece.[55] A clarification it was not. There was something in it for everyone—sometimes in the same sentence. "Counting by race in order to remedy past wrongs or rewarding special groups by taking from others perpetuates and even deepens the divisions between us, but race-based politics is even more wrong and must be repudiated by men and women of civility and compassion," Kemp wrote.[56] This kind of obfuscation would not serve Proposition 209 well, Steinberg feared. In the campaign, Kemp would need to defend Proposition 209 on its merits, so Steinberg attempted to appeal to Kemp's intellectual side—the one that liked big ideas.

To do this, he enlisted the help of Thomas L. (Dusty) Rhodes.[57] The former partner at Goldman, Sachs, and Company had taken over the *National Review* from William Rusher in 1992, and, like Rusher, he disliked affirmative action and enjoyed influencing policy. He founded Change-N.Y., an anti-tax group, in 1991 and helped elect George E. Pataki governor of New York in 1994. Unlike many of the other monied men who damned affirmative action, Rhodes had experienced poverty. He looked like the son of a Boston Brahman, but he was actually the child of Welsh blue-collar immigrants. His was the Horatio Alger story: public schools in Spanish Harlem, scholarships into the Ivy League, and, after attainment of a master's degree at the University of Pennsylvania's Wharton School of Business, a lucrative life on Wall Street. His interest in affirmative action seemed to come from his dislike of any government regulation—from taxes to employment reports.

Rhodes wanted Kemp to signal an eventual endorsement of Proposition 209 by highlighting the Fourteenth Amendment in his acceptance speech. The Fourteenth Amendment provided a classic example of the problems inherent when politics and policy collide. The Fourteenth Amendment guarantees "equal protection under the laws" and was ratified in 1868 to counter state laws limiting the civil rights of slaves who had been freed three years earlier. The drafters recognized the disconnect between intent and practice by giving Congress the power to "enforce, by appropriate legislation, the provisions of this article." Essentially, the amendment underscored the government's commitment to ensuring equality to recently freed slaves.

More than a century later, however, whites invoked the Fourteenth Amendment to argue that affirmative action programs violated their right to "equal protection under the laws." Indeed, the Supreme Court decided in its 1978 *Bakke* decision that the university had violated the equal protection clause by establishing two separate committees to review applications—one for whites and one for minorities. But the Court upheld the legitimacy of guaranteeing equal protection while considering race as a factor in admissions. To do this, the university had to have one committee review all the applicants. Race, like geography, could be considered a plus factor, but no slots could be reserved for one group. Up until the 1989 *Croson* decision, the Court strengthened the notion that affirmative action and equal protection were compatible. But *Croson* and the 1995 *Adarand* decisions made the grounds for compatibility more tenuous by cautioning that state and federal affirmative action programs had to meet the test of "strict scrutiny."

This judicial history gave the constitutional doctrine of equal protection meaning, but in politics it could be ignored. Strategists such as Rhodes or anyone else could replace the complex legal history with a cleaner plot line that went like this: The Fourteenth Amendment guarantees equal protection under the law, and affirmative action gives preferences to different groups: ergo affirmative action is unconstitutional.

Delving into the Supreme Court's decisions interpreting the Fourteenth Amendment, however, proved beside the point in San Diego. Kemp didn't need big ideas to support Proposition 209. All he needed was an offer to join Dole's presidential ticket. Just hours before Powell gave his opening night address, Kemp was interviewed by NBC anchor Tom Brokaw. "Are you opposed to 209 or not?" Brokaw asked impatiently after Kemp tried to avoid a direct answer. "I am going to be a supporter of Bob Dole's position on CCRI, the California Civil Rights Initiative," he finally acknowledged. "The usually ebullient Kemp looked as if he had swallowed the new Republican platform whole, which in a sense he had," wrote Richard Cohen.[58]

Kemp later explained that his main problem with the attack on affirmative action—that it failed to offer any new solutions—had been resolved. "With enterprise zones and educational opportunity and access to credit and capital and housing, I think we can say we have a better civil rights initiative than liberals," he said. Many viewed his epiphany with suspicion. "Before he got his bell rung in San Diego, the old Jack Kemp used to believe that it was premature to cut off such aid to victims of historic discrimination without having effective programs to replace them," a *New York Times* editorial noted. "His blithe assurances that he and Mr. Dole will come up with such alternatives defies belief, given the Republican Party's current ideological makeup."[59]

Steinberg was also nervous—but for different reasons. "We had been working with Kemp for over a year. He needed to do this in a principled way, but Dole's people started pressuring him and then he makes a total reversal, and then the way he does it makes it seem like he cut a deal, like he was going to support Dole's position on 209 because he wanted to be part of the ticket."[60] Steinberg understood that this could mean trouble on the campaign trail. Connerly, however, believed that the conversion was genuine. "It has been an evolution in his thinking," he explained with obvious delight.[61]

Kemp's conversion had so lifted Connerly's spirits that he got over his disappointment at not being asked to address the convention to speak against affirmative action and sat in the audience to listen to Powell endorse it. "It is our party, the party of Lincoln, that must always stand for equal rights and fair opportunity for all," Powell declared on Monday night. "And where discrimination still exists, or where the scars of past discrimination still contaminate and disfigure the present, we must not close our eyes to it, declare there is a level playing field, and hope that it will go away by itself." If that wasn't an explicit enough support of affirmative action, later in the speech he made it perfectly clear: "You all know that I believe in a woman's right to choose, and I strongly support affirmative action."

Connerly had previously threatened a walkout during Powell's speech and published a blistering open letter to the ex-general that appeared in the *San Diego Union Tribune* during the convention. Having received Kemp's endorsement, Connerly's attitude toward Powell had brightened noticeably: "It was one of the greatest speeches I've ever heard. I was the first one up on my feet."[62] Connerly explained that Powell's support of affirmative action was unimportant: "He did not make any reference at all to Proposition 209. That was my overriding concern."

Kemp's speech on Thursday night failed to mention the Fourteenth Amendment or lay the groundwork for using affirmative action in the campaign. Instead, Dole made the case in his acceptance speech. "He had help from a lot of people,"

Steinberg said, referring to others who helped Dole write his speech.[63]

In his acceptance speech, Dole referred to Lincoln, not only in calling for an inclusive party, as Kemp and Powell had done, but also in criticizing multiculturalism. "Though I can only look up, and at a very steep angle, to Washington and Lincoln, let me remind you of their concern for the sometimes delicate unity of the people," he said. "The notion that we are and should be one people rather than 'peoples' of the United States seems so self-evident and obvious that it is hard for me to imagine that I must defend it. . . . When the blood of the sons of the immigrants and the grandsons of slaves fell on foreign fields, it was American blood. In it, you could not read the ethnic particulars of the soldier who died next to you. He was an American. And when I think of how we learned this lesson, I wonder how we could have unlearned it." He called on "every American to rise above all that may divide us and to defend the unity of the nation for the honor of generations past and the sake of those to come."[64]

Having set the stage, Dole then moved to the language of the Fourteenth Amendment, implicitly calling for an end to the use of race and gender in hiring and education. "The Constitution of the United States mandates equal protection under the law. This is not code language for racism, it is plain speaking against it. And the guiding light of my administration will be that in this country we have not rank order by birth, no claim to favoritism by race, no expectation of judgment other than it be evenhanded. And we cannot guarantee the outcome, but we shall guarantee the opportunity in America."

At the end of the convention, leery of any fight over affirmative action, Kemp tried to soften the message. "Whatever we do in California," he said, "I promise you Bob Dole and Jack Kemp are not going to be divisive, we are not going to use wedge issues."[65] But that would prove a difficult promise to keep.

5

Feminists, Minorities, and the Democratic Party

Democrats Search for a New Identity Politics

> Our challenge is twofold, first to explore the
> American dream of opportunity and the American
> value of responsibility; and second, to bring our
> country together amid all our diversity in a stronger
> community, so that we can find common ground
> and move forward as one.
>
> PRESIDENT BILL CLINTON
> *July 1995, in his major policy*
> *address on affirmative action*

The Northern California Coalition's failure at the end of 1995 to put its alternative Equal Opportunity Without Quotas initiative on the ballot was equivalent to watching a carefully constructed house of cards collapse. The opposition in the north had taken a vow of pragmatism in their battle to save affirmative action, and when the polls told them that the only way to beat CCRI was to put a competing initiative on the ballot— already a proven tactic in California's initiative wars[1]—they held to that promise. A team of lawyers spent much of 1995 drafting an initiative, and it was clever. It took advantage of what the polls showed voters wanted but in fact offered what was already the law of the land: equal opportunity and no quotas. It didn't matter to the electorate. Voters liked it better than CCRI, according to the opposition's polls.[2]

But the tactic proved to be *too* clever. The state legislative analyst concluded that the alternative initiative would end education programs designed for minorities—programs the analyst interpreted as having quotas. By then it was too late for the northern coalition to file a lawsuit contesting the analyst's interpretation of quotas, and it was too late to rewrite the initiative that they had thought harmless. So the northern coalition dropped it, and as David Oppenheimer, the law professor who had worked long hours to draft the alternative, put it, they promised "to continue to fight the good fight." But the defeat of the alternative was still too fresh, and no one was sure what to do next.

To decide, more than three dozen coalition members and activists met in the conference room of the ACLU's San Francisco office on Mission Street on January 26, 1996.[3] Aleita Huguenin, the manager of governmental relations for the California Teachers Association, reported first. The news wasn't good. After being off the streets for three weeks because they lacked funds, CCRI's advocates were again collecting signatures. And they were paying top dollar. Thanks to the nearly half a million dollars pumped into CCRI by Governor Pete Wilson's fund raising, workers were earning $1 a signature.[4] "Suddenly, they are all over," Jan Adams, the grassroots organizer for Californians for Justice, reported. The group slumped collectively.

Then David Salniker, a lawyer, offered a suggestion. Jerome Karabel, the U.C. Berkeley professor who had helped with polling and strategy for the alternative initiative, had raised the issue of sending out so-called bigot busters to trip up the CCRI signature gatherers. In lay terms, the tactic was known as voter education: A team of people, well versed on affirmative action, would go to the places where CCRI backers were gathering signatures and attempt to educate voters about the petition they were being asked to sign. Adams and Rebecca

Gordon, a financial consultant to nonprofits, had suggested such a strategy much earlier in the campaign, but the statewide campaign officials never acted on their proposal. Now was the chance. If effective, the tactic could prevent CCRI from collecting enough signatures to get on the ballot. Huguenin's CTA had almost ambushed the signature-gathering effort for the school voucher initiative in 1994 in this way. If the opposition were to do this against CCRI, they had to act fast. CCRI's deadline was February 21.

Unknown to the coalition members, this was just the maneuver that worried CCRI's signature gatherer, American Petition Consultants. They were further behind than most knew. Not only had they lost time off the streets, but the rainy season had started, making it more difficult for the signature gatherers working outside grocery stores and along commercial strips to persuade people to stop and sign petitions. In truth, the prospect of reaching the goal of one million signatures was looking worse than it had for any signature drive managed by Bill and Michael Arno, the brothers who owned American Petition Consultants.[5] The last thing they needed was to have the opposition out on the streets, discouraging people from signing. "We would have been screwed," said Bill Arno.[6] "We were very worried about an harassment campaign."

Unaware of CCRI's precarious situation and discouraged by the news of its new deep pockets, the opposition gave short shrift to the proposal for "bigot busters." "We came close to blocking a petition, but it took six months of advance work," said Huguenin, referring to her union's efforts to stop the school voucher initiative. "It's just not something most people feel comfortable doing. You have to train them." Adams agreed, adding that it would take lots of money to get up to speed. No one appeared interested. In less than ten minutes an opportunity had been lost. The meeting moved on to discuss press conferences, the message the group was going to convey, and how it could work with the coalition in the south.

Efforts there were moving at a decidedly different tempo. The Feminist Majority's Third Avenue offices on the edge of Beverly Hills had been the south's war room for almost a year. The place buzzed. Katherine Spillar, the Feminist Majority's national director, was spending nearly all of her time on the campaign to defeat CCRI. Connie Rice, Western Regional Counsel for the NAACP Legal Defense and Education Fund, and Molly Munger, also a regional counsel with the fund, were there whenever work permitted. Peg Yorkin, the co-founder of the Feminist Majority, was always ready to help, as were Ellie Smeal, the president of the Feminist Majority, Patricia Ireland, the president of the National Organization for Women, and their newest friend, Lorraine Sheinberg.

These were the kind of women others noticed. When they met at a restaurant to drink coffee and plan, they radiated energy. "Three different men came up to a group of us at a table one day," Rice recalled, "and made comments like 'Whoa, something is going on.'"[7] And it was. When the new year rolled in, Spillar and the others had a master plan to defeat CCRI: a $5 million advertising campaign aimed primarily at drumming home CCRI's impact on women, a grassroots get-out-the-vote campaign to mobilize minority voters and a massive education campaign. The latter had already been launched by nonprofit educational organizations such as the Mexican-American Legal Defense and Education Fund and the Equal Rights Advocates.

The campaign's task was daunting. The numbers varied according to who did the calculations, but the estimate the coalition used in early 1996 looked like this: To defeat CCRI, the opposition needed the votes of 25 percent of white males, 60 percent of white women, 70 percent of African Americans, and 60 percent of Latinos. Recognizing the need to court women, the coalition in the south had already begun reframing the debate.

When CCRI first began making news, political writers focused on the race issue—what the initiative would take away from blacks, Latinos, and other minorities. By early 1996, however, the women's groups had been able to turn media attention to the impact that CCRI would have on women. They did this by talking about Clause C of CCRI to anyone who would listen. Clause C reads, "Nothing in this section shall be interpreted as prohibiting bona fide qualifications based on sex which are reasonably necessary to the normal operation of public employment, public education, or public contracting." In op-ed pieces and press conferences, the women's groups began referring to the thirty-one-word sentence as the "stealth" clause, one that would extinguish women's legal protection against discrimination so that even the right to maternity leave would be eliminated.

Poppycock, said CCRI's proponents, but they were worried. The focus on Clause C was beginning to turn the public's attention from race to gender—a development that could broaden the opposition's base significantly. When NBC featured the opposition to CCRI on a nightly news broadcast, it hardly mentioned race. Instead it highlighted Spillar and women business owners. Arnold Steinberg, the campaign manager for CCRI, warned his colleagues. "We consider Clause C the focal point of the attack on CCRI. . . .We recognize ultimately the campaign for CCRI could lose if the opposition could use Clause C to impeach the message of the initiative. . . . We cannot give an inch on this issue," CCRI's campaign plan concluded.[8] In another section Steinberg wrote, "The opposition will try to turn attention from race to gender, in an attempt to appeal to the largely white electorate, especially females. In turn, we would rather, in the limited attention span afforded by a campaign, focus on race, than gender."

Despite Steinberg's concerns, the opposition recognized that women had yet to be convinced to vote against CCRI. Polls showed that many women failed to link their professional success to affirmative action, and others believed the programs actually diminished job prospects for their husbands and sons. What's more, the women's groups were accustomed to fighting battles in which they already held the edge in public opinion. "Since the mid-60s, we've had a majority on our issues and it's just a matter of mobilizing our supporters," said Patricia Ireland, president of the National Organization for Women. "On this issue we are leading, not following public opinion."[9] The women's groups had not yet figured out if it was possible to make women accept what NOW and the Feminist Majority believed—that if CCRI was approved, women had a lot to lose.

The narrowness of a campaign based on women worried Karabel, the U.C. professor who had analyzed reams of polling data. For this strategy to work, "we would need a huge gender gap," Karabel said. "That would be astonishing. Some in the opposition have a gut level feeling that women will come to see that affirmative action is as much about gender as race—that will be the first time. It's not enough that there are interests at stake and that these interests will be trampled on; what we need to do is to move beyond the civil rights and the feminist groups to include labor and the Democrats."

Karabel's reservations were shared by others. But in early 1996 Karabel and others up north were not yet at the table with their counterparts in the south. And this split was uppermost in everyone's mind.

The first priority of the opposition campaign in early 1996 became what would later be described as "the forced marriage" between north and south. The merger was dicey. Feelings had been hurt. Spillar, confident and determined, had delivered many of the barbs. She was an unlikely conciliator, and everyone agreed it would be best to hire a professional to run the statewide campaign. Robert Shrum, a Washington political consultant who had long worked for Democrats and who had already volunteered to run the media campaign, recommended Patricia Ewing. A thirty-four-year-old graduate of the University of Delaware, Ewing had been running candidate campaigns for more than a decade.

Ewing interviewed with Spillar, Smeal, and others, and by the end of February she was on board. With the blessing of the women who had hired her, Ewing set off to reconcile with the north. She traveled up the California coast to visit with the exiled members: Eva Paterson, with the San Francisco Lawyers Committee for Civil Rights; Dorothy Erlich, director of the San Francisco office of the ACLU; Hari Dillon, of the Vanguard Foundation; and others, including advisors such as Oppenheimer and Karabel. By April Ewing had negotiated a reconciliation.

One of the first requests made by the new members of the coalition was to restart the process of hiring a campaign manager. Ewing was likely to be in the mix, but many in the north felt it would be wise to consider other options. Smeal and Spillar refused, and Paterson and others backed down. With the benefit of hindsight, it was a decision many would regret.

Ewing stayed, and by May she had moved the campaign out of the Feminist Majority's offices and into the low-rent section of Beverly Boulevard in Los Angeles. A young man with a knitted cap on his head and gold rings through his ear answered the phones, and a poster of Rosie the Riveter—"We Can Do It!"—was nailed to the wall. Ewing, dressed in a black leotard and jeans, was not so sure. Her misgivings came from the immediate: her problems in bringing the numerous egos in the statewide coalition together to raise money and come up with a message.

Coalition Politics, or the Road to Hell

In May the Feminist Majority and NOW dominated the twelve-member board of what was then called "Women Won't Go Back: The Campaign to Save Women's Rights & Civil Rights." It was flush with big donors. In addition to Yorkin, who had given $10 million to the Feminist Fund in 1991, it included Lorraine Sheinberg, who ranked thirty-fifth among Hollywood political contributors—(thirty places below her husband,

Sidney Sheinberg, a former MCA chairman), and Carol Leif, the daughter of former MCA chairman Lew Wasserman.[10] Early on some believed that Yorkin and her Hollywood connections would provide the bulk of the cash needed to beat CCRI. Indeed, Mayor Willie Brown told some of the coalition members in the north that he expected as much.

The money, however, wasn't immediately forthcoming. Most of what Yorkin and Sheinberg had given by May consisted of "in-kind" contributions of staff and office space. Yorkin said she had made it clear from the outset that she would not bankroll the campaign. And as she watched Ewing in action, she became increasingly disturbed. No campaign plan materialized. No direct marketing plan was started. Instead, Ewing turned on the women who had hired her. She complained that Spillar's constant requests for information were beginning to feel like harassment. Feminist Majority staffers on loan to Ewing reported that Ewing was spending most of her time on the telephone badmouthing Spillar, the Feminist Majority, and NOW. Handwritten signs began to appear on the walls at the campaign's headquarters. "The road to hell is paved with feminists," one of them read.

"There was nothing in the nature of the campaign that should have created the types of tensions that materialized in three weeks," said Patty Bellasalma, the director of research, who was on loan to Ewing from the Feminist Majority. "She came up to me and said she didn't realize how hated Kathy Spillar was, and that's just not the case. Ewing had no idea who the players were, but she quickly decided that the Feminist Majority, the leader of the campaign, and its main financial contributor had to be eliminated." Although coalition members may have had their differences with Spillar, they credited her with taking the lead when no one else was focused. Moreover, they worried that Ewing might alienate Yorkin and Sheinberg. The worry was well placed.

Yorkin had wanted her contributions to be the seed money to attract the really big money. But as Yorkin became more frustrated with Ewing's lack of fund raising and tired of the attacks on Spillar, she became less willing to write any checks at all. Moreover, she was unhappy with the lack of progress on a campaign plan. Yorkin was a multimillionaire who tried to get the biggest bang for her buck. She didn't just write checks; she investigated to make sure the money was well used. What she saw on Ewing's ledger did not make her happy. "All the money was going to payroll," she said.[11] "The reason I didn't put more money into it than I did was that the payroll was so large."

Despite her inability to raise funds elsewhere, Ewing was unconcerned about the increasing coolness from Yorkin and Sheinberg. In fact, everything the women's groups did irritated Ewing. They liked media events; she hated them. "This is a factor of being bomb throwers and never working from inside," said Ewing.[12] Typical of how Ewing differed with the Feminist Majority and NOW was her reaction to NOW's national "Fight the Right" rally in San Francisco in March 1996. The women's groups liked such events because they highlighted an issue for donors and brought them new volunteers. Months later, Ewing cringed when reminded of the rally. "It hurt us," she said.[13] To Ewing, it diverted energy from the coalition's main task of raising money, and it put an us-against-them spin on the campaign. "The NOW march created an environment in which [women] have an enemy," Ewing said. "It doesn't make mainstream Democrats look at the issue again." Ewing was equally unhappy with the Feminist Majority's plans for a "Freedom Summer," in which young college students were being recruited to travel to California to campaign against CCRI and join a bus tour with Jesse Jackson, Ellie Smeal, and Patricia Ireland. "Talk about people who are talking to themselves," she said. By summer, Ewing was sick of feminists. "They wake up every morning hating men," she said.[14]

But most disturbing of all, Ewing said, was the time she was squandering on coalition politics. Nonetheless, Ewing took seriously her role in the drama, which one member referred to as "the cat fight in the sky." "They have all done battles for the last 20 years and they like or don't like one another based on how they have treated one another," Ewing said.[15] "There are a lot of egos and I have to build trust so that I can count on them in October when it really counts." But it was unclear if there would be any campaign in October if she failed to raise money. By September Ewing had already lowered the campaign's goal to $2 million from $5 million.

"The air power is television," said Ellie Smeal, the president of the Feminist Majority. "Television can bring us close, and then the grassroots troops can go in for the cleanup, but we need money to do ads." And the money wasn't coming in. "It's much worse than I ever thought," said Smeal. "It's like raising money for abortion in 1979–80, and I know how bad that was."[16]

Others were concerned as well. Munger, Rice, Spillar, and allies up north such as Eva Paterson at the Lawyers' Committee for Civil Rights worked the phones. Munger put in $25,000 of her own money and raised another $100,000 through her corporate legal connections, but she became frustrated with the lack of a plan. "We needed to take advantage of the enormous amount of time available at the outset to focus on fund raising, but instead it got down to an internecine focus," Munger said.[17] She and others wanted to see a fund-raising plan that put rainmakers on the phone.

Paterson said she watched Ewing try to assemble a high-powered fund-raising committee, but no one stepped forward. "People thought this was a loser," Paterson said.[18] It didn't help, she added, to have the governor browbeating corporations and big donors to stay away. Nor did it help to have President Clinton virtually ignoring the campaign on his visits to California. State Democratic officials, who often make such fund-raising calls, knew that Proposition 209 wasn't a priority with the president or the party, and so most never called in their chits with their big supporters. Louis Caldera, a Democratic assemblyman from Los Angeles, said that assembly Democrats who made calls to raise funds to defeat Proposition 187 in 1994 were not making calls to defeat CCRI. And why should they, he asked. "The issue is a loser for Democrats; there's no money in it for us or the assembly and no credit to be taken."[19]

One minority businessman who had given generously to the campaign to defeat Proposition 187 in 1994 and had donated $10,000 to the Clinton-Gore campaign in 1996 said he never got a phone call on Proposition 209. "This is the season," he said as the election approached. "I'm getting calls from everyone and I only give to those who call." There was, he said, nothing subtle about the approach politicians used to get their favorite projects funded. "We got a call from Gloria Molina on 187, and we couldn't get the check over there fast enough; and on Clinton-Gore, Willie Brown got on the phone, told us exactly how much he needed, and we sent it by messenger." [20]

None of the fund raisers Ewing hired seemed to have the magic Rolodex either. To change her luck, she placed a Mexican votive candle in the office and lit it.

One Step Forward, Two Steps Back

The opposition's one big break came in late spring after Connie Rice began a letter-writing campaign. The opponents to CCRI needed firepower, and Rice began to focus on the only American politician able to deliver it: retired general Colin Powell.[21] When he actually replied to her first letter, the women were ecstatic. Not only had he not rejected Rice's request for help, "he said he was interested in her work," said one of her coalition colleagues. Rice and her boss, Elaine Jones, set up a meeting with Powell at his Virginia home.

When she was growing up, Rice had watched her father, an Air Force colonel, prepare final reports. He used a blue binder, dividers, and a razor-sharp outline. Rice remembered this as she prepared for her meeting with Powell. When the retired general greeted Rice and Jones at his house, Rice was armed with her blue binder and an icebreaker: She brought greetings from her cousin, Condoleezza Rice, provost of Stanford University and a friend of Powell from her days on the National Security Staff, when Powell worked as President Ronald Reagan's advisor. Powell made no promises to Rice and Jones. But less than a month later he gave a speech at Maryland's Bowie State, in which, for the first time, he explicitly condemned the "misguided" efforts of Proposition 209's promoters.

Powell's speech and Dole's increasing gender gap slowed the Republican nominee's attack—never more than lukewarm at best—on affirmative action. Even some California Republicans were advising against a political campaign that stressed the party's opposition to affirmative action. The political dynamic had changed everywhere—everywhere, that is, but Sacramento. There Governor Wilson was still in charge, and in the summer he reminded the opposition what that meant. Republican Attorney General Dan Lungren's office was busy attending to the ballot summaries that would explain to California's fifteen million voters the twelve initiatives on the November ballot. The one-hundred-word title and summary represented the sum total of what many voters read about an initiative. If they want to know more, they could flip through the thick voter pamphlet for the legislative analyst's full report and arguments and rebuttals from both proponents and opponents. The summary, however, set the tone, and most Californians cast their ballots without looking beyond it.

It was through the summary that the opposition wanted voters to understand that Proposition 209 would end most of the state's affirmative action programs. The legislative analyst's report had concluded as much, and the initiative's authors had said so publicly. The opposition believed that the summary would contain this clarification because state law requires the attorney general to be impartial. To avoid a conflict of interest, the legislature prohibits an attorney general from writing the summary if the official is also the initiative's "promoter" or author. It does not, however, prevent the attorney general from writing the summary and also acting as an advocate of the initiative or an "agent of the promoter." Lungren fell into this category. Like Governor Wilson, he strongly believed in the principles endorsed by Proposition 209 and had spoken often and candidly about his position. In fact, he signed the ballot pamphlet's rebuttal to the argument against the initiative.

When Lungren issued the required summary in July, the opposition went ballistic. Just as the earlier title and summary failed to mention affirmative action, nowhere did the summary inform voters that the initiative would have any impact on affirmative action. Instead it mirrored the initiative's language, stating that CCRI would prohibit local and state government entities from "discriminating against or giving preferential treatment" based on race, sex, ethnicity, or national origin. This was devastating to the opposition, because although polls showed that voters hated preferences, they were friendlier toward affirmative action.

The opposition campaign took Lungren to court. On August 1 Sacramento County Superior Court Judge James T. Ford ordered the attorney general to rewrite the ballot language because the omission of "affirmative action" was misleading to voters. "The court is satisfied by clear and convincing evidence that the attorney general has not fully stated the main purpose and the chief point of the initiative," Ford said. "The determination by this court is that the chief purpose of this initiative is to effect change with respect to affirmative action programs in the state of California." Lungren's office immediately appealed the decision. In a unanimous decision, the Third District Court of Appeal in Sacramento stayed Ford's order.

"The title and summary inform the public of the general purpose of the measure," wrote presiding justice Robert K. Puglia. "The title and summary need not contain a complete catalogue or index of all the measure's provisions and if reasonable minds may differ as to the sufficiency of the title, the title should be held sufficient." Puglia decided that "affirmative action" was an ill-defined concept: "Even if we assume that much, most of all of the impact of the prohibition will be borne by programs commonly associated with the term 'affirmative action,' we cannot fault the Attorney General for refraining from the use of such an amorphous, value-laden term from the ballot title and the ballot label."

If Ewing felt crushed, CCRI's campaign manager, Arnie Steinberg, was euphoric. On the same page of the campaign plan where he wrote about Proposition 209's conundrum—that "most affirmative action programs *do* include discrimination and preferences" and would therefore be outlawed by Proposition 209—he demonstrated graphically why he advised against an attack on affirmative action. "Notice the results for these two successive questions," he wrote in bold letters. When Steinberg polled voters in April 1996 and read CCRI's language using the reference to preferences, it won 72 percent support, but when he asked how many would vote yes because "it will end affirmative action programs that use quotas and set-asides based on race and gender," support plummeted to 45 percent.[22]

Clinton and Affirmative Action

In a presidential election year money, issues, and the strategy of every other campaign are affected by the sweep and power of that reelection effort. Just as Ward Connerly and his campaign to end race and gender preferences would get caught up in the dynamics of the Republican primaries and the Dole-Kemp ticket, Ewing and the opponents of CCRI could not escape the impact of Clinton-Gore: Their efforts could be energized by the ticket's popularity or dulled by its rejection. And their fund-raising capabilities could be enhanced by a nod from the right Clinton-Gore operative, or they could be diminished by disapproval or silence.

Clinton's reelection effort and the opposition to CCRI began at different points. Women's rights and civil rights leaders were determined to defend affirmative action. Clinton, weakened after his party's loss in the mid-term elections, was just as determined to depoliticize it. George Stephanopoulos, Clinton's senior advisor, recalled that in March 1995, the White House feared the issue would "race through America."[23] That was an alarming prospect. If Democrats had learned anything in the last thirty years, it was that playing the race card worked well in electoral politics—but it worked against them.[24] No one understood this better than Clinton.

Until 1964 blacks considered neither political party an ally; the odds of getting help from either were poor. Then, in 1964, the Republicans nominated Senator Barry Goldwater as their candidate. Goldwater had voted against the Civil Rights Act of 1964, and his opponent, Lyndon Johnson, had championed it. Neither Johnson nor Goldwater campaigned much on the issue of civil rights; a discussion of war and peace dominated the campaign.[25] Nonetheless, their respective votes on the Civil Rights Act became symbolic of where their parties stood, and the election marked a turning point in how blacks and working-class whites viewed the two political parties.[26] The election also provided a platform for Governor George Wallace of Alabama, on which he demonstrated how to use race to attract northern voters. Running in the 1964 primaries in the north and then in a full campaign in 1968, he talked about states' rights and law and order. "Wallace provided the Republican party with tools for reaching Democratic working-class voters," wrote Thomas and Mary Edsall in their 1991 book, *Chain Reaction.* "Wallace's conservative populism, his conceptualization of a privileged, coercive liberal Democratic establishment, and his redefinition of racial conflict—painting the opponents of integration as victims of an overbearing, dictatorial, and arbitrary central government—proved essential to the building of a new, conservative Republican presidential majority."[27]

Increasingly, blacks saw allies in Democratic presidential candidates, who favored poverty programs and civil rights legislation, while working-class whites, once safe Democratic constituencies, saw a new enemy. Stanley B. Greenberg, a pollster for the Democratic Party who would later work for Clinton, traveled to Macomb County in the mid-1980s to help the Michigan Democratic Party understand why the Detroit suburb's white working-class residents were fast abandoning the party. By 1984 Macomb's residents—many of them autoworkers and many of them Catholic—had become the archetypal Reagan Democrats. Greenberg concluded they made this change because they believed the Democrats no longer cared about them—the white working class.

> Many sensed that the federal government itself had come down directly and personally to block these workers' opportunities. This was not an abstract or an analytic position; it was a deeply felt personal slight that shaped the individuals' whole perception of the government. One of the union men failed to get a business loan because, he reported, "I was an average American white guy," and his views resonated through the group.
>
> The federal government that had once helped create their world was now wholly biased against them. For the men, particularly those over thirty, the feeling took on a special intensity. When asked who got a "raw deal" in this country, they responded successively and ever more directly: "It's the white people"—"white, American middle-class male."[28]

Like-minded Democrats wanting to recapture these voters formed the Democratic Leadership Council in the mid-1980s. Clinton was one of its board members and its most formidable leader. Most important, Clinton's history with the civil rights community gave him the credibility that allowed him to reach out to the white working class. His credentials were good. His grandfather had run a store in Arkansas that gave credit to blacks; Eva Paterson's grandfather was one of them. David Maraniss noted in his biography, *First in His Class,* that as governor of Arkansas, Clinton appointed more blacks to state boards and commissions than had all previous Arkansas governors combined.[29] A southerner, Clinton felt comfortable with blacks and he understood their history. Martin Luther King, Jr., was his hero. But Clinton also had a certain appreciation for the political longevity of Arkansas Governor Orval Faubus, an unabashed protector of segregation.

Clinton began to transform Democratic politics with new language. In contrast to Lyndon Johnson's call for a Great Society and an appeal to Americans to help those less fortunate because it was right, Clinton talked of personal responsibility, the middle class, and empowerment. The Democratic Leadership Council's 1990 manifesto, the New Orleans Declaration, offered a revised yin and yang between government and citizens. The DLC's version of government promised "equal opportunity, not equal outcomes." It would protect civil rights to move minorities "into America's economic and cultural mainstream," but not "race, gender, or ethnic separatism." The Democratic Party's mission would be "to expand opportunity, not government."[30]

It was a message that Clinton was unafraid to take to blacks and whites. "I'll give you your values back, I'll restore the economic leadership, I'll help you build the middle class back," Clinton told the white suburban voters of Macomb County in 1992. "But in turn, you've got to say: Okay, let's do it with everybody in this country."[31] The following morning Clinton talked to black voters in Detroit: "I went to Macomb County in Michigan and I said something politicians don't normally say in Macomb County: I said I want your votes to come home to the Democratic Party. . . . I want to tell you that we didn't do right by middle America for awhile, but I have a program that will restore the middle class, without regard to race." This was the language of unity, and it worked. In 1992 Clinton began to reclaim Macomb County and its Reagan Democrats. After giving Ronald Reagan 53 percent of the vote in 1980 and nearly 70 percent in 1984, Macomb's residents handed George Bush only 43 percent of the vote in 1992.[32]

This history of balancing white and black interests served Clinton well in devising a strategy after his party lost the 1994 mid-term elections, and some Republican strategists and politicians began looking at affirmative action—a linchpin of civil rights—as the issue that could return Reagan Democrats to the Republican Party and clinch the 1996 presidential election. Although civil rights and women's rights leaders played a significant role in persuading Clinton to stand by affirmative action, he had only to look for guidance to his own success in muting racial politics. In some ways Clinton's approach to the angry white males who emerged as a Republican voting bloc in 1994 was the same one that any dime-store psychologist would recommend: Instead of condemning them as selfish or racist, he acknowledged their pain. He defended affirmative action, but with a different tone.

Clinton's July 1995 televised speech on civil rights was an example of his ability to defend the importance of civil rights programs while reaching out to those who disagreed. He began by putting the challenge of equal opportunity in a context that echoed the DLC's New Orleans Declaration: "Our challenge is twofold: first to restore the American dream of opportunity and the American value of responsibility; and second, to bring our country together amid all our diversity in a stronger community, so that we can find common ground and move forward as one."[33]

He then gave his audience a history lesson on how affirmative action developed—with bipartisan support—and where it failed—with quotas that were deemed unfair and unlawful. The advances made by minorities and women, he said, indicated to some that affirmative action was no longer needed. With regard to this conclusion, he asked Americans to consider the facts: an unemployment rate for African Americans that remained twice that of whites, and the findings of the Republican-sponsored Glass Ceiling Report showing that 95 percent of the senior management positions in the nation's largest companies were held by white males. But even in defending affirmative action, Clinton carefully avoided a pitched battle.

"Some question the fundamental purpose of the effort," he said, referring to affirmative action. "There are people who honestly believe that affirmative action always amounts to group preferences over individual merit, that affirmative action always leads to reverse discrimination, that ultimately, therefore, it demeans those who benefit from it and discriminates against those who are not helped by it. I just have to tell you that all of you have to decide how you feel about that, and all of our fellow countrymen and women have to decide as well. But I believe if there are no quotas, if we give no opportunities to unqualified people, if we have no reverse discrimination, and if, when the problem ends, the program ends, that criticism is wrong. That's what I believe. But we should have this debate and everyone should ask the question."[34]

In fact, Clinton made it clear that he was more interested in muting this debate than in amplifying it. "Affirmative action has not always been perfect, and affirmative action should not go on forever. It should be changed now to take care of those things that are wrong and it should be retired when its job is done. I am resolved that day will come. But the evidence suggests, indeed, screams that that day has not come. . . . So here is what I think we should do. . . . We should have a simple slogan: Amend it, but don't end it."[35]

By refusing to stand in complete opposition to the fears of the white middle class, Clinton left the door open. Most important in terms of the upcoming election, he didn't alienate opponents to affirmative action or challenge them to a duel that history strongly suggested he would lose. Unlike Dole, who appeared uncomfortable as he campaigned in 1995 and 1996 with his new stance against affirmative action, Clinton was eminently at ease with his. But that was cold comfort to the opponents of CCRI.

Spinning Wheels

Clinton had the luxury of concentrating on winning over white males because he had already charmed their wives; his gender gap with Senator Dole was growing. Moreover, he could count on blacks and Latinos. Civil rights and women's rights leaders, however, had no reliable base when it came to defeating CCRI. June polls showed that white women were not yet buying the argument that Clause C meant a return to the stone age or even to the kitchen.[36]

Even minority communities could not yet be counted on to vote against Proposition 209. Confused by the language of the California Civil Rights Initiative, a majority of L.A.'s residents were still ready to support it, according to a June *Los Angeles Times* poll. It showed that in the city of Los Angeles—where blacks and Latinos make up the majority of the population— 69 percent of the voters supported Proposition 209, including 56 percent of the blacks who were polled and 68 percent of the Hispanics.[37] "We had to reverse those numbers," Rice recalled.[38] All the polls showed that Proposition 209 would win, but for it to win among minorities would deal a devastating blow to civil rights advocates. "My boss told me just make sure that the black and Latino community doesn't vote for this thing," Rice said. "We didn't go into this thinking we could win, but if minorities voted for it, it would have created a civil rights emergency."[39]

Trying to figure out how to rally women and minorities, as well as the swing voters the opposition needed to win, would have stirred debate no matter what the internal relations. But by midsummer, the opposition to Proposition 209 was at wit's end. Ewing was rarely speaking to anyone from the women's groups, and the women were digging in their heels. Earlier in the year Diane Feldman and Louis Harris had been hired to do more polling to find the right message, but board members disagreed on their findings. The conference calls became increasingly contentious. "You'd have Harris saying one thing,

Feldman arguing for another, and Ewing trying to manage both," said one participant.[40] "It was wild." Bob Shrum, the media advisor, recalled "endless conference calls that got very theological about the content of the message."[41]

The differences were apparent in the confidential analyses Harris and Feldman each prepared on the same poll. "When asked about 'affirmative action programs which ensure equal opportunity for women,' a substantial 69 percent to 26 percent majority of voters statewide come down in favor," Harris wrote, reiterating the poll's findings. "Perhaps even more significant, on the presumably far more difficult 'affirmative action programs to ensure equal opportunity for minorities' a solid 61 percent to 32 percent majority favors such a law. However, it should be pointed out that when asked if they favor or oppose 'affirmative action,' without any other qualifying clauses, a narrower 50 percent to 37 percent plurality supports affirmative action. A substantial 11 to 19 points are added to the pro–affirmative action column when the key words 'programs to ensure equal opportunity' are amended to explain what affirmative action means. The lesson from this series on affirmative action is that whenever the connection is made between affirmative action and efforts to 'ensure equal opportunity,' support for affirmative action takes off."

The problem, Harris found, was that "a majority of 59 percent do not yet make the connection between passage of CCRI and a weakening and ultimate ending of affirmative action for women and minorities. Only 41 percent of the state's voters believe 'if passed, CCRI will end affirmative action in California.'" The measure, read without qualification, enjoyed a resounding 70 percent majority.

"The gender gap is real and must be the major concentration of this campaign," Harris concluded. "With women it will be effective to emphasize the truth that high on the priority list of the extreme right are plans to cut back on and even wipe out choice on abortion and measures to weaken and ultimately to wipe out affirmative action programs."[42]

Harris concluded that for the opposition to win, 57 percent of all women had to vote no on Proposition 209 including 50 percent of all white women. Overall, Harris believed that with a well-financed and well-orchestrated campaign, 48 percent of whites would vote no, along with 69 percent of all blacks and 60 percent of Latinos.

Women, he concluded, were worried that "a woman's choice on abortion is threatened," and that 75 percent of all women support "affirmative action programs which ensure equal opportunity for women." Accordingly, Harris concluded:

> The basic campaign theme becomes this: We will not let it happen. We will not allow America to turn its back on giving women the right to choose in the case of abortion. Adoption of the Republican plank on abortion will criminalize abortions. We will not allow California to turn its back on giving women and minorities the chance to achieve equal opportunity through affirmative action programs. Prop 209 will do that. Stop Gingrich, Buchanan, and Wilson from getting away with it. Vote 'no' on Prop 209.[43]

Feldman's analysis of the same data was decidedly less focused on women:

> The campaign's message must be disciplined because it needs to run through an opening between voters' doubts about an initiative which harms the value of equal opportunity. The message must reach a broad audience because the campaign is unlikely to dominate in any demographic group (with the possible exception of African-Americans). There is a gender gap in the ultimate opposition to CCRI, and women are the campaign's principal target. Nonetheless, the campaign is unlikely to win without some broad scale and across-the-board movement because the predictable movement among women is not sufficient to defeat the initiative. . . .

Ultimately, the campaign's persuasion materials must include three elements of message: (1) the value of equal opportunity; (2) the argument that the initiative goes too far by wiping out programs designed to ensure equal opportunity for women and minorities like outreach and tutoring programs; and (3) the consequence that the initiative will lead to further division among people of different races and ethnic groups. If the campaign can establish that the initiative goes too far, it can then add that it eliminates protections for women. Voters do not now believe the consequences of the initiative's Clause C. . . . Voters support affirmative action to the extent that it is about ensuring equal opportunity for women and minorities. Equal opportunity is the value to which they subscribe; the programmatic elements of affirmative action are suspect to them. Then, just 50 percent of voters favor affirmative action, but support climbs above 60 percent when affirmative action is linked with equal opportunity for either women or minorities.

Rather than linking Proposition 209 to efforts to end a woman's right to choose, Feldman recommended moderation.

Fundamentally, the arguments that move voters most are about moderation. Language like "goes too far," "mend it don't end it," and "we are not where we have got to be" are each more convincing than language about trickery or conspiracy. . . .The most credible and negative consequences of the initiative are elimination of outreach and tutoring programs, and racial divisiveness. Voters' tentativeness on affirmative action means that the elimination of affirmative action programs cannot stand alone as the principal consequence of the initiative. Some of the consequences that are least acceptable to voters are

also not credible, and the campaign will not sound
like the voice of moderation if it makes claims voters
view as incredible. The elimination of tutoring and
outreach programs are both undesirable and believ-
able consequences of the initiative.

The least credible of the consequences, according to a chart in
Feldman's memo, were Clause C, the end of maternity leave,
and the end of rape crisis centers.[44]

Predictably, the Feminist Majority emerged as the strongest
proponent of the Harris analysis. Others agreed with
Feldman, including Ewing, their campaign manager; Rice and
Munger, with the NAACP Legal Defense and Education Fund;
Dorothy Erlich and Ramona Ripston, with the ACLU; Aleita J.
Huguenin, with the California Teachers Association; Eva
Paterson, with the San Francisco Lawyers' Committee for
Civil Rights; Jan Adams, with Californians for Justice; and
Anthony Thigpen, with AGENDA.

Even though the women's rights leaders were becoming increasingly isolated, they argued vociferously against mend-it-
don't-end-it, taking a position that would influence the
Feldman group all the way through the campaign. To Ireland,
mend-it-don't-end-it was like "throwing the baby out with the
bath water." Her cohort at the Feminist Majority, Smeal, offered an even more potent argument. She reasoned that just as
Clinton's promise to "end welfare as we know it" produced legislation that cut rather than reformed welfare, his slogan on affirmative action would abolish rather than mend affirmative action. "She was very persuasive in arguing that it was something
that could come back and bite us in the butt," said Paterson.[45]

Virtually no one—except Bob Shrum, the opposition's
media advisor—wanted the mend-it-don't-end-it message,
which virtually all the polls indicated was a winner. "There
was fear on the part of some people that a 'mend it don't end
it' strategy said that we could fix it or that a mainstream strategy that tied into Powell and Clinton invited the legislature to

go back next year and change affirmative action," Shrum said. To him it looked like a winner—especially since funds were so tight. "Instead of trying to create your own message, it made sense to hook on to something that was already out there," Shrum said. As Shrum argued, coalition members began raising the point that winning with the wrong strategy would be as bad as losing with integrity. That kind of talk made Shrum nervous. The point, he believed, was to win.

The Forced Marriage Falls Apart

Just as many couples do when a marriage is going bad, the statewide coalition failed to deal directly with big issues, such as money and message. Instead, their response was the equivalent of rearranging the furniture: they expanded the board. Anthony Thigpen, the black organizer in south Los Angeles, had been added, and so had Eva Paterson, director of the Lawyers' Committee for Civil Rights. But the board was still controlled by the Feminist Majority, and the black community wanted a bigger representation. With tensions rising, a full board meeting was scheduled for the weekend of August 10— the weekend before the Republican Convention opened in San Diego. Several days before the board meeting Rice, Thigpen, and Ewing decided to elect two new board members—both well-respected black leaders from Los Angeles—by taking a vote on a conference call.

Hari Dillon, director of Vanguard Foundation and a member of the coalition from the north, got word of the plan, and he knew immediately that Spillar, Smeal, Ireland, and Yorkin would feel ambushed. "I tried to get Ireland on the phone before the conference call because I wanted to warn her that this was no big deal, that we should all just let it go through and be open and receptive, but I couldn't get her. The phone kept ringing busy."

The conference call was a disaster. As Dillon expected, the women were taken by surprise. They had already agreed to expand the board, and they were unclear why it needed to be done before the meeting. "They sandbagged us on the telephone," said Yorkin.[46] "We wanted to wait for the board meeting and they wanted to push through the new members, and when we wouldn't do it, they went around calling us racist." When the call ended, no one felt good. Talk of the phone call got back to civil rights organizations in Washington, and they were aghast. "We kept waiting for this to come out in the press," said Ralph Neas, executive director of the Leadership Conference on Civil Rights.[47]

When the board meeting opened on August 10, everyone was on edge. "No one talked about what was on everyone's mind," said Jan Adams, the grassroots organizer in the Bay Area. "Instead we talked about the board and the bylaws and then the staff." But there were minefields everywhere, and the ground rules didn't help. The staff was invited to the meeting but could not participate in the discussion. One person who attended said that the staff sat in a line, nearly twitching with anger when the discussion turned toward them. The Feminist Majority wanted a full report on how much everyone on the staff was getting paid. Ewing balked. Rice, Thigpen, Paterson, and others supported her. Someone called for a break, and minutes later the entire staff, "five blonde women, were out in the hall crying and talking to Anthony Thigpen," said one board member.[48] "It was a circus." Thigpen, an exceedingly private person whose emotions were always in check, wasn't quite sure what to do. "It was hard to know what we were arguing about, the issues or the personalities," Thigpen said.[49]

When everyone returned to the room, the staff was allowed to vent. Eventually, the board members managed to get through the encounter session and moved on to business. Again they debated message. Somehow the meeting finally came to an end. "When I woke up the next day, I thought, this is crazy, something has got to happen," said Ewing.[50]

On Monday Spillar, gaunt and on the edge of tears, watched the Powell speech from the Feminist Majority's headquarters.

Ellie Smeal called in from San Diego, where she had just participated in a protest march. "I haven't heard anything," Spillar told her. "There's nothing new to report."

On Friday Spillar got a call from Molly Munger. She, Ramona Ripston from the ACLU, and Anthony Thigpen wanted to come over for a meeting. Spillar knew something was up. Spillar, Yorkin, and Smeal met with the three emissaries. Munger opened the meeting. "We were invited to leave the coalition," Yorkin said.[51] "It was one of the worst things I have gone through since my divorce 12 years ago."

The Feminist Majority, NOW, and Hari Dillon broke off to become the Stop Prop 209 campaign. Ewing, Rice, Munger, Paterson, Erlich, Thigpen, Adams, and everyone else stayed with what was now called the Campaign to Defeat 209. The announcement to the press referred to the break-up as an "expansion" of the campaign against Proposition 209.

With Friends Like These

With Spillar and the feminist faction out of the way, Ewing hoped to attract some money from the Clinton-Gore campaign. And why not? They were on the same side. The opposition marveled at the president's ability to drop into town and pick up $4 million in one night. Liberal Democrats such as David Geffen were writing checks for $100,000 to the Democratic National Committee. The Campaign to Defeat 209 was getting $1,000 to $5,000 from the same sources. "It's a little like you giving us $1," said Yorkin. But these donors weren't anxious to give more, not even after receiving appeals from Yorkin and Sheinberg.

The members of the Campaign to Defeat 209 began to believe that the Democratic Party and Clinton in particular owed them. They were on the front lines defending civil rights. Where were the Democrats? The opposition's campaign needed visibility, but Clinton rarely mentioned affirmative action on his trips to California. "The president's first responsibility was to

make sure that he carried California," said Bill Carrick, a senior advisor to the Clinton-Gore campaign.[52] "And to do that
he tried to deal with the themes and messages that were specific to his presidency and his reelection." Proposition 209,
Carrick said, "was not a universal theme." The president's
polls indicated that it consistently had 55 percent of the vote,
but that less than 1 percent of the state's residents mentioned
affirmative action as a major concern. California voters in this
election cycle had simple concerns," said Carrick. "They were
worried about jobs and the environment, and 209 was not on
their radar screen."

The opposition could almost swallow that, but they failed
to understand why Clinton refused to spread some of his
money around. And worse still, they began to suspect that
Clinton's California campaign staff was telling donors to stay
away from the battle over affirmative action. "There were people in the California party operation and some people in the
Clinton campaign who wanted this issue to go away," said
Shrum, who kept in touch with George Stephanopoulos
throughout the 1996 campaign.[53] "I wish that people would
have told the big givers in Los Angeles that this is something
we care about. I have no reason not to think that there were
people in the California Clinton campaign who probably said
that this is not important to us so don't give to it. Do I think it
came from the center of the campaign? No." But Shrum knew
as well as anyone else that it didn't have to come from the center of the campaign. Some of the peripheral players were powerful enough.

One of them was Bill Wardlaw, a multimillionaire lawyer
who had chaired Clinton's 1992 campaign in California. "Bill
Wardlaw, campaign colleagues say, was the principal architect
of a strategy to recapture California's Reagan Democrats for
Clinton," the *Los Angeles Times* reported in early 1995.[54]
"Deeply conservative, Bill is known in the councils of the state
Democratic Party as a consistent voice for white working
men—the key swing group that deserted the party in droves to

become so-called Reagan Democrats. Bill feels a kinship to the group and wants its members back"[55]

Wardlaw had managed Republican Mayor Richard Riordan's campaign, and both he and Riordan were good friends with Steinberg, the campaign manager for CCRI. Although Wardlaw had advised Riordan to oppose Proposition 209—he needed minority support to remain in the mayor's office—he wanted Clinton to stay away from the issue. "There was an understanding very early on," explained Joe Gelman, who was fired from CCRI's Los Angeles office in late 1995.[56] "Arnie and I went to meet with Wardlaw even before we opened our campaign. Wardlaw was enthusiastic about the initiative. He supported it ideologically and point blank was extremely concerned about the effect it would have on the Clinton campaign." Wardlaw and Steinberg had common interests. Wardlaw didn't want Clinton in the middle of an issue that would alienate Reagan Democrats, and Steinberg was willing to leave Clinton out of the campaign's attacks on preferences as long as the president didn't pour money into the opposition's campaign.

Although nothing was put in writing and there was no formal agreement, Steinberg agreed that there was a tacit understanding that if Clinton stayed away from the issue and its campaign, the Proposition 209 advocates would refrain from attacking Clinton. "I think that people on the Clinton side understood that I viewed my client as 209 and not Bob Dole, and I had no interest in taking on Bill Clinton," Steinberg said.[57] "I think that there was a congruence of interests there and an overlapping of objectives." Wardlaw explained, "Were we concerned about the impact on the reelection of the president? Absolutely yes, and therefore we had certain views as to the interrelationship between the president's reelect campaign and 209 . . . but that doesn't mean there was any agreement. My view early on, and I told people who had any interest in my view, was that we had to monitor the campaign and that it wasn't in the president's interest to have his campaign intimately involved in the 209 campaign."[58] Wardlaw added that he had many friends in the Proposition 209 campaign. "Arnie Steinberg and I talk with great regularity, and obviously we had discussions on 209 but there was no agreement as far as I'm aware." Wardlaw said he gave money to the opposition campaign, but when asked if he voted against Proposition 209, he replied, "That's a private matter."

Steinberg pointed out that he kept Clinton out of the campaign as long as he was in charge. When Pamela Lewis, a statewide co-chair of Proposition 209, wanted to run an open letter to President Clinton denouncing his support for affirmative action, Steinberg refused. "I think that it was entirely possible that if anyone other than myself had been running the campaign, it would have taken Clinton on and tried to goad him into a fight."

Steinberg was right. There were others in the state Republican Party exceedingly anxious to draw Clinton into a debate on Proposition 209. And as summer turned into fall, one of them, John Herrington, a former Secretary of Energy and chairman of the state Republican Party, was getting ready to do just that.

6

The Ground War at Ground Zero

An Attempt to Revive the Grassroots

> I want to figure out how you make community po-
> litical work part of someone's routing, like church.
>
> ANTHONY THIGPEN

The Mexican Flags

When 70,000 young Latinos marched through Los Angeles on October 16, 1994, to protest Proposition 187, it was one of the largest demonstrations in the city's history. But what many Californians remembered were the flags—the Mexican flags. The green, red, and white Mexican banners unfurled above brown faces were captured on film and were stamped indelibly on the minds of outraged whites. "If they want to be part of this country, they should carry this country's flag," Jarron Holland, a drugstore clerk, told a reporter at the time.[1] "After that march, we watched the spread on 187 widen by two points a day," said Steve Smith, the political director for the state Democratic Party.[2]

The flags reminded white Californians that however much Governor Pete Wilson might rail against illegal immigrants, the state was heading toward a time when it would be majority Latino. But the vote for Proposition 187, which was supported by 63 percent of all whites, reminded Latinos that their time had not yet come. At some point in the near future, whites would make up less than 50 percent of the population, but in 1994 they still represented 78 percent of all voters.[3]

Even those who sensed a political awakening in those flags cautioned against reading too much into them. Any upswing in Latino voting rates would have the greatest impact on local congressional or municipal elections, where Latino voters represented a clear majority. In statewide elections Latinos would make a difference only if voting rates surged far beyond anyone's expectations and if they voted in a bloc with other minorities. The inability of minority nonvoters to make a difference had been noted in 1989 by William Galston, who was then with the University of Maryland, and Elaine Ciulla Kamarck of the Progressive Policy Institute, the research group aligned with the Democratic Leadership Council. In "The Myth of Mobilization" the authors observed that some Democrats believed the party need not alter its message to recapture the presidency; it had only to get current nonparticipants to vote. "The facts do not support this contention," they concluded, and gave three reasons why: at the end of the 1980s nearly as many people identified themselves as Republicans as Democrats, people who tended to vote only in high-interest elections were no longer necessarily Democrats, and increasingly Republicans were becoming the party of those who worked for a living.[4] "If only voters with family incomes of under $50,000 per year had participated in the 1988 election, George Bush would still have won."[5] Recognizing these political realities, Clinton had recaptured the presidency for the Democrats by appealing to white middle-class voters. In political speak he talked about "putting people first." Translated into policy, this meant "ending welfare as we know it" and declaring the "era of big government" over.[6]

In this environment, grassroots electoral activism in poorer communities had all but dried up. So had the votes. South Los Angeles was a case in point. Earlier voter registration drives had bolstered its rolls to nearly 300,000, or some 25 percent of the city's registered voters.[7] In the 1992 presidential election, however, little more than half of its voters went to the polls.[8] Voter turnout in one South Los Angeles council district was so dismal that Councilwoman Rita Walters was elected in 1991 by winning only 6,251 votes out of a population of 250,000.[9]

With voters scarce and potential voters difficult to excite, most political operatives running statewide races never bothered with such neighborhoods. The coalition opposed to Proposition 209 did not have that luxury. Even if minority voters couldn't defeat the proposition, they had to go on record as opposing it. If they voted yes on election day, it would be the equivalent of a beneficiary rejecting the benefit—and to civil rights leaders, that would have dire consequences. It would indicate to conservatives that minorities, unwittingly or by default, accepted a retreat in government-sanctioned civil rights programs. And if the impossible should happen—if, for example, a big media campaign succeeded in narrowing the opposition's thirty- to forty-point gap in the polls to five points—educating and getting out nonvoters could make the difference.

These political calculations aside, Anthony Thigpen, a former Black Panther, and Jan Adams, an organizer for César Chávez in the 1970s, were unlikely to let the statewide coalition ignore nonwhites. From their point of view, political leaders willing and able to manipulate California's racial tensions for political gain punished poor minority communities most. This analysis failed to embitter Thigpen and Adams. They understood that the political assaults on minorities for political gain would continue as long as poor communities failed to participate in the political process. Thigpen and Adams found this situation unacceptable. The abandoned political wastelands of South Los Angeles, Bell Gardens, Richmond, and Oakland had to maximize their potential strength. But how did the powerless become a new source of power?

Neither Bolsheviks nor saints, Thigpen and Adams sought
real-world solutions. In 1996 voting provided part of the answer. They mapped these vast territories like political cartog-
raphers, drawing up lists of potential voters (unregistered but
qualified to register), occasional voters (those who had voted
at least once in the last six years), and likely voters (residents
who voted consistently). They would use Proposition 209 as a
divining rod to test political interest in minority communities.
Once they sensed even the slightest interest, they dug down. "I
want to figure out how you make community political work
part of someone's routine, like church," said Thigpen.

Adams and Thigpen knew their chances of defeating
Proposition 209 were slim, but they were building for the future—for a time when minority communities would take
their place among California's decision makers. They weren't,
however, naive. Both Thigpen and Adams had done political
work longer than nearly anyone else in the statewide coalition against Proposition 209, and it was realism, not roman-
ticism, that distinguished them. They understood the need
for alliances and had little patience for coalition infighting.
Just as President Clinton could appreciate the political skills
that kept segregationist Arkansas Governor Orval Faubus in
office, Thigpen and Adams, far to Clinton's left, could admire
the president's political acumen. "He really knows how to
speak to people," Adams said.[10] They understood the president's need to focus first and foremost on his own reelection,
but while Clinton was worried about winning in 1996, Adams
and Thigpen were more concerned about an election some
time in the future. They read political tea leaves differently.
Whereas the Democratic Party saw disaster in those Mexican
flags, Adams and Thigpen saw hope.

Anthony Thigpen and South Los Angeles

March 23, 1996, was that rarity in Los Angeles—a bright
clear day. The downtown buildings of granite and glass were

etched in sharp lines against the blue sky. Traffic moved efficiently. The air actually smelled good. It was exactly the kind of morning community organizers wanted for election day. Early in the election cycle, however, this was the kind of day that could keep volunteers away; there were better places to be on such a splendid Saturday morning than inside a church listening to speakers talk about a political battle nearly nine months away. Worse still, the regional finals of the NCAA basketball championships were on television, and the game pitting Kentucky against Wake Forest promised to be a good one.

But Thigpen, who was organizing a morning rally and training session at St. Brigid's Catholic Church in South-Central, was unperturbed. Six-feet-four and as lithe as a basketball player, Thigpen wandered between the church and the classrooms, where glazed donuts and hot coffee had been laid out for prospective volunteers. Except for the clipboard in his hand, it was difficult to tell that Thigpen was in charge. Like others on the staff, he prepared the seminar rooms, emptied boxes filled with flyers, and checked who had arrived. By 8:30 A.M. cars began to turn into the church's asphalt parking lot; when it filled up, they began parking up and down Western Avenue and along 52nd Street. By 9 A.M. 250 volunteers, mostly African Americans, were seated inside—ready to start on time, just as Thigpen liked.

The forty-three-year-old organizer had worked in this community for years. He was born not far away, on 103rd Street in Watts, where his grandparents owned a duplex and where he lived with his parents, brother, and sister until he was thirteen. When Watts exploded in flames in 1965 his father swept up the family, threw a tent in the trunk of the car, and took them camping. "It was something we didn't want to be a part of," said James Thigpen, Anthony's father.[11] "We didn't want to watch our community getting a bad name and getting destroyed." When they returned, thirty-four people lay dead and 200 buildings had been destroyed.[12] The National Guard patrolled the streets. A guard stood in their back yard. What had been 103rd Street became known as Charcoal Alley.[13]

The Thigpens moved to Pacoima, in the San Fernando Valley, and the elder Thigpen commuted to his job in South Los Angeles as a meter reader for the Department of Water and Power. He watched as white families, and some African American families, packed up and moved away. Although he was disturbed by the growing isolation of South Los Angeles, Thigpen was happy to have his family in Pacoima. On Saturday mornings he would gather his three children together and read to them from Plato and Aristotle or listen to Martin Luther King, Jr., on the radio.[14]

His son Anthony thrived and graduated from San Fernando Valley High School in 1971, the same year President Richard Nixon announced a "new American Revolution." A different insurrection called to Anthony. "Something happened to him there at Northridge," said his father referring to California State University at Northridge, where his son had enrolled.[15] "I don't know what it was, he started reading books like *Black Rage*," he said. Thigpen left Northridge to join the Black Panthers in Oakland. In less than two years, he returned to Los Angeles, disillusioned with the Panthers but committed to doing community work. "The rhetoric didn't match the reality," said Thigpen of his Panther experience.

When Thigpen returned to Los Angeles in 1974, Tom Bradley, the city's first black mayor, had been in office for a year. Bradley was elected by a coalition of West Side liberals and South Los Angeles activists, but most of the mayor's development plans focused on downtown. When the new skyline emerged, developers skipped over the mayor's core constituencies in South Los Angeles and continued building on the West Side. What was left behind receded even further from mainstream Los Angeles.

During the following decade Thigpen worked as a machinist by day and with the Coalition Against Police Abuse at night;

two of his friends had been killed in incidents with the police. It was a time when the LAPD could get away with almost anything. The epidemic of crack and gangs frustrated the city's civil rights leadership as much as it did its most conservative whites. In hopes of controlling gang violence, they refrained from pressing the police for accountability and inadvertently insulated Chief Daryl Gates and his force.[16] "Chief Gates was only emboldened. . . . Following a rash of LAPD 'chokehold' killings of young black men in custody, he advanced the extraordinary theory that the deaths were the fault of the victims' racial anatomy, not excessive police force."[17] Anthony's younger brother, Ron, who would later become an executive vice president of the Family Savings Banks in Los Angeles, worried that Anthony would become another police fatality. "It was happening a lot back then and with him being politically active, I knew he was at risk," Ron Thigpen said. "He was the type who didn't care. He wasn't going to back down."[18]

No political movement in the 1980s in Los Angeles—not Thigpen's modest work or the boom years of Mayor Bradley's 20-year regime—could rival the longer-range changes that were happening in the state and in Los Angeles in particular. "Some 400,000 migrants per year poured in during the 1980s (versus 300,000 births). . . . The human flash flood completely transfigured the face of California's people and cities. . . . From one of the whitest states in the U.S. in the 1960s, California became the most polyglot. . . . School districts found themselves trying to educate millions of new children, as enrollment grew from 3.1 million in 1980 to 5.1 million in 1990."[19] These changes were particularly sharp in Los Angeles. Nearly one and a half million new residents moved into the county, and 93 percent of them were Latino.[20] Neighborhoods in South Los Angeles that were once majority African American were becoming majority Latino.

The newest California rush coincided with a severe statewide recession. Seventy thousand manufacturing jobs had left South Los Angeles by 1990, and the area was already scraping bottom when the state economy collapsed.[21] The high-paying union jobs created by the auto industry had left. In their place entrepreneurs set up nonunion shops, and African Americans competed against the influx of immigrants for low-paying jobs. Thigpen said he could feel the tension building. Unlike his own family, residents there did not have options or a safety net. Daily life grew steadily more brutal. Gangs turned 18th Street, Central Avenue, and Broadway into combat zones. Drive-ins that had once served up hamburgers and fries were abandoned, and the new squatters operating behind boarded-up windows sold crack, cocaine, or heroin. South-Central had the feel of an armed camp. Virtually the only people willing to run legitimate businesses there were Korean immigrants, who often operated their small corner grocery stores from cash registers sheltered behind thick bulletproof glass.

In this environment, residents could not summon any response but rage. "There was a tendency in any community meeting you'd hold for people to just vent and vent about how bad things were and how they would never change and how they were frustrated with the political system and nearly every elected official," Thigpen said.[22] Instead of pursuing development projects that had been proposed, or developing their own, residents vehemently opposed everything. Something was bound to happen, and the LAPD provided the spark. On March 3, 1991, an amateur video photographer filmed Rodney King, a twenty-five-year-old part-time groundskeeper on parole for second-degree robbery, being beaten by members of the LAPD. South Los Angeles watched this grainy video over and over on television, and when an all-white jury acquitted the officers of wrongdoing on April 29, 1992, the city exploded. This time Thigpen stayed and watched the worst civil disturbance in the city's history. The toll was far greater than in Watts: forty-five people were killed, thousands were injured, and damage exceeded $1 billion. Two hundred liquor stores, many of them owned by Korean immigrants, burned to the ground.

When it was over, Thigpen headed to the Montana mountains to clear his head and figure out what his role should be in Los Angeles after Rodney King. He returned six weeks later with plans for a new organization, AGENDA—an acronym that gave urgency to its longer iteration, Action for Grassroots Empowerment & Neighborhood Development Alternatives. As he had hiked through the Montana wilderness, Thigpen decided that although plenty of social service agencies tried to serve South Los Angeles, no one—other than political leaders with private electoral agendas—actually organized residents to help themselves. "There is a need for an independent entity or institution that really pays attention to grassroots organizing and that both keeps established leaders accountable and also builds the kind of alliances that need to be built," Thigpen said.[23] "People need to organize, but around an agenda and not just in reaction to what others propose."

Before South Los Angeles had time to develop an agenda, however, Governor Pete Wilson launched a barrage of initiatives that ended up aggravating rather than healing the tensions among its African American, Latino, and Korean residents. Initially, African Americans were inclined to support Proposition 187 and its promise of cutting off illegal immigration, and Latinos and Koreans—many of them recent immigrants—resented them for it. Another initiative, known as three-strikes, which was designed to keep repeat felons behind bars, was equally divisive. Latinos and Koreans tended to support it, and African Americans were divided.

All of this bitter history—Watts, Bradley's benign neglect, Rodney King, and the ethnic infighting—had brought Thigpen and the 250-odd volunteers to St. Brigid's on that brilliant Saturday morning. Something needed to change, and Thigpen hoped that organizing against Proposition 209 would be a turning point. He sat on the hard pew and watched as the meeting began.

"What is at issue is respect. Those with power only respect power," said Councilman Mark Ridley-Thomas. Dressed in a white shirt and sports coat, Ridley-Thomas looked more professorial than political; in fact, he was both. He had linked up with Thigpen years earlier when both were working with the Coalition Against Police Abuse. At the time, Ridley-Thomas was studying toward a master's degree in religious studies from Immaculate Heart College. Both men liked to talk philosophy and politics, and they were both committed to doing something for the city's black community.

It was Thigpen who convinced Ridley-Thomas to run for office in 1985, and it was Thigpen who ran his field operation.[24] After narrowly winning the first time around, Ridley-Thomas returned to office in 1995 with 89 percent of the vote, the highest approval rating in the city. "He makes a habit of doing good work," said a staff member of a local state senator.[25] What Ridley-Thomas did that Saturday in March was tell the assembled men and women the truth: The powerful would never pay attention to South Los Angeles unless residents demonstrated their power in the voting booth.

Connie Rice, Western Counsel for the NAACP Legal Defense and Education Fund, followed Ridley-Thomas with a message at least as blunt. "The future of civil rights lies in your hands. Mother Rosa Parks asked me 'Are you gonna beat this thing in California? If not, I refused to give up my seat for nothing.'" The crowd answered, "Amen." Rice, however, was not there to preach. She told them straight: "The black population in California is small," she said. "We cannot beat this alone. We need to make a strategic alliance with women and others of color. We are in the majority when we link with Latinos, with white women, and with the 25 percent of white men who will support us."

Rice's talk of strategic links wasn't just theoretical. The previous summer Thigpen had joined with Ridley-Thomas and a number of churches to form the South Los Angeles Affirmative Action Project, known as SLAAAP. To extend SLAAAP's reach in Los Angeles, Thigpen helped create the Metropolitan Alliance, an umbrella organization that linked South Los Angeles to white, Latino, and Asian organizers in West Los Angeles, Pasadena, San Pedro, Huntington Park, Inglewood, and elsewhere.

Although there had been considerable rhetoric about inter-minority unity, real collaborations were rare and often controversial. But the one that really riled other black leaders was Thigpen's decision to ally with the Feminist Majority and the National Organization for Women. Black leaders in Los Angeles were still smarting from remarks made by NOW's Los Angeles director, Tammy Bruce, after the O. J. Simpson acquittal. "What we need to teach our children is . . . not about racism but is about violence against women," Bruce told Ted Koppel on ABC's *Nightline* after the verdict. Although her remarks were condemned by Patricia Ireland, the president of NOW, they did not endear feminist groups to black leaders.

Thigpen, however, believed Katherine Spillar and the Feminist Majority to be among the few progressive leaders and organizations with the money and the focus to run a campaign. He knew that Proposition 209 was not going to be defeated by minority voters alone. "All you had to do was look at the voting patterns to see that we couldn't beat 209 with just people of color," Thigpen said.[26] "The logical allies were women." Those who opposed the alliance, he said, "weren't looking at the numbers."

At St. Brigid's Thigpen handed out pie charts illustrating how such alliances could make the black community stronger. Then he got to the point: what South Los Angeles needed to do. He told his audience that he'd "been out walking precincts since November" and that "residents were largely unaware of" the California Civil Rights Initiative. "At this point our community is not organized. There are no mysteries, no shortcuts about what has to be done. We have to walk the precincts. We need you to multiply your vote by fifty. It's our watch. To win will require us to do more than we like, more than we want to do."

Thigpen wasn't being theatrical. There was nothing easy about grassroots precinct work—least of all in South Los Angeles, where walking door to door during the day was dreary and at night was downright dangerous. Thigpen's plan envisioned organizing as many as 500 precincts in South Los Angeles and 1,000 citywide. The goal was to find seventy-five "occasional" voters in each precinct and make sure that on November 5 they got to the polls and got there with plenty of information on Proposition 209. "If anyone can do it, it's Anthony," said Steve Smith from the state Democratic Party.[27] "He's the best in the business. We'd love to have him."

Thigpen's early precinct walks and talks to church groups were disheartening. Many of the residents were too isolated from the mainstream to understand the connection between affirmative action and their lives—if indeed there was one. Most had never competed against whites for jobs or for places at the state's elite universities. "First we had to convince people that affirmative action had something to do with them," Thigpen recalled.[28] "It wasn't obvious to them, so we had to do a huge education drive. I'd ask, 'Who knows anyone working for the post office or police,' and hands would go up. That was affirmative action. And then I'd talk about their children in schools. Still the degree that it touches them in their daily lives is small." Nevertheless, Thigpen believed that saving affirmative action was important. "There is a need to draw the line," Thigpen said.[29] "All of this is part of a right wing agenda to ignore these communities."

Nearly every weekend from March on Thigpen, his staff, and Councilman Ridley-Thomas would go to churches, sign up more volunteers, and train them to walk precincts. House by house, block by block, an electoral machine was being assembled. But progress was slow. "People are still so confused," said Thigpen in the early summer.[30] "The challenge of educating so many people is daunting." Every day Thigpen's precinct workers had the same frustrating experience. Voters were confused; many believed CCRI was a civil rights initiative that would be good for them. "If we don't go to their doors, we're going to lose them, but the numbers say that we aren't getting to enough people," Thigpen said.[31] By summer organizers were in 50 to 100 precincts, but a *Los Angeles Times* poll showed that the majority of black and Latino voters in Los Angeles County still favored the proposition.[32]

To increase their numbers faster, Thigpen added smaller meetings during the week to the large weekend meetings at churches. If an AGENDA worker found a resident interested in doing precinct work, a staffer would offer to go to the recruit's house and give an evening training session with anyone from the neighborhood. The house meetings worked well, and Thigpen began to feel the momentum grow. The word coming back from others in the Metropolitan Alliance was also positive. The organizers decided to call a mass meeting of the alliance for late September to test the validity of those reports. Was the alliance a true vehicle for organizing, or was it, like so many of its predecessors, an empty shell?

A couple of evenings before the meeting Thigpen brought together twelve representatives from the alliance at his offices on Vermont Street to prepare. Precinct maps, with colored pins stuck in the blocks that had been covered, hung from the conference room's walls. Thigpen, who generally dressed casually in an open-neck shirt and khakis, wore a tie for the meeting. He went quickly through the Saturday program. When someone at the meeting pointed out that the new buttons printed for the alliance had accidentally used New York City's skyline in the background and not L.A.'s, Thigpen laughed, pinned one on proudly, and moved on to the numbers. The goal was to get 500 "screaming and activated" volunteers from across the city to attend the alliance's kickoff. Only 394 potential recruits had responded positively, and everyone offered excuses as to why they had not reached their goal. "We've got a lot of work to do," Thigpen said calmly. He urged everyone to get to the telephones, and he adjourned the meeting to make sure they had time.

It was a leadership style that worked. On September 28 nearly 600 volunteers appeared at Holman United Methodist Church on West Adams Boulevard. They mached Thigpen's vision of a new Los Angeles political base: a mix of young and old, Latino, African American, and Asian. The prospective recruits came from as far away as the West Side and Bell Gardens, and they were full of hope and humor. Roger Ponce, a junior from San Fernando Valley High School, wore a Cleveland Indians cap on his head. "If we can just make people aware of the issue," the young Latino said, fiddling with his cap, "we're going to beat this thing." Asked about the fears of white voters and the Mexican flags, he grinned. "They were beautiful, weren't they?"

By October 19, a little more than two weeks before the election, it was clear that even in the most distressed neighborhoods of South Los Angeles some progress had been made.

Matlie Jones, a sixty-four-year-old retiree who lived in an L.A. precinct just off Slauson Avenue, was attending her second training session. Rain threatened, but she straightened her glasses, tied a scarf around her head, and listened closely to Ng'ethe Maina, an AGENDA staffer, explain the tactics of talking to residents. "If they are a certain age," Maina said, "remind them about Jim Crow. They'll remember that and they'll know what you're talking about if you tell them this will send us back to the time of Jim Crow. If they're younger, talk about how it's important for their children to get into special school programs or college."

After getting an explanation on how to ask residents to sign a pledge card and how to mark the voting list, Jones was ready to go. "It's a great beginning, a new beginning," she said, sliding into her beat-up sedan. "I've never witnessed this kind of thing before—all these people working together. It's not a black thing or a brown thing, but a human thing."

Mrs. Jones's walk along 58th Street just off Slauson Avenue met with both hope and despair. At one house two preschool children came to the door and looked out cautiously through the screen. "Oh, I'm feeling sick today," their mother moaned from the dark living room as her children stared out. "Just leave what you have there."

"She's having a bad day," Mrs. Jones said, shaking her head and moving on to the next house, only to find that she had to walk a distance before an address matched one on her list of registered voters. "We've got a lot of work to do here to register these people," she said.

At another house, an older Latina answered the door and invited Mrs. Jones in. She had hoped Mrs. Jones was the repairman who the landlord had promised would fix the large hole in the middle of the living room ceiling, but when she found out otherwise, she quickly fetched her daughter. Yes, they knew about Proposition 209, and yes, they planned to vote against it. The daughter would even volunteer on election day.

At another house thirteen-year-old Curtis Phelps sat on the porch steps sharing a bag of chips with ten-year-old Brenden Funches. "Hey baby, who are you gonna vote for?" Mrs. Jones said as she walked up the steps and rapped on the door.

"Bill Clinton," Curtis said and then asked what Mrs. Jones was doing.

When she mentioned affirmative action, the ten-year-old looked confused.

"You know, affirmative action," the thirteen-year-old jumped in before Mrs. Jones could explain. "It helps us to get into schools because sometimes you know we don't test so well maybe because we're too nervous or something."

The boy knew about it only too well. He was in an outreach program for minority students, and if 209 was approved, it was likely to be cut.

Californians for Justice

By the time she declared war against Proposition 209, there weren't many progressive causes Jan Adams hadn't served. The only child of a bookkeeper and a preschool teacher in Buffalo, New York, Adams had gone west in 1965 to attend the University of California at Berkeley. She was taken with the activist promise of the 1960s, but when she graduated from Berkeley she headed to Harvard to study modern European history. "I never really knew what I was doing there, but it made the relatives happy," she recalled.[33] Being the kind of person who finishes what she starts, Adams stayed in Cambridge long enough to get her master's degree, but it wasn't long before she had gravitated back toward progressive causes—the Catholic Worker newspaper, the Farmworkers Union, and some consulting work for anti-apartheid groups in South Africa. For much of that time Adams—a tall, big-boned woman with graying hair shaved close to the scalp and several earrings piercing each lobe—financed her political life retrofitting Bay Area house foundations to make them earthquake secure. "I lived through the development of the art," she recalled, rolling her eyes.[34]

By the time construction work had become too hard on her body, Adams's political skills had become marketable. Although she appeared the quintessential outsider, Adams had come to understand the political system as well as any suit-and-tie professional, and she felt as at ease in that world as she did in San Francisco's gay community. "She's one of the more versatile people I know," said Angie Fa, who hired Adams to run her successful 1992 campaign for the San Francisco school board. "She's comfortable with the grassroots volunteers, the PTA types, and the donors."

After Fa was elected, Adams landed a job at the Applied Research Center, a progressive research group based in Oakland. She was at her desk one day in 1994 when Emily Goldfarb, the executive director of the Coalition for

Immigrant Rights, walked in and told Adams's boss Gary
Delgado that she needed support organizing the growing
number of volunteers who wanted to help defeat Proposition
187. Delgado promptly lent her Adams. "A lot of people who
do campaigns spend a lot of time in meetings and debating
and discussing and arguing and trying to decide who is going
to be out front," said Goldfarb. "Jan is extremely results oriented, and she wants to see action right away. Even though
that sounds logical, not many people do it." Goldfarb had
more high praise for Adams. "I've been doing this work for 20
years, and it's rare to meet anyone as skilled and talented who
also wants to stay in the background—and not in that annoy-
ing or self-sacrificing way."

Adams spent three months organizing in San Francisco's
minority communities to defeat Proposition 187, and when
the election was over she thought long and hard about the results. To Adams Proposition 187 was a precursor of electoral
battles that would be about nothing less than "California's
growing pains." The experience with Proposition 187 taught
her that even traditional media campaigns would have difficulty persuading white voters to kill initiatives that scape-
goated immigrants and other minorities. The opposition to
187 had spent nearly $2 million on media to move white vot-
ers to their side. Countless mainstream religious, labor, and
community groups had supported their efforts. None of it had
swayed whites. The initiative remained as popular with them
on election day as it was when it was first introduced.

Initially minority groups had also supported Proposition
187, but a strong educational and get-out-the-vote effort had
turned Latinos, African Americans, and Asians around. These
communities, Adams decided, had potential. They could be
organized. In the San Francisco precincts with strong grassroots organizing against Proposition 187, the no vote was especially high: 83 percent in the Latino Mission District, 70
percent in Chinatown, and 70 percent in the black neighborhood of Bayview and Hunters Point. "These results suggest

that something more happened in San Francisco than merely the city's ordinary liberal voting," Adams concluded.[35] People who normally failed to vote could be moved. But it was hard work, and as she looked at the lay of the electoral land she knew that no matter how good the field operation in San Francisco, it meant nothing unless the same was done in the southern part of the state. Two-thirds of the voters lived in the south; voters in Los Angeles County alone cast 23 percent of the total votes on Proposition 187. To beat any initiative, she concluded, "progressives have to raise the margin of victory in populous Santa Clara County in the north (where only 52 percent voted against Proposition 187), win in Los Angeles County, and lower conservative margins in San Diego, San Bernadino, Orange, and Riverside Counties."[36]

During the Proposition 187 campaign one of the offices where Adams and her volunteers did phone work at night was the San Francisco Lawyers' Committee for Civil Rights. When Eva Paterson, its executive director, started gathering people in early 1995 to organize around the impending battle on affirmative action, Adams and her partner, Rebecca Gordon, a financial accounting consultant for nonprofits, volunteered for the grassroots organizing committee. They were just the kind of recruits organizers hope will walk through the door. They thought big, they were analytical in their approach, and, best of all, they worked long hours for little or no money.

Soon Adams and Gordon were reporting back to Delgado about their plans for organizing a statewide grassroots campaign in targeted precincts, where the voter turnout was traditionally low but could be increased sharply with the help of door-to-door volunteers. The two women had identified 6,000 such precincts out of some 25,000 in California, and they figured they could organize 1,500. Delgado liked the idea, and he had a name for it: Californians for Justice, or CFJ. While the statewide coalition continued with its interminable debates over message and strategy, Adams and Gordon, backed by

Delgado, moved single-mindedly to form a separate political action committee to raise money. They met with Los Angeles organizers to see if they would be welcome there. Thigpen was delighted and quickly made Adams part of the Metropolitan Alliance.

In no time at all Adams produced a ninety-five-page campaign plan that covered everything from the precinct organizing programs to fund raising and media. Adams envisioned get-out-the-vote operations in 1,500 precincts with the objective of turning out in each precinct seventy-five voters who would otherwise not have voted against Proposition 209 and, in many cases, wouldn't have voted at all. She hoped to net 112,500 no votes that otherwise wouldn't have been there. Gordon crunched the numbers. Recruiting and training precinct leaders and 20,000 volunteers would cost $180,000, or $120 a precinct. It was doable, Adams and Gordon agreed.

Writing the campaign plan was the easy part. It would be considerably harder to find volunteers for 1,500 precincts. CFJ's device became the Million Voices for Justice petitions. By June 1995 several dozen volunteers, petitions in hand, began collecting signatures wherever likely recruits could be found—Oakland's Festival at the Lake, Berkeley's Juneteeth, and San Francisco's Gay Pride Parade. The petitions were translated into Spanish, Tagalog, and several other Asian languages. Anyone who signed one was called to volunteer—for phone banking or data entry—and if they agreed, they were called again for a training session. People who displayed any competence were put in charge of a precinct before they knew what had happened to them. By August Adams had a director in Oakland, Mimi Ho; one in Los Angeles, Joselito Laudencia; and the backing of a number of Asian, Latino, and black groups.

As quickly as Gordon logged in the money, Adams printed up the campaign paraphernalia—bumper stickers, buttons, T-shirts—that she believed would generate momentum and interest. Precinct walkers began asking residents to put posters in their windows or bumper stickers on their cars. Like Thigpen, Adams and her volunteers spent the weekends out walking precincts. "We tend not to work as deep as Anthony," Adams said.[37] "We go for numbers, and we work in places where people are probably not as alienated because many are Latino and Asian and they feel more possibilities." To Adams, the Mexican flags waved in the protest against Proposition 187 reflected not resentment, but promise. And organizing against Proposition 209 was proving her right. In Los Angeles CFJ was signing on volunteers who spoke only Spanish, as well as bilingual high school students.

By mid-September CFJ was a happening thing. In the Oakland office, abuzz with young men and women coming through to pick up campaign materials, Adams expressed delight with the activity. "If you organize, it works," she said, grinning as she packed some boxes to send to Los Angeles. Californians for Justice was close to meeting its $180,000 target, and checks from a direct mail campaign and private fundraisers kept coming in. Adams summed up their progress: "We're strongest closest to our main offices in Los Angeles and here—that means were strong in Alameda County and Richmond in the north. In L.A. we're very strong in Pasadena, not bad in Long Beach, and very strong in Bell Gardens."[38] San Francisco, she added, was so easy they didn't have to make much of an effort. "The Democrats are begging to move into our offices there," she said, enjoying the irony of having the attention of a state party that had been reluctant to support their efforts. "It's not that they want to help," she explained. "It's just that they want to be around the activity. It helps build morale."[39]

Despite the polls, Adams was beginning to believe in the possibility of beating Proposition 209. "There's been this whole change in the political climate," she said.[40] "The world is quite a different place than it was in early 1995." The economy had improved, Governor Wilson's bid to ride the initiative into the White House had failed, and Los Angeles Mayor Richard Riordan, sensing that he could not win reelection without support from the minority community, had come out against Proposition 209. Still, Adams was a realist. She didn't expect President Clinton to climb on board the opposition's bandwagon. "It wouldn't make sense for him to go off message, even with that kind of lead," Adams said flatly.[41] "You never know what could happen to that lead." Moreover, she had no idea where the coalition would come up with the money it needed for a media campaign.

But this was not Adam's first concern. Win or lose on Proposition 209, she meant to make a lasting difference. Adams, Gordon, and Delgado wanted to set up a statewide grassroots organization that would data-bank volunteers and be ready to move on any issue. "We have the demographics on our side," Adams said.[42] "If we bring the people who are not in the electorate into it, we can have an impact. We want to build a permanent organization to deal with all this junk." Her campaign plan made that clear: "We are building for the long term, not to 'win' some tiny piece of turf for a moment," it stated.[43] "The one important respect in which the CFJ effort differs from an ordinary electoral campaign is that we are seeking to work in a way which builds for the long term empowerment of the people who have been pushed to the margins of California society: the communities of color, young people, low income people."

That September day gave an indication of the extent of work that needed to be done. After dropping the L.A.-bound boxes off at Greyhound, Adams continued down Interstate 880 to visit CFJ's newest office in San Jose. Someone had promised to open an office in San Jose earlier in the year, but although he looked and sounded legitimate, he turned out to be a flake. Only recently had they found the money to send down two young staffers. The two women, Gina Acebo and

Rona Fernandez, worked out of offices on loan from Janitors for Justice and retired at night to the Grail, a boarding house run by a local Catholic church. Adams needed to lend them moral support and run through plans for a voter registration effort the following day at the San Jose Arena, where nearly 11,000 people from 104 countries would be sworn in as U.S. citizens.[44]

While Adams cased the arena with Acebo, the office director, Fernandez walked precincts. The precinct walk was a harsh reminder of how slow the process can be and the importance of a media campaign. Fernandez, a third-generation Filipina who graduated in 1995 from U.C. Berkeley in marine biology, was still learning how to get from one side of the city to another. She had trouble sleeping at night if she started thinking about all the work to be done, but her experience in student protests at Berkeley had made her a convert to door-to-door campaigning. "On campus people are operating from the notion that we can stop this by protesting," she said, shaking her head. "That's not going to happen. We have to do field work."

This became painfully clear at one of the first houses. A twenty-seven-year-old white woman named Christine came to the door. A child clung to her side, and a television blared in the background. When Fernandez asked the young woman if she was registered to vote, she said she wasn't sure. "I voted once," she said, "but then I had my kids, and its a pain to take them anywhere."

Fernandez politely explained that she could register to vote by mail and handed her the form. "If I can't make it, do I have to show up?" the woman asked.

Such responses, Adams said later, were all too common. "The level of participation is unbelievably low if left to itself," she said. "People don't have any information. You can never underestimate how little they have. It's terrifying."

Even if voters could be reached by foot, many had already been won over by the air war that Arnold Steinberg, the cam-

paign manager for Proposition 209, launched on the radio
after Labor Day. Fernandez tried at one house to explain affirmative action to an elderly Latino man, but he cut her off gra-
ciously. He had already heard about the proposition on the
radio.

"I heard on the radio that it won't discriminate against anyone," the man said, referring to Proposition 209.

Fernandez headed down the street, shaking her head in
disgust. "I heard that same commercial," she said. "And when
I heard it I thought, 'wow, we have radio spots' because it
sounded so much like it was for civil rights and then I heard
Ward Connerly's name." The opposition campaign had no
money to counter Proposition 209's radio advertisements, so,
by default, the air war had been conceded to Connerly and
Steinberg.

With this kind of political disadvantage, Adams had to think
beyond 1996 and imagine the future. The Mexican flags
helped, and they weren't just a memory. At the Los Angeles office of CFJ, evidence abounded that the anger over Proposition
187 had been turned into political action. The local Spanish-
language press was writing more about Proposition 209 than
the mainstream press, and organizers were finding the Latino
community surprisingly familiar with the campaign against affirmative action. The same was true of the Korean-language
press and the Korean community. These communities were
less concerned about the ins and outs of affirmative action
than with Proposition 209's supporters. All these communities
needed to know, explained CFJ staffer Nicole Davis, was that
Proposition 209 was being promoted by the same man who
had championed Proposition 187—Governor Pete Wilson. "If
you mentioned 187 in connection with 209," Davis said, "that
was enough to get Latinos agitated."

7

Countdown

A Defining Moment, or the Color Bind

You get what you settle for.
THELMA AND LOUISE POSTER
in the Feminist Majority's
Los Angeles Office

The Search for Financial Independence

At the end of August 1996 Arnold Steinberg, the campaign manager for Proposition 209, was banking on mood. The polls for Bob Dole looked dismal, but Steinberg hoped the festive air of a national convention would turn otherwise shrewd businessmen into guileless optimists ready to sign checks. The Republican National Convention in San Diego tried. The clear sea air, the balloons, the nostalgia evoked by Nancy Reagan, and the intimacy of Elizabeth Dole all worked a kind of magic on the money men who attended the convention at night and dropped in on private parties held afterward. "There was a certain euphoria," Steinberg recalled.[1] "I hoped to capitalize on it and the fact that Dole donors wanted him to win and were willing to give to the issues that might help him." Such donations, Steinberg calculated, would make Proposition 209 independent—most important, from the losing Dole-Kemp ticket. Steinberg saw little irony in exploiting any false hopes inspired by the GOP convention to free him of its presidential nominee.

His job was to promote Proposition 209, and in August his focus groups told him that 209 was a winner; Dole-Kemp was not. If he failed to make the initiative financially independent, it would be at the mercy of the Dole campaign for funds. This was fine if the candidate unexpectedly surged in the polls and made a convincing case for the initiative—Steinberg had been working on him to do as much for months. But if Dole slipped further and then grasped at Proposition 209, he could pull the popular initiative down with him.

The convention's magic was not as compelling as Steinberg would have liked, but he did collect enough checks to unveil his first radio commercial.[2] The sixty-second advertisement, which started after Labor Day, played the race card, but it differed sharply from the way in which the Republican Party had previously used race for political advantage. Whereas the 1988 Willie Horton commercials or the later immigration ads exploited white fears of "them," this commercial was soft in tone, moral in stance, and unifying in theme. "The worst possible campaign for CCRI," Steinberg advised in his campaign plan, "is a negative, angry, strident campaign . . . the kind we will not have."[3] Instead, the commercial, featuring Proposition 209 chair Ward Connerly, appealed to an idealized notion of common sense and fair play. And as Anthony Thigpen and Jan Adams were finding in their door-to-door canvassing, it worked—even with the presumed supporters of affirmative action.

The ad begins with a tug of heartstrings for Connerly—his friend has died.

Connerly: "Last year, one of my closest friends died. *(pause)* In eighteen years, we had never discussed race or color. It never came up that he was white and I'm black. That wasn't important. For me and millions of other minorities and for women, what is important is that we all have an equal chance to compete.[4]

Through the device of the dead friend who was white, Connerly identifies himself as African American and at the same time

discounts the significance of racial identity. His self-identifica-
tion, however, invites listeners to presume that Connerly could
be a recipient of government preferences but instead opts for
equal treatment.

Connerly: I thought equal treatment is the *law*. But if equal
  treatment is the law, why is the government so involved in
  giving preferences to *some* people—just because of their
  race or *sex*? Goals, timetables, set-asides: everyone knows
  we're talking about quotas. Race and sex discrimination
  are wrong, regardless of who's favored. Proposition 209
  would prohibit discrimination *and* preferential treatment .
  . . in public employment, education, and contracting. . . .
  For men *and* women of *every* race, Proposition 209 keeps
  all existing protections against discrimination. If it didn't,
  I wouldn't be its campaign chairman.
Female Announcer: Equal opportunity *without* quotas. Yes!
  Proposition 209. Bring us together.[5]

Steinberg relies on the moral capital of a successful black businessman while channeling white resentment of affirmative action programs toward feelings of virtue rather than anger or
fear. A vote for Proposition 209, the ad implies, is not a vote
against minorities and women, but a vote for fairness. Although
the ad accentuates the positive, it also hits a negative chord by
emphasizing that a vote for Proposition 209 is a vote against
"quotas" and against government preferences for *"some"* people.
The tag line "Bring us together" ends the ad on an upbeat, positive note of unity. It also inoculates Proposition 209 against
charges of divisiveness.

Days after the commercial aired, however, the campaign's
attempt to gain the high ground was undercut by House
Speaker Gingrich and Governor Wilson. They had invited
sixty or so California executives to participate in a September 6
confidential teleconference on Proposition 209. Unbeknownst
to them, Rick Orlov, a reporter from the *Los Angeles Daily*

News, had mistakenly received an invitation as well. He listened in as the Speaker and the Governor hawked Proposition 209 as a wedge issue that could help Republicans win the presidency and retain control of Congress.

"It's become a partisan issue," Wilson enthusiastically told the prospective donors, ". . . that works strongly to our advantage."[6] The initiative, he went on, "has every bit the potential to make a critical difference in the race for president and House members. There is a real analogy between the experience two years ago in 1994 when I was seeking reelection and Proposition 187 was on the ballot."[7] For his part, Gingrich reminded listeners that if Republicans rode Proposition 209, "Clinton has to take his time and money out of the Midwest to put in California. He can't win the presidency without winning California. I think this is as important as any single resource in the campaign."

It was a spin on Proposition 209 and presidential politics that was dated. Polls showed that Clinton's fortunes had changed considerably from 1995, when California had been considered a must-win state. Few of the donors responded to the appeal, and Steinberg was aghast as he read the press reports. It was, he said sarcastically, another product of "the much vaunted" Wilson organization. "You had the worst of both worlds," said Steinberg.[8] "You didn't raise much money, but you got bad press."

The Search for a Campaign

Patricia Ewing, the campaign manager for Defeat Proposition 209, was delighted by the snafu. Her fund-raising wasn't going any better than it had in the summer, and increasingly she relied on the Proposition 209 campaign to fumble. Meanwhile Ewing tried to raise money, but liberals kept their checkbooks closed and the Proposition 209 campaign continued to effectively block corporate donors from getting to her. That summer, pressure from Wilson ended any plans Pacific Gas and Electric had to fund the opposition's campaign. "We heard that his phone call was even stronger than his letter," said Thomas Wood, the initiative's co-author, referring to Wilson's public "Dear Stan" letter to PG&E chairman Stanley Skinner. In that two-and-a-half-page letter Wilson chastised Skinner for coming out against Proposition 209.[9]

Without corporate funders the opposition depended on traditional Democratic Party sources, but none of the party's leaders took on Proposition 209 as their mission. Mayor Willie Brown, an ally and a formidable fund-raiser—probably the best that the opposition or the party had—did not seem to have his heart in the campaign. The popular mayor had been key in getting the Business Round Table and PG&E to oppose Proposition 209, but their opposition did not produce money. And as Wood remarked, who cared if PG&E opposed Proposition 209? "People have a love/hate relationship with it anyway," he said.[10] "We were only concerned about it giving money." Brown said that he did everything the opposition requested, including making all the fund-raising calls he was asked to make. It probably didn't help, however, that Brown felt that the initiative was unbeatable. "There was no way to raise $35 million for this kind of issue, and that's what it would have taken," Brown said, naming a figure that no one in the campaign had ever imagined raising.[11] "You needed Huffington coverage," he added, referring to Michael Huffington, who spent that amount in his unsuccessful 1994 Senate race against Senator Dianne Feinstein. "That means wall-to-wall on every station with every clever propaganda technique in existence. Then you may have had a shot, but short of that you had no shot at all."

Ewing's coalition was unhappy with the lack of an opposition campaign or any visibility at all. With the women's groups out on their own since mid-August, the opposition coalition was smaller, but anything but trim. Ewing's advisors or wanna-be advisors far outnumbered those for a candidate campaign. In the south, they included Connie Rice and Molly Munger from the NAACP Legal Defense and Education Fund, Ramona Ripston at the ACLU, and Anthony Thigpen at AGENDA. In San Francisco Dorothy Erlich at the ACLU, Eva Paterson at the Lawyer's Committee for Civil Rights, Jan Adams at Californians for Justice, and Jerome

Karabel, a sociology professor at U.C. Berkeley, kept abreast of the campaign's progress on Thursday morning conference calls. Few of these advisors had great political expertise, but they had been with the coalition from the outset. No one was paying them to participate in an endless stream of weekend rallies, evening debates, or after-work strategy sessions. To them the opposition to Proposition 209 wasn't just a political campaign; it was a line in the sand: it called into question their life's work.

Some of them tried to raise money, but they wanted to do more. It was difficult for them to sit idle and accept Ewing's argument that money was the only thing that mattered—especially when money was not forthcoming. They had all spent too many hours planning strategy to completely let go. Some took on speaking engagements; others suggested campaign tactics. Typical of these attempts was Karabel's idea that the opposition try to ride Clinton's coattails. On its face the idea made sense: Clinton was popular, as was his mend-it-don't-end-it message on affirmative action. Therefore, if they could get him to talk about affirmative action and attack Proposition 209 during a visit to California, the opposition would benefit. Such press coverage might even help fund-raising. But, the Clinton-Gore campaign in California had spurned a connection. That operation felt it wasn't Clinton's job to help the opposition to 209—he had an election to win—and his campaign staff wasn't going to make it easy for anyone to trade on his popularity. The campaign staff had already made sure that during his trips to California Clinton never raised the issue of affirmative action or Proposition 209. Nevertheless, Karabel thought it was worth a try.

He recalled that in the spring of 1995 Paterson had visited Clinton at the White House to impress on him the importance of what was then known as the California Civil Rights Initiative. The two shared some history. Her father had grown up in Hope, Arkansas, and Paterson remembered that Clinton's grandfather was one of four white merchants who served blacks. "We bonded," Paterson told the *Plain Dealer* in Cleveland as she recounted the meeting.[12] Karabel believed that it was time for Paterson to take advantage of this connection. She agreed and wrote a letter to the president. To Paterson's surprise, she received a reply in late August at her home address in Oakland. "Proposals such as Proposition 209 that are designed to eliminate all affirmative action programs in public education, employment, and contracting are inconsistent with our national goal of ensuring equal opportunity and contrary to all of our interests. I assure you I will actively oppose this measure. . . . Sincerely, Bill Clinton."[13] Karabel was as excited as someone who had just felt a sharp tug at the end of his fishing line. It was the strongest statement Clinton had ever made on Proposition 209. Karabel wanted to make the letter public.

At the very least, Karabel believed, it would make the news for one day, and it might encourage reporters to question Clinton on his views about Proposition 209. Suddenly, however, Ewing became timid. It was a personal letter. Did their campaign have the right to release it? Karabel was baffled. "It's a letter from the president, it's signed by him, he's a big boy, he probably assumes we are going to release it and suddenly we're worried about protecting the president," said Karabel, incredulous at the campaign's reluctance to act.[14] "This is supposed to be the party that supports affirmative action. Why are we worried about releasing a letter that says exactly that?" Weeks later a quote from the letter was included in the middle of a long press release about other opposition campaign business. Karabel, Paterson, and Erlich would look back on Ewing's reluctance and wonder if she had been thinking of the president's best interests more than those of her campaign.

But in September they faulted their own political inexperience, and, when Ewing failed to release the letter, Karabel proposed a more traditional move. He wanted the campaign to take out full-page ads in the *New York Times* and the *Los Angeles Times* highlighting the opponents of Proposition 209. By mid-September, however, Bob Shrum, the opposition's Washington, DC, media advisor, and Ewing were no longer returning his phone calls. "I got 400 faxes a day from people who knew what would work," said Shrum, obviously finding the free advice tiresome. "If we do X, everyone promised we would get 51 percent of the vote." For her part, Ewing was wearying of coalition campaigns. "It was thirty people who thought they should be the person making the decisions," she said. The advisors, however, were frantic. To find the 209 campaign, all they had to do was turn on the radio. They had nothing to counter Connerly, and, if they didn't fault Ewing for failing to raise money, they did want some evidence of a campaign.

Attorney General Dan Lungren
and the Wellness Foundation

By late summer Steinberg was confident the opposition would not get any big money from traditional Democratic Party or corporate sources. But he knew that one possible white knight remained—the California Wellness Foundation. A not-for-profit foundation with assets of $800 million, Wellness was created in 1992 as a condition of HealthNet's decision to change its tax status from a nonprofit to a for-profit health maintenance organization. The foundation was a way for HealthNet to repay taxpayers for the benefits it had enjoyed as a nonprofit. Wellness's charter directed it to use its money to improve the health of the state's residents. Generally this had meant funding health treatment and disease prevention programs. But in 1994 Wellness broke with the convention of what a private foundation did with its money and became a major player in initiative politics. Steinberg felt that if it made a similar move in 1996, Proposition 209 could fall.

Wellness was drawn to the political arena in 1994 and again in 1996 for the same reason—voters were confused and health was at issue. In 1994 the tobacco companies put on the ballot Proposition 188, whose title—Statewide Regulation Initiative—suggested it would tighten restrictions on smoking. In fact, however, it would have weakened them. But voters in California, who are vociferously antismoking, responded favorably to the implication of tightened smoking restrictions. Early polling showed that 70 percent supported the initiative. But if the public had truly understood Proposition 188, most opponents felt, it would easily be defeated.

Herb Gunther, Wellness's media advisor, believed that alerting voters to Proposition 188's true intent was exactly the kind of public service Wellness should provide. Gunther, who ran the Public Media Center, was a fixture in San Francisco's progressive community. He had a national reputation for political ads that were factual, smart, and attractive. He believed that the same style would work in a public education campaign on Proposition 188. Gary Yates, Wellness's president, agreed. Yates and his board had already ordered up a poll about the proposition and, after reviewing its results, asked Gunther to come up with a proposal for a media campaign.

To enter any campaign, Wellness had to be aware of two hurdles. First, it had to convince the attorney general, who oversees public charities, that they were not violating their mission to improve the health of Californians, thus putting in jeopardy the foundation's charitable status. Second, the media campaign had to satisfy the Internal Revenue Service's prohibitions against political lobbying by private foundations. Wellness's advertising campaign had to be nonpartisan and purely educational. The $4 million television and print campaign created by Gunther was exactly that. One ad stated rhetorically, "Who supports Proposition 188—You have a right to know." The list of supporters and opponents, pulled from the ballot pamphlet that few voters bother to read, followed. Philip Morris and other tobacco companies fell under the Yes side, and the American Cancer Society and health care groups on the No side. In the end, Proposition 188 lost with 70 percent of the electorate opposing it, and Wellness got the credit.

Gunther's campaign on Proposition 188 had successfully pushed the envelope of a foundation's ability to impact the political process, and he was eager to try again with Proposition 209. As an Asian American, he believed strongly in affirmative action and he believed that Proposition 209 was similar to Proposition 188 because voters were unsure of what the initiative would actually do. It called itself a *civil rights initiative,* but voters were unaware that it would eliminate affirmative action. Would they still support it if they knew? Yates and his board had become interested in the issue after reading the May issue of the *New England Journal of Medicine.* In it, the authors concluded, "Black and Hispanic physicians have a unique and important role in caring for poor, black and Hispanic patients in California. Dismantling affirmative action programs, as is currently proposed, may threaten health care for both poor people and members of minority groups."[15] Yates said that after reading the article the board authorized some market research to look at attitudes toward the initiative. "What we found is that like almost every ballot initiative, the public didn't understand it very well," said Yates.[16]

Gunther believed the link between affirmative action and health was real—every major national and state medical association eventually came out against Proposition 209. Yates and other members of the board, however, were not as sure. Everyone agreed, however, that Proposition 209 supporters were likely to challenge the link between health and affirmative action. Gunther's planned educational campaign for Proposition 209 was even flatter than the one he had run for 188. First, he would inform voters of the bare fact that Proposition 209 would change the state constitution. It wasn't sexy, but it was effective. Steinberg knew from his own work that heightened awareness of the initiative's impact on the state constitution could cost his side three to five percentage points. In addition, Gunther planned to run spots that would simply amplify the ballot pamphlet's summary from the legislative analyst. It clearly stated what the attorney general's summary had failed to do: the initiative would have a significant impact on state affirmative action programs. Again, Steinberg was aware that this strategy would cost Proposition 209 some votes. In his campaign plan, Steinberg underscored the success of the Wellness strategy on Proposition 188 and warned, "A similar approach in this campaign could seek to frame the issue in a way which would help the other side. This is an awesome strategy, which could be devastating."[17]

All summer Steinberg waited for Wellness to emerge. In late August a network source tipped him off. Someone, the source told him, was asking about a big education buy. Steinberg knew exactly who it was, and he pounced. Wood, who was one of Proposition 209's co-authors and who had been researching ways to prevent a Wellness campaign, had determined that Attorney General Lungren had plenty of power to stop Wellness. "He can tell a public charity not to do something, and then the burden of proof is on the charity," Wood said.[18] "It didn't take much prodding," he added, to get Lungren to fire off a letter to Wellness. Even before the foundation's board of directors met on September 16 to make its final decision, Gunther could feel Yates pulling back. "It was the first time that I would not be making the presentation," Gunther said.[19]

When the board gathered at the Ritz Carlton in Laguna Beach, a letter signed by Deputy Attorney General H. Chester Horn, Jr., was faxed to them. It informed the board that Lungren's office was aware of its plans "to support an advertising campaign opposing passage of Proposition 209" and noted its concern that "expenditures by the Foundation for such advertising might constitute improper attempts to influence legislation and fall outside of the ambit of the Foundation's charitable charter."[20] The letter continued, "Such actions could subject the Foundation to excise tax penalties or possible loss of tax exempt status and its directors to personal liability for any improper expenditure of the Foundation's charitable assets." The letter then asked for a complete description of the foundation's plans to become involved in the 209 campaign.

For board members already reluctant to endorse the campaign, this was reason enough to pull back. Those in favor of going ahead argued that Gunther's campaign was nonpartisan and was not lobbying—the IRS restricted the foundation from political lobbying. Lungren, they argued, supported Proposition 209 and was using his position as attorney general to improperly restrain the foundation's freedom of speech. In the end the board voted five to three to authorize Yates to look at Gunther's proposal and to consult with lawyers. Gunther's legal counsel, Silk, Adler & Colvin, a San Francisco-based firm specializing in nonprofit tax law, had already approved the campaign as a legitimate and defensible expenditure. "Looking at the articles of incorporation and trust law in California we thought it was absolutely clear that this campaign and the nexus between health and affirmative action was not a stretch at all," said Gregory Colvin, the attorney who advised Gunther. Colvin added that Wellness had given grants to minority health concerns before and that the first major Supreme Court decision on affirmative action, *Bakke,* concerned admission to a medical school.[21] In addition to the approval from Silk, Adler & Colvin, Gunther had a letter from the IRS giving Gunther pre-approval of his campaign.

The foundation had commissioned two academic studies documenting the nexus between health and affirmative action, but Yates maintained, "We had no strong supporting document for the health connection, and our charter is to improve the health of people in California."[22] Indeed, the foundation's legal counsel had strongly advised against any Proposition 209 campaign because the nexus between health and affirmative action was not sufficiently supported. In a conference call the following week Wellness's board agreed with its legal counsel and voted six to three against going forward. Gunther, however, believed it was more a matter of politics than a lack of research. "We knew there was a compelling health issue, and we didn't want to sit this one out," said Gunther.[23] Yates, he added, merely got cold feet. Colvin said it was not surprising. "I have never heard of the attorney general's office attempting to exercise prior restraint in the area of free speech," said Colvin.[24] "It has a tremendous chill-

ing effect. Foundations are highly sensitive and easily intimidated."

The Opposition Finds Duke

By September the opposition's campaign was languishing.
Donors might give to a cause with an outside chance of winning, but that wasn't the opposition to Proposition 209. It had
no momentum, no charismatic spokesperson like Connerly,
and no air time. Then, in early September, Ewing found an
image, a message, and at long last a campaign. It came from
the most unlikely of sources—Vladimir Cerna, an immigrant
from El Salvador. Cerna was Senate President of the student
body at California State University, Northridge, a strong advocate of affirmative action, and an immigrant with a flair for
the theatrical. He was watching the Jerry Springer show on
television one night when the guest was David Duke. The former Klansman from Louisiana railed against affirmative action. Cerna was intrigued. After he turned off the television, he
checked out Duke's web page. The following week he discussed his idea with others on campus, and in no time at all
the students decided to sponsor a forum on affirmative action.
They would invite prominent speakers from both camps. And
they would invite David Duke.

Suddenly, Cal State, Northridge, was ground zero of
Proposition 209. It was an odd place to take center stage.
None of California's campuses had been particularly fertile
ground for large demonstrations against Proposition 209 or in
support of affirmative action. When the U.C. regents met to
end affirmative action in July 1995, nearly as many reporters
as protesters attended the meeting. Elsewhere at the U.C. campuses, protests had taken place as students returned to classes
in the fall, but the marches were puny compared with the
crowds generated by the antiwar or free speech movements.
In fact, the chancellors seemed more upset about the loss of
affirmative action than the students. A faculty advisor to the

students at U.C. Irvine said that she was supposed to work at a table on campus for students opposed to Proposition 209. "The truth was," she said, "I could never find the table." Bob Shrum, the campaign's Washington media advisor, concluded early on, "this was not going to be a movement campaign."

For most U.C. students, little was at stake: they were white and affirmative action affected them only indirectly, by creating a diverse student body. Neither their lives nor their civil liberties were at stake, and no leader like Martin Luther King, Jr., or John or Robert Kennedy rallied them to the cause. State campuses such as Northridge and Sacramento State had more activity, but then they also had more minority students. Even at these campuses, however, activity was muted and generally inspired by activist faculty members. "You can't compare it to the 1960s," said Anthony Platt, a former Berkeley activist and a professor at Sacramento State who helped organize students and faculty on his campus to oppose Proposition 209. "You are talking about the difference between a grassroots spontaneous movement of the sixties and the seventies and a student body 30 years later that has come of age during the Reagan and Bush administrations and regards the civil rights movement as history."

Most campus activities failed to attract any attention, but David Duke at Northridge was a national story. More significant, Duke inspired Ewing. Duke, she reported with excitement in the Thursday morning conference calls with her advisors up north, would reveal the Proposition 209 campaign as the work of racists. It would give the opposition the direction it needed. Some were leery, but they had to admit that Ewing was right about one thing: Affirmative action was again in the news. "It took a freak show to get national attention on this," said Rice of the NAACP Legal Defense and Education Fund.

Both 209's supporters and opponents might have done well to ignore the ex-Klansman, but both sides seemed intent on using Duke's presence to raise the issue's profile. Connerly went ballistic. Accusing the opposition of McCarthy-like conspiracy, he tried to secure all of the telephone records from Blenda Wilson, the African American university president of the Northridge campus. When that failed, Connerly asked the courts for a gag order on Duke. Editorial writers, at first critical of the invitation to Duke, began to remind Connerly of the right of free speech. For a moment it looked as if all the opposition had to do was stand by and watch Connerly self-destruct.

Instead Ewing jumped into the fray with both feet. "In any party there are extremists, and this is an extremist measure," she proclaimed. She explained, "Anyone who says 209 is about ending discrimination—the moment David Duke steps across the state line, that's a bald-faced lie."[25] The same campaign manager who had been worried about the Feminist Majority as bomb throwers now tossed her own molotov cocktail, calling the debate "a defining moment in the campaign. . . . Duke puts the lie to their claim that this proposition isn't about affirmative action."[26] All the months of polling and research about the need for a moderate message were cast aside as Ewing poured kerosene on the fire. Proposition 209 supporters, she implied, were racists of the worst order. This, however, was the shouting match that Clinton had warned in April 1995 that Democrats could not win. It antagonized rather than reached out to mainstream voters.

Duke's presence in California on the eve of the nation's most important referendum on civil rights in more than three decades did more to sidetrack the state's conversation about race than enrich it. No one doubted that some of Proposition 209's supporters were racist, but to imply that anyone who supported 209 was a racist was considered by many to be ineffective politics. "I was kind of surprised by their focus on Duke," Steinberg said.[27] "It showed an inside the Washington beltway mentality where this could be reduced to racism, and it was wrong." This was fine with Steinberg: Not only did the opposition seem shrill and extreme, but all the attention on Duke centered the campaign on race, not on gender, and race was exactly the focus he wanted. Connerly felt the same.

Publically, he denounced Duke's visit, but privately, he thought "Alleluia," he recalled after the election.[28] You see, he explained, Duke returned the public's attention to race.

Even before he arrived at Northridge, Duke was obligingly newsworthy. He could be heard on California radio damning affirmative action and minorities, and accusing blacks and Latinos of raping white women "by the thousands."[29] Recognizing that it was Mexican immigration, not blacks, that unsettled Californians most, Duke tailored his message to his audience. "I don't want California to look like Mexico," he said. "I don't want to have their pollution. I don't want the corruption. I don't want their disease. I don't want their superstition. I don't want us to look like that country. If we continue this alien invasion, we will be like Mexico."[30]

On the day of the Duke debate, the proponents of Proposition 209 once more denounced his visit and repudiated his support for their measure. "David Duke has no place in California," declared Connerly at a sparsely attended event in a Van Nuys community center designed to attract the media already gathered a few miles away for the Northridge debate. "He is anti-diversity, anti-integration. David Duke stands in opposition to everything Proposition 209 is about." When the few reporters who bothered to attend Connerly's press conference finished writing down his remarks, they rushed back to campus. There cameras had been set up early in the morning. Northridge was the story that the media, particularly television, wanted: angry demonstrations, confrontations with the police, blood.

Inside the hall, a multi-ethnic group of 800 spectators listened politely as Duke debated Joe Hicks, the executive director of the Los Angeles-based Multicultural Collaborative. Duke continued his harangue against affirmative action, which for him meant "discrimination against white people." In a time of diminishing job opportunities in a demographically diverse society, he declared, whites would suffer, and he appealed openly to what he saw as the self-interest of whites:

The founding elements of this country, the Constitution,
the Declaration of Independence, the basis of this nation
was created primarily by white Europeans. And we
should not be second class citizens in our own country.
We should not face discrimination in the nation the fab-
ric of which we created. I will stand up for equal rights
for all in America, including white people in our society.

Hicks offered a competing vision:

[Martin Luther] King [Jr.] was interviewed in 1965. . . .
[He was asked:] "If a nationwide program of preferential
treatment in terms of employment for Negroes were to
be adopted, how would you propose to assuage resentment of whites who already feel their jobs are being
jeopardized by the influx of Negroes resulting from desegregation?" King responded: "We must develop a program of public works, retraining and jobs for all, so that
none, white or black, will feel threatened. At the present
time," King said, "thousands of jobs a week are disap-
pearing in the wake of automation and other production
efficiency techniques. Black or white, we will all be
harmed unless something grand and imaginative is
done. The unemployed, poverty stricken white man
must be made to realize that he is in the very same boat
as the Negro. Together . . . they can exert massive pressure to get jobs for all. Together . . . they could form a
grand alliance. Together," Dr. King said, "they could
merge all people for the good of all."

Meanwhile, things were considerably livelier outside the
hall. Initially, another 800 students milled around as about 100
protested the debate. When some of the protesters from the
Berkeley-based Coalition to Defend Affirmative Action by Any
Means Necessary started to pound on the windows, the campus police sprayed the crowd with Mace. Thirty officers from
the LAPD's critical response unit and a contingent on horses

were called in from the campus perimeters. Soon batons and pepper spray were flying. In the end, six people—only one of whom was a student at Northridge—were arrested.

After almost a month of news stories and editorials, the debate itself was hardly covered. Instead television stations and newspapers statewide focused on the demonstrators and the baton-wielding police. They portrayed violent protests that never really materialized. The *Sacramento Bee* ran more than 1,500 words on the Duke story and the *Los Angeles Times* ran nearly 1,400 words, but both gave short shrift to the debate. The editorials and next-day analyses uniformly damned Northridge student leaders and the opposition to Proposition 209. Typical was a column by Dan Walters in the *Sacramento Bee* that described the opposition as "shooting itself in the feet." "If Duke's invitation to represent Proposition 209 was a sophomoric trick to turn sentiment against the measure, it may have backfired," Walters wrote. "Voters who watched accounts of the incident now correlate the opposition to the measure with violent demonstrators and stupid students. Wilson and Connerly come off seeming reasonable and sympathetic. The legitimate opponents of Proposition 209 look bad, meanwhile, because they refused to join Wilson and Connerly in denouncing the invitation to Duke and, while denying any involvement in bringing Duke to Northridge, clearly hoped that it would help them with their uphill campaign against the measure by equating Wilson and Connerly with Duke."[31]

Some in the opposition looked at the coverage and worried that Duke had done more harm than good. Ewing disagreed. She talked about using Duke's visit in their paid media campaign—if, that is, they could raise the money.

The Feminist Majority and NOW Go It Alone

When the main coalition dumped the Feminist Majority and NOW in mid-August, Katherine Spillar, the national director

of the Feminist Majority and the lead person on the affirmative action campaign, took it hard. She had worked closely
with Rice and Munger for months, and she took personally
their decision to go along with the others. "It was difficult for
Kathy," said Peg Yorkin, the co-founder of the Feminist
Majority and a long-time contributor to women candidates.[32]
"They had all become friends."

Spillar was, however, the kind of person who took seriously
the old adage, Don't get mad—get even. After a short lull she was
back organizing, anxious to show nonbelievers that women
could be convinced to vote against Proposition 209. Yorkin and
Lorraine Sheinberg, another big Democratic Party donor, were
ready to back her up, and suddenly they were writing checks for
more than $100,000 each. Sheinberg was also busy going
through her Rolodex to call other heavy hitters. Women, she
said, could be counted on. She suspected that others, however,
were being told not to give to the campaign because it would
hurt Clinton. No one said this directly, she explained. "They
talked in code."

"That was clearly the issue," Sheinberg said.[33] "After I
spoke with them they would say they were going to talk to
someone about it and name someone very high up in the party
and then never get back to me. I was not dealing with political neophytes." Sheinberg also talked to Clinton directly at an
exclusive fund-raising dinner in June at the home of former
chair of MCA Lew Wasserman—one of those affairs where
everyone had already spent a night in the White House's
Lincoln bedroom. "I told him he needed to speak out more
clearly (about affirmative action) in California, and then I was
going to move on and he pulled me back. 'You know the only
way to run a campaign on this issue is to put a woman's face
on it,' he advised," Sheinberg added.[34] "Then he said he would
speak out publicly, but he never really did."

Sheinberg wasn't one to wait for Clinton to act. She wrote
more checks to the campaign and loaned Spillar the third
floor of a building on Wilshire known as the Bubble Factory.

The Sheinbergs had their own production company on the second floor. On the third floor, Spillar's Freedom Summer for college students working against Proposition 209 turned into Freedom Fall. At almost any time of day or night, the large open space was the command post of a small Lydian army— women out plastering the city with posters, visiting college campuses, and carrying out small demonstrations on busy urban intersections.

Justine Andronici, a twenty-four-year-old graduate of Colgate College, was in charge of the student organizing. She focused on state and community colleges and tried to hook up with already existing student organizations. "We'd get a call from a community college and we would be out there with fliers, information, anything they needed," Andronici said.[35] By midsummer her troops had already been on 50 campuses. The lack of a women's campus network, Andronici said, was disappointing, but once again the state's growing Latino population was emerging as a player. The Movimiento Estudiantil Chicano de Aztlán, a student organization known as MEChA that had been around since the late 1960s, had grown impressively in the wake of the 1994 Proposition 187 campaign. In 1997 its members proved critical in aiding Andronici efforts, but again the gatherings were small events—more like pep rallies than protests.

On September 28 a Freedom Bus set off from Los Angeles to visit churches an schools across the state. The bus was packed with Jesse Jackson; Patricia Ireland, the president of NOW; Ellie Smeal, the president of the Feminist Majority; Dolores Huerta, the secretary-treasurer of the United Farmworkers Union; and a group of college volunteers. The Freedom Bus speakers may have been preaching to the converted, as Ewing believed, but they were also getting a fair amount of positive press coverage. Typical of the campus rallies was a late morning event at Santa Rosa Junior College, in Northern California. About 300 students gathered on the lawn to hear Huerta and Smeal. While the two headliners spoke, the campaign staff and volunteers fanned out and signed up students to work on election day. Omar Gallardo, a twenty-one-year-old sophomore active in MEChA, had helped to organize the rally. Like others in MEChA, his activism was personal. He credited his success in college to affirmative action. In high school he had been part of the Puente (Bridge) program designed to help Mexican American students in English and math. "If it wasn't for that program I wouldn't have stayed in school," he said flatly.

By October 9 the Freedom Bus was back in Los Angeles for a fund-raiser with Senators Dianne Feinstein and Barbara Boxer and Anita Hill, the law professor who accused then Supreme Court nominee Clarence Thomas of sexual harassment. The day began at Mount Saint Mary's, a women's college in West Los Angeles. No more than 200 students gathered to hear the traveling caravan. Smeal was undaunted by the size of the crowd. "Can you give us election day?" she bellowed as if she were addressing thousands. "Can you give me a baby sitter," a cheerful woman responded, explaining that she had four children. Smeal knew how to persuade the reluctant, and in no time the prospect had signed up to walk precincts on election day. She would take her children along.

Later that evening donors paid $150 to attend a fund-raiser at a large private home in the Wilshire District. At times it was unclear if some of those snacking on chicken and beef fajitas were at the right affair. Cary Davidson, an attorney from Reed & Davidson, CCRI's early law firm, said he was there "on business." From his point of view, "There isn't any way 209 loses." The assembly democrat Louis Caldera, who had many misgivings about affirmative action programs, also attended the fund-raiser. He believed assembly Democrats needed an initiative issue to run with, but opposing Proposition 209 was not the right one. "I suggested No on 211," he said, referring to the high-profile securities initiative, "but I didn't get enough backing." Carol Leif, the daughter of former MCA chair Lew Wasserman, tried to remain upbeat. They had done pretty well, she said, explaining that the fund-raiser was competing with the Kemp-Gore debate and the first game of the National League championship series.

The Republicans Divided

With no advertising campaign, both camps—the coalition led by Ewing and the one led by Spillar—were desperate to get their message across. Apart from the Freedom Bus and Grandmaster Duke, affirmative action was not a television story. Nevertheless, Proposition 209 received a lot of attention from the print media, and the campaign was being taken to voters in an antiquated form of American politics—the community forum. By the end of October more than twenty-five Proposition 209 debates or forums a week were being held around the state. Each was attended by anywhere from five to five hundred people. Comparatively few, however, were covered by the press, and fewer still got much play. Some debates were broadcast on radio. Others were shown on cable television, and a few, notably those sponsored by media consortiums called "Voice of the Voter," were broadcast regionally on network television. One televised debate, carried by ABC network affiliates in San Francisco and Los Angeles, was broadcast statewide two weekends before the election.

More than changing anyone's mind, the debates offered a glimpse of how difficult it is to talk about complex issues in a political campaign. Rather than exploring issues of race and discrimination, each side tried to make points with the voter. The Proposition 209 campaign understood that it was imperative to stay on message—which meant highlighting the simple issue of fairness and ignoring the complexity of ongoing discrimination. The opposition's task was more difficult. They had to explain how Proposition 209 violated fairness and how using race and gender preferences helped to ensure it. A typical exchange was one between Connerly and Rice in a mid-October debate.

Connerly: Civil Rights. They are individual rights. . . . Civil
Rights are those things that we defend, we cherish, we
preserve at all expense because they are the essence of
democracy. . . . [T]here is one principle that we have to
decide whether we agree with, and that's the principle
of equal treatment under the law.[36]

Rice: Yes, the ultimate expression of equal treatment under
the law and the ultimate expression of civil rights is our
constitution, but that wasn't enough. We've had to actually amend our constitution with the Fourteenth
Amendment, we've actually had to go further than that
in the 1960s. Mr. Connerly is absolutely right. The
crowning expression of civil rights in today's society is
the 1964 Civil Rights Act, Title 9, and the Voting Rights
Act of this country. Proposition 209 is not a civil rights
bill. It is in fact a decoy. Like a duck decoy it is put
there to actually destroy the real thing. . . . The purpose
is to make currently legal affirmative action programs
illegal. . . . It was crafted as a wedge issue. . . . It's not
about civil rights. There's nothing right about it, and
there's nothing civil about it. We have not arrived at a
time in this country when we can afford to replace
equal opportunity with the empty rhetoric of color
blindness.

Rice attacked the notion of "simple" principles. "The First
Amendment is eight words," she said. "It's taken us 200 years,
and we still don't know what it means." Still, Connerly
doggedly returned to the principle:

Connerly: The principle here is whether the state shall be
allowed to discriminate against or grant preferential
treatment to any individual or group on the basis of
race, sex, color, ethnicity or national origin. That's the
principle. If there's not one person that you can prove
has been the victim of reverse discrimination or whatever, the principle is still valid.

If Connerly was comfortable with the principle, others in the Republican Party were having trouble. Although Steinberg had held out hope at the Republican convention that Dole and Kemp might be able to frame Proposition 209 as an initiative that ensured equal opportunity for all, he was quickly disabused of the notion. Dole failed to mention Proposition 209 in his California tour that followed the convention, and Kemp actually promised reporters that he and Dole had no plans to take it on. "We are not going to campaign on a wedge issue," Kemp told reporters at a breakfast in late September. "We are not going to let this issue tear up California."[37] Not that Kemp was above playing racial politics, but it was a radically different kind of racial politics than Republicans generally practiced. Speaking to minority voters in Fillmore, the southern Santa Clara Valley town where his wife was born and raised, Kemp said that the country's capital "is locked up in the hands of white people," and promised to "remove the barriers that stand in the way of low-income people and particularly minority men and women."[38] Whose side was Kemp on, Steinberg wondered.

Steinberg's sense of wonder grew when Tim Russert asked Kemp about affirmative action on *Meet the Press* in early October. Instead of rejecting racial preferences, Kemp embraced them. "Race is a legitimate issue to take into consideration for entrance to college," he said, in direct contradiction to Connerly, Wilson, the U.C. regents, and the 209 campaign. He added, however, "It is one of many. It's not the only one. I have always opposed and always will any affirmative action program that leads to a quota."[39]

Three days later in the vice-presidential debate held in San Diego and moderated by PBS's Jim Lehrer, Kemp tried frantically to avoid the issue altogether when it was raised by Al Gore.

Gore: There is a specific measure on the ballot in California.
It was embodied in legislation introduced by Senator
Dole to apply to the whole nation.

Mr. Kemp campaigned against it, spoke against it,
wrote letters against.it, went to California to fight against
it, and now has endorsed it. I don't think it's a minor matter. I think this is one of the most important challenges
that our country has to face in the future. And I hope that
Mr. Kemp will try to persuade Senator Dole to adopt Mr.
Kemp's position instead of the other way around.

Lehrer: Mr. Kemp, what is your position?

Kemp: Does that red light mean we're supposed to stop?

Lehrer: That means—yes, he's—right.

Gore: You thought that was going to be your problem and
not mine.

(laughter)

Kemp: Yes, right. I can't believe I'm keeping within the time
limit.

(laughter)

Lehrer: Mr. Kemp, do we have a serious race problem in the
United States right now?

Kemp: Yes, we really do. This country has yet to deal with the
type of inclusionary politics. It is so very important for
Americans—white and black, Jew and Christian, immigrant and native born—to sit down and talk and listen
and begin to understand what it's like to come from that
different perspective. Our country is, as the Kerner report suggested a number of year ago, being split. . . . We
really have two economies. Our general economy, our
national economy, our mainstream economy is democratic, is based on incentives—a small *d*, Al. . . .
Unfortunately, in urban America—and I was glad to
hear the vice president talk a little bit about it—they
have abandoned the inner cities. There's a socialist
economy. There's no private housing. It's mostly public
housing. You're told where to go to school. You're told
what to buy with food stamps. . . . That must change.

"I was disgusted," said Steinberg.[40] He began to feel that
"the momentum was moving against" Proposition 209.[41]

8

Stumbling to the Finish Line

Dole Grasps for Proposition 209 and the Opposition Reaches for David Duke

We've got to get to the point in this country where
we can let some of this stuff go.
PRESIDENT BILL CLINTON
October 31, 1996, in
Oakland, California

Set to Risk All

On the weekend of October 12 Senator Dole's campaign team
huddled in Washington to figure out how a victory could be
fashioned from what looked like certain defeat. To win the
White House a candidate needed 270 of the 538 electoral college votes. The campaign team calculated that Dole had 123
and Clinton had 195. Many analysts had already given the race
to Clinton, but it was too early for Dole to accept that finality.
The campaign team developed a game plan. The discussion focused on two blocs of electoral votes. One included New
Jersey's 15 electoral votes, Pennsylvania's 23, Delaware's 3, and
Connecticut's 8, for a total of 49. The other consisted of
California's 54 electoral votes. The campaign couldn't go for
both; that would cost too much money. But winning either
bloc along with a string of states where the media spots were
not as expensive could put Dole over the top.

At first it was a coin toss. The states included in the two blocs of electoral votes polled about the same. But slowly Dole's numbers for Pennsylvania and New Jersey started to slip while California remained steady, at around a 10 percent gap. The Republican hold on Congress was also looking weak, making California's many congressional races the trove that could best help to secure the GOP's majority in the House of Representatives. California was an increasingly favored option for another reason as well: Proposition 209. "Given the matrix of issues that was left to play, it was one of the few that looked as if it might help," said Tony Fabrizio, Dole's pollster.

Dole staffer Dennis Shea had been pushing the candidate for months to take up affirmative action. So had California advisors Governor Pete Wilson and Ken Khachigian. But Dole had been reluctant to embrace either Proposition 209 or illegal immigration. He knew the rhetoric surrounding both issues, but he lacked the passion that gave the rhetoric zing. Sources close to him said Proposition 209 was too overreaching for his taste. He wanted to get rid of set-asides and, like every other American, he disavowed quotas, but ending all affirmative action? That was another matter. Kemp was even more ambivalent. Until he was tapped to be Dole's running mate, the former HUD secretary had advised against acting too hastily to eliminate affirmative action. And depending on the day of the week, Kemp still supported race-based preferences. Nevertheless, Dole and Kemp acquiesced to their advisors' urging. The *San Francisco Chronicle* announced on Monday, October 14, that Dole was set "to risk all" on California.

Even if Dole and Kemp could stay on message supporting Proposition 209—and evidence to the contrary quickly emerged—the strategy was risky at best. First of all, California in 1996 was a far different place from California in 1994. The economy was on the rebound. In 1994 it had been easy for Wilson to make anxious voters feel that if the state wouldn't spend $3 billion on illegal workers, there would be more money and jobs for unemployed Americans. Economists and political analysts felt in early 1995 that unemployed white workers could be made to feel equally shortchanged by the perceived benefits minorities received from affirmative action. But by 1996 many of the unemployed had found work.

Moreover, Dole was not Wilson. The governor retained the discipline of a marine. He began his attacks on undocumented workers years before Proposition 187 had been introduced. And from late 1991 on the governor consistently stayed on message, questioning the money California spent to educate and care for undocumented workers. By the time Proposition 187 emerged, Wilson was identified with its provisions. "The California electorate had spent the previous two years debating immigration outside of an election context," said Dan Schnur, Wilson's former aide.[1] In contrast Dole supported affirmative action until March 1995. When he switched sides, he did so unenthusiastically. And when he turned to it in mid-October to salvage his presidential campaign, he appeared desperate. "Lots of times issues become good issues because you make them good issues," said Lyn Nofziger, a Republican political consultant.[2] "Dole should have been on 209 from the very beginning and certainly from the start of the fall. When you get into something in the last two or three weeks that you have deliberately been ignoring, it looks like panic."

Given their situation, Dole and Kemp had to be especially convincing. They had to hit hard. They had to sound like true believers. But there was also a legitimate concern that, if they hit too hard, they could alienate voters in other states. "There were two schools of thought," said Fabrizio.[3] "One said that if you are going to play California to win, you had to do 209 early. The other mind-set said that if you play 209, it may hurt you in some marginal states like New Jersey and Pennsylvania because it was clearly not as deeply supported in those states. Those states had not had two years of media about affirmative action, and there was the feeling that you could shoot yourself in the foot in places like Pennsylvania and New Jersey." Despite Dole's diminished prospects in those states, they continued to concern him. Nevertheless, he pushed ahead with the California strategy, and on Monday, October 14, he arrived in San Diego and gave his first major campaign speech on affirmative action and Proposition 209. "A hundred years ago, defending against the unjust Supreme Court decision that affirmed segregation, Justice John Harlan wrote that the law regards man as man and takes no account for his color. And that was the spirit and the promise of the 1964 Civil Rights Act, which I voted for as a member of the House of Representatives, guaranteeing equal access to opportunities—not equal results, but equal access. And opportunity to participate."[4] Even if one disagreed, it was a coherent argument.

On the following night, however, Dole debated President Clinton in San Diego, and the confidence and moral authority he had projected the day before disappeared. When asked about affirmative action on national prime-time television, he was sheepish—failing to clearly endorse Proposition 209 by name, offering a muddled explanation for his turnaround on affirmative action, and managing to sound both wistful and flippant as he joked about a disability preference in the presidential race:

Dole: Well, we might not be there yet, but we're not going to
   get there by giving preferences and quotas. I supported
   that route for some time and again, I think it gets back
   to experience—a little experience, a little age, a little
   intelligence. And I noticed that nobody was really benefiting except a very small group at the top. The average
   person wasn't benefiting. People that had the money
   were benefiting. People that got all the jobs were
   benefiting. It seems to me that we ought to support the
   California Civil Rights Initiative. It ought to be not based
   on gender or ethnicity or color or disability. I'm disabled
   and I shouldn't have a preference. I would like to have
   one in this race, come to think of it. But I don't get one.
   Maybe we can work that out. I get a 10-point spot.

These were the words of no clear-eyed believer, but they were more in line with the nature of Dole's campaign—a random set of thoughts and asides. On some days, Dole attacked Clinton's character, on other days the press, and on still other days illegal immigration. Proposition 209 became the Dole campaign's stepchild—sometimes fought over, mostly ignored. "The campaign was completely inept," said Mike Schroeder, then vice chair of the California Republican Party.[5] "The Dole campaign never had a message on 209 or anything. They never developed any traction on any message, and when they adopted 209 no one believed them. It was too late, and their message had a very hard-edged racist approach."

Collision at the California Border

Arnold Steinberg, Proposition 209's campaign manager, had long wooed Dole, but when Dole finally came around, his belated presence was irritating at best—and "best" was rarely the case. If Dole had been more convincing about 209, Steinberg might have been happy to see the candidate cross the state line. He was, after all, coming with money, a commodity that Steinberg desperately needed. But Dole equivocated, and Steinberg was no longer anxious to do business with his team. The Republican National Committee had asked Steinberg in early October to make Proposition 209 commercials pitting Dole against Clinton, and Steinberg refused. "It would have compromised the campaign—my interest was in 209 and not Bob Dole, and there was no reason for me to diffuse 209 with something about the presidential campaign," Steinberg said.[6]

Instead, Steinberg had been running a nonpartisan radio campaign for Proposition 209. The first ad, which began to appear after Labor Day, featured Ward Connerly. The second ad, appearing in early October, cleverly undercut the gender arguments against the initiative. It featured Janice Camarena, who purported to be a young white female victim of reverse discrimination. The ad was timed to start running just as the

Claremont Institute released a study on white victims of reverse discrimination and as Assemblyman Bernie Richter geared up to hold hearings on discrimination against whites in higher education. These stories turned emotional anecdotes into potent political messages. And despite the power of personal stories, the opposition never countered the dozen or so cases of reverse discrimination that the Proposition's supporters had at their disposal with any of the hundreds of thousands of discrimination cases civil rights advocates had at theirs.

Steinberg's ability to make the most of the available cases of reverse discrimination was apparent in the Camarena ad. At twenty-six, Camarena was not glamorous. She was a sad, blue-eyed blond whose life in San Diego, and later in Crestline, had been touched more than once by tragedy. A working single mother with three young children, she enrolled in San Bernardino Valley Community College to realize her ambition to become a nurse. In January 1994 she was denied entrance into an English 101 class reserved for students in the Bridge Program, a remedial course designed for African American students. The teacher, she said, told her to leave because she was white, and as she walked out the other students laughed. A year later she sued the college, and in 1996 the case was settled. The college reimbursed her legal fees and agreed to remove any language in course descriptions implying that a certain class was "designed" for any specific group of students.

College officials disputed key facts, including the classroom scene, and argued that the Bridge Program, as well as a similar program designed for Latino students, did not exclude any students. Camarena was not accepted in that particular class, they said, because she had not preregistered, nor had she taken the prerequisite class. Moreover, they argued, another English 101 class, open to all students, was available in the same time slot. The settlement, they insisted, was a financial decision rather than an admission of wrongdoing.

From Camarena's story, Steinberg produced the following ad.

Male Announcer: The following actually happened January 19th, 1994.

Camarena: The teacher said to me, "You have to leave."

Male Announcer: Because you're white.

Camarena: Yes. Then I left. *(door slams shut—sound undercurrent)*

Male Announcer: As she went out the door, students laughed. *(laughter fades)* But for this young, widowed mother trying to enroll in a class at a public college, racial quotas were no laughing matter.

Camarena: I thought that discrimination was illegal.

Male Announcer: But the law allows preferential treatment.

Camarena: Another class was for Mexican American students only.

Male Announcer: These programs are based *not* on merit, or even on need, but on race. Janice Camarena Ingraham is white. Her deceased husband was Mexican American.

Camarena: Recently our public school asked the race of my children. I said the human race.

Male Announcer: Janice now is one of many women *and* men leading the campaign *for* Proposition 209. Proposition 209 prohibits discrimination and preferential quotas. It protects men *and* women of *all* races.

Female Announcer: Equal opportunity *without* quotas. Yes! Proposition 209. Bring us together.

The Camarena story, a classic example of reverse discrimination, set white women off from racial minorities and undermined the opposition's argument that women and minorities had a shared interest in maintaining affirmative action. The commercial stresses that Camarena's "whiteness" excluded her from educational opportunities. The radio spot also heightens its emotional appeal to a white audience by showing Camarena not only excluded, but humiliated by the minority students, who laugh as she leaves the classroom. Camarena does not claim racial superiority but moral superiority ("I said the

human race"). The advertisement promises that Proposition
209 will protect victims against any such future incidents.

Nonpartisan ads did not interest the Dole campaign, and
when the candidate was ready to spend money in California
the Republicans did not bother to ask Steinberg again for
help. To cut the ads the RNC wanted, John Herrington, chair
of the state Republican Party, called Sal Russo, a Sacramento-
based Republican media consultant. Within days, Russo had
prepared two ads—one with Herrington as the spokesperson
and the other with an unknown middle-aged woman. When
focus groups nixed Herrington, the second commercial went
out to television stations to begin running October 23.

The commercial opens with a montage of faces.

Female Narrator: We should be judged on merit, not by
gender or the color of our skin.

A solo piano melody plays in the background as a middle-aged
white woman with blond hair steps out from a group of thirteen people, including some Latinos and Asians. The camera
focuses on the woman.

Female Narrator: Job quotas and preferences are wrong.
Proposition 209 ends quotas and special treatment.
But Bill Clinton opposes Proposition 209, just like he
opposed Proposition 187.

As she speaks of Clinton, his image comes on screen in grainy
black and white. It is the image of a callow Bill Clinton, in shirt
sleeves, sitting in front of a microphone, crossing his arms. He
looks like he's listening to someone else talk and he doesn't look
happy. The commercial then cuts to footage of Martin Luther
King's 1963 speech at the Lincoln Memorial in Washington.

Martin Luther King, Jr.: . . . where they will not be judged by
the color of their skin but by the content of their character. I have a dream today!

The ad cuts back to a close-up of the woman.

Female Narrator: Martin Luther King was right. Bill Clinton is wrong to oppose Proposition 209. Let's get rid of all preferences.

The commercial ends with a plug to vote "Yes" on Proposition 209 in white letters against a backdrop of the Declaration of Independence and a waving American flag.

As soon as word leaked out that the California Republican Party was to run a television commercial linking Proposition 209 to Martin Luther King, Jr., civil rights leaders exploded. Many who had previously avoided Proposition 209 now spoke out with bitterness and anger. "Those who suggest that [King] did not support affirmative action are misrepresenting his beliefs, and indeed, his life's work," Coretta Scott King said in a joint statement with her son, Dexter Scott King. Even Proposition 209 co-author Thomas Wood—who along with Glynn Custred, Connerly, and others speaking for the campaign had been using King's line in debates—acknowledged that the ad crossed the line of propriety. "The problem is that there is plenty of evidence that King thought that blacks were entitled to preferences," Wood said, adding that there was also evidence that King would have included poor whites.[7] "He probably would have been somewhere around 'mend it don't end it.'" Worse than the misinformation the commercial conveyed, Wood said, was its tactical error in shifting the debate on Proposition 209 to Martin Luther King. "That couldn't possibly be to our advantage."

Steinberg was furious. He had lost control of the campaign he had shepherded for nearly two years. Compounding his problems was his lack of leverage. None of the state Republican officials who had supported him before could help now. Earlier in the Proposition 209 campaign Wilson had directed money from the state party to the Proposition 209 campaign because he had been responsible for raising it and because Herrington, the party's chair, agreed. Now the former Secretary of Energy's loyalty was to the Dole campaign. If Dole won, Herrington hoped for a cabinet position. If Dole lost, he wanted Haley Barbour's seat as chair of the RNC. Such goals made him eager to curry favor with the Dole campaign and the RNC. "Whatever was needed to be done, Herrington would do it," said a high state Republican Party official.[8]

Moreover, Herrington had reason to feel that the California Republican Party owned the Proposition 209 campaign. It had been responsible for nearly half of the initiative's bankroll, with much of the balance coming from national Republican donors. If Dole wanted to use the proposition to salvage his campaign or if the RNC believed it could increase their congressional victories, Herrington felt it was theirs to use. If Govenor Wilson disagreed, he would not win in a showdown with Herrington. "The chair has the power to make unilateral decisions and that's it," said Schroeder, who became chair in 1997.[9] Although Wilson might have been able to persuade a close political ally to listen to Steinberg, Herrington did not fit that bill. Their differences went back to 1976, when Wilson endorsed Gerald Ford for president instead of Ronald Reagan, and it continued into the 1990s with Wilson's tax hike and his support of gay rights. Nor was Connerly able to help Steinberg. The U.C. regent had been a compelling spokesperson, and his access to the governor had been critical in promoting Proposition 209, but his political influence within the state Republican Party was only as strong as Wilson's.

Steinberg, however, refused to back down. Making Proposition 209 partisan so late in the game, Steinberg feared, would lose it votes. The initiative's financing may have come primarily from Republican Party sources and donors, but its popular support came from Democrats as well.[10] When Wilson failed to dissuade Herrington, Steinberg attacked. He fired off faxes to officials in the state party calling for Herrington's resignation. Then he jumped into a public shouting match with Scott Taylor, the liaison with the RNC. "I cannot stress enough how strongly we feel that Prop 209 has been mismanaged by the staff," Taylor told the *Los Angeles Times*. He praised Connerly and damned Steinberg.[11] The "only decision we have made is that we would never give the money directly to the initiative campaign because we're afraid of how it would be managed," he added. Steinberg retaliated. "The use of King was juvenile at best and counterproductive at worst," Steinberg told the *Sacramento Bee*.[12] "People who don't know the issue probably shouldn't be creating ads about the issue. . . . This was an unnecessary controversy." To add punch, he filed a defamation lawsuit against Taylor.

Steinberg, party officials decided, was out of control. Connerly asked him to lie low, but Steinberg refused and Connerly was insulted. "The chair of the campaign was telling him to do something and he was rejecting it," Connerly said, referring to himself in the third person. Such insubordination was "unforgivable," he said.[13] "I fired him." Technically, Connerly lacked the authority to fire Steinberg, but he didn't even bother to ask Custred and Wood for their opinions. Dismayed, for a few short days they considered firing Connerly. But how would it look? Two white men firing their black spokesperson? They let it pass.

Steinberg, however, had made his point, and after all the bad press the RNC and Herrington sent Russo back to the studio to revise the commercial.

As before, a white woman steps out of a multi-ethnic group of people, and the same Clinton image appears on the screen. But King has been eliminated. Instead, the commercial cuts to the initiative's text, which is shown in black letters on a piece of ivory paper. The first words of the proposition, "The State shall not discriminate," are extracted from the text and shown in blue against a stark white background.

Female Narrator: Proposition 209 is only 37 words and it says
we shall not discriminate. It's right for California.

Again there is a close-up of the woman as she finishes speaking.

Female Narrator: Bill Clinton is wrong to oppose Proposition
209. Let's end all discrimination. Vote yes on
Proposition 209.

The commercial concludes, as before, with the message to vote
"Yes" on Proposition 209 in white letters against a backdrop of
the Declaration of Independence and a waving American flag.

Steinberg didn't like the revised ad any better; mentioning
Proposition 187 showed that Herrington was "in a time warp,"
he snapped. More significantly, voters were revising their
views on Proposition 209. The field poll released on October
30 showed that the race had narrowed to 46 percent for 209,
41 percent against, and 13 percent undecided. The following
day Connerly, echoing Steinberg, asked the state Republican
Party to pull its television ad. "We have ads that are more powerful, that are nonpartisan, and that accentuate the fact that
this is about preferences," Connerly pleaded.[14] Herrington refused and told reporters, "Ward Connerly is a very good
spokesman for Proposition 209, but he doesn't run the
Republican Party."[15] Connerly retorted that if 209 lost, it
would be Herrington's fault. "To the extent that our lead might
have diminished a few points it is directly a response to an ad
that, to be charitable, does not accentuate the core of this debate. And to the extent that this initiative is endangered, let it
be at the doorstep of John Herrington."[16] Connerly, however,
didn't matter to Herrington, and the ad stayed on through the
end of the campaign.

Clinton Ducks

While Dole bounced around on the issues, Clinton consistently kept his distance from Proposition 209. Tom Umberg,

who was in charge of the Clinton campaign in California, re-called that Dole was "constantly trying to goad us into making the campaign into one about 209."[17] Clinton, however, refused to advise voters against the proposition. If opponents were distressed, Republicans admired the president's political savvy. "When we hit him with 209," said Fabrizio, "Clinton came back with medicare—he was attacking us on more salient issues."[18] On his own, Clinton never brought up Proposition 209. When a voter asked him about affirmative action during the San Diego presidential debate, Clinton made the civil rights program sound like one for the disabled:

> I am against quotas. I'm against giving anybody any kind of preference for something they're not qualified for. But since I still believe that there is some discrimi-nation and that not everybody has an opportunity to prove they're qualified, I favor the right kind of affirma-tive action. I've done more to eliminate programs—affirmative action programs—I don't think were fair. And to tighten others up than my predecessors have since affirmative action's been around. But I have also worked hard to give people a chance to prove that they are qualified. Let me just give you some examples. We've doubled the number of loans from the Small Business Administration, tripled the number of loans to women businesspeople. No one unqualified—everybody had to meet the standards. We've opened 260,000 new jobs in the military to women since I've been president. But the joint chiefs say we're strong and more compe-tent and solid than ever. Let me give you another exam-ple of what I mean. For me, affirmative action is mak-ing that extra effort. It's sort of like what Senator Dole did when he sponsored the Americans with Disabilities Act and said to certain stores, OK, you've got to make it accessible to people in wheelchairs. We weren't guaran-teeing anything—anybody anything except the chance to prove they were qualified, the chance to prove that

they could do it. And that's why I must say I agree with
General Powell that we're not there yet. We ought to
keep making those extra affirmative action programs
the law and the policy of the land.

The president had understood from the beginning that an
aggressive stand against Proposition 209 could cost him too
many white voters. This was reflected in the constituency outreach reports for ethnic groups that Clinton's deputy chief of
staff, Harold Ickes, prepared in early 1995. Only the documents for white ethnics mentioned affirmative action. Along
with abortion, Ickes pointed out, it was a "hot button issue" in
white ethnic communities.[19] Better not to mention it. The
message in California was jobs, education, and the environment. Period.

Although the early signs from the Democratic Party had
never been encouraging, the opposition campaign was se-
verely let down. Connie Rice, from the NAACP Legal Defense
and Education Fund, recalled a conversation she and Donald
Fowler, co-chair of the Democratic National Committee, had
in early 1995. "I asked him whether they were going to sell us
down the river," she said. "I should have asked him how far. I
had no idea the Democratic Party was this corrupt in representing its constituencies."[20] At least Custred and Wood, she
noted, could depend on the Republican Party for funds.

San Francisco Mayor Willie Brown and other African
American leaders said they asked Clinton's campaign staff for
help but got none. "No, I don't think they did enough," Brown
said, referring to the Clinton operatives.[21] They listened politely and said 'We do what we can.'" But neither Brown nor
other African American leaders chose to pursue the issue with
much vigor. "The formal civil rights movement is in disarray,"
said Roger Wilkins, a professor at George Mason University.
"The only good thing you can say is that the NAACP didn't do
much because they were trying to get out of bankruptcy."[22]
Black executives took credit for Clinton's mend-it-don't-end-it

policy but did little or nothing to raise funds or contribute their own to defeat Proposition 209.

The quiescence of prominent African Americans was startling to one member of the opposition, who listened in on a teleconference Clinton had in early October with some forty African American leaders in as many cities. Five cities enjoyed two-way communication with the president; in San Francisco Mayor Brown was on the line. "Brown didn't mention 209 by name," said the opposition member. "He said he was deeply grateful to Bill Clinton for 'mend it don't end it' and nothing about the Democrats helping us with funds. He gave the administration a complete pass. What it says is the African American leadership is so weak they couldn't do anything— about affirmative action or the welfare bill."

Hope flared briefly when George Stephanopoulos, Clinton's senior advisor, agreed to appear at an anti–Proposition 209 fund-raiser. But the affair gave new meaning to the term *lip service*. Peter Barker, one of the sponsors, read his *Wall Street Journal*. Asked what had interested him in the issue of affirmative action, he barely looked up from his stock tables. "Molly," he said, referring to Munger, at the NAACP Legal Defense and Education Fund, who had called in chits with all of her friends. Bill Wardlaw, the other sponsor, and Clinton advisor, appeared only on the printed announcement. Most of the forty or so people gathered to hear Stephanopoulos and eat the lox, bagels, and fruit were Democratic Party officials. "They're probably all here to make sure we don't get any money," said Rice, plainly disgusted.[23]

Stephanopoulos put a brilliant spin on Clinton and Proposition 209. Because the president had omitted Proposition 209 from his campaign speeches, the young man reached back to July 1995 to remind those assembled of the president's support. It was on that day, in his mend-it-don't-end-it speech, that Clinton defended affirmative action. "Something memorable happened then," Stephanopoulos said with wonder. "Bob Dole stopped talking about it." By Stephanopoulos's account, the debate over affirmative action had died fifteen months ear-lier. Fund-raising etiquette prevented anyone from reminding the honored guest that, following Clinton's speech, the U.C. regents had ended affirmative action at the University of California, Dole had introduced legislation in Congress to end it at the federal level, and the state Republican Party had poured enough money into Proposition 209 to put it on the ballot.

Stephanopoulos did call Proposition 209 a "critical issue in a critical state" and promised that the president would soon unveil a commercial to address it. The new commercial, he ex-plained without embarrassment, featured Jim Brady talking about Clinton and gun control. No one asked him to explain the logic.

Following Stephanopoulos, Pat Ewing, campaign manager for the opposition, also alluded to a new commercial. "The campaign has designed a nuclear bomb," she told the poten-tial donors. "We've got money for four days. If we can get the ad up for seven days, we can win. " It was a hard sell, and few were buying. When Assemblywoman Marguerite Archie-Hudson got up to call for checks, it felt as if the room were filled with bidders at an auction and Proposition 209 was the item that no one wanted to buy.

Nuclear Fusion, Southern Style

In a different world, the trajectory of the Dole campaign, the infighting, and the fiasco with the King footage would have helped the opposition. But Ewing had on blinders. Instead of taking advantage of the controversies in the 209 campaign, she kicked up one of her own. The "nuclear bomb" she re-ferred to at the Stephanopoulos fete was Klan Grandmaster David Duke.

Using Duke wasn't what their polling material advised the coalition to do. "Fundamentally, the arguments that move voters are about moderation," wrote Diane Feldman, the opposition's Washington, DC, pollster in June.[24] "Language like 'goes too far,' 'mend it don't end it,' and 'we are not where we have got to be' are each more convincing than language about trickery or conspiracy. African Americans respond to the language of conspiracy but other voters do not. The No on CCRI must be the voice of moderation."

Earlier Bob Shrum, the campaign's Washington media consultant, had argued unsuccessfully that the coalition should follow this advice. But with funds for only a week's worth of television, he was starting to come around to the view that moderation wasn't enough. He agreed with Ewing—Duke was their man.

The Duke ad, cut in early October by Shrum, was anything but moderate. It began and ended with burning crosses and Klan regalia. Colin Powell and President Clinton were wedged in between—both had rated high with voters in the list of Feldman's arguments against Proposition 209—but the enduring image was the burning cross.

(David Duke walks onto a stage waving and smiling)
Male Announcer: He's not just another guy in a business suit.
(cut to a burning cross with Duke in front wearing a white robe)
Male Announcer: He's David Duke, former head of the Ku
   Klux Klan. And he's come to California to support
   Proposition 209.
*(cut back to Duke speaking, then to a series of quick images of
   work and classroom)*
Male Announcer: Proposition 209 would close education and
   job opportunities to women and minorities, close magnet schools, lock women out of government jobs, end
   equal opportunity.
(cut to photos of Newt Gingrich, Pat Buchanan, and David Duke)
Male Announcer: Newt Gingrich, Pat Buchanan, and David
   Duke want you to vote Yes on 209.

(cut to photo of Colin Powell and Bill Clinton at the White House)
Male Announcer: President Clinton and Colin Powell say you should vote No.
(cut back to Duke speaking, then finish with the burning cross)
Male Announcer: Don't be fooled. David Duke didn't come to California to end discrimination. Vote No on 209.

Playing the "race card" generally means appealing to white voters' fears and resentment of minorities. In this ad, the roles are reversed; Shrum evokes the fear of virulent white racism. The most shocking image, a burning cross, graphically evokes the Klan's atrocities as well as the recent wave of arson against Southern churches. Nothing is left to the viewer's imagination. Lest there be any mistake, film clips of Duke, Gingrich, and Buchanan receive special lighting effects to emphasize their "whiteness." The primary targets for this commercial were minorities and white liberals who believe themselves to be racially tolerant. Liberals, however, are least receptive to negative advertising, which may explain the almost universal condemnation this ad received.[25]

Many in the coalition were ambivalent about the Duke commercial. Jerome Karabel, the U.C. Berkeley sociology professor, was one of them. "But what did I know," Karabel said.[26] Instead of relying on his own judgment, Karabel arranged to have UCLA political science professor Shanto Iyengar, a leading expert on the political effects of television commercials, test the Duke ad for free. Ewing, however, would have none of it. Iyengar, she argued, wanted to publish his results after the election.

As the day to run the Duke ad approached, however, Ewing's coalition members became insistent about dumping it. Wasn't the King disaster in the other camp an opportunity? "It seemed like an opening to take the high road," said Dorothy Erlich, director of the ACLU in San Francisco.[27] Ewing, however, was adamant. Rice backed her up, and Ewing reassured others. "We were told that if we didn't like the commercial we could pull it and put something else on the air," said Eva Paterson, executive director of the Lawyers' Committee for Civil Rights.[28] The ad began running on October 28, and the reaction was almost uniformly negative. "When we wanted to pull it, we were told there was no way to do it," said Paterson. "It was one of the things that pissed me off most."

Ironically, the Duke ad found its greatest support at the Democratic National Committee. The commercial accomplished precisely what the Democrats had envisioned in early 1995, when Ickes wrote his constituency outreach proposals. The report on African Americans noted that "Democrats only win statewide elections in California when they maximize black voter turnout."[29] The report never mentioned affirmative action or the California Civil Rights Initiative as rallying points, but it noted, "In the 1996 Presidential election, we might find that some blacks may well be more inspired to go to the polls in greater numbers to vote against the 'enemies of civil rights' than for the Democratic candidate."[30] Duke's effectiveness had been tested with blacks and Latinos and, as Ewing said, "the response was off the charts." To African Americans and Latinos Duke was a clear "enemy of civil rights." If he insulted moderate voters, that was okay with the Democrats; they already had a goodly number in the Clinton camp. They needed to ensure, however, that blacks and Latinos dispirited by the welfare bill would get angry enough to go to the polls. Duke could do it. The DNC even came up with money that kept Duke on the air.

In retrospect the Stephanopoulos fund-raiser took on new meaning. Stephanopoulos and the president's California advisor, Bill Wardlaw, knew then what the opposition's commerical looked like, and by Stephanopoulos appearing at the event and Wardlaw sponsoring it, they were telling donors that it was finally okay to give money to the opposition. There was, after all, a logic to Stephanopoulos's claim about the compatibility of the Jim Brady commerical on Clinton's support of gun control and the Duke ad. An election was about winning, and Brady would appeal to Reagan Democrats and Duke would rally minority voters.

From Kitchen Chats to Striptease

The high road hadn't been completely forsaken. Around the time that the Duke ad began running, the Feminist Majority and NOW began running a series of six radio spots targeted at different audiences. The ads, thematically similar, emphasized gender and called explicitly for a defense of affirmative action programs.

Unlike the Duke ad, the radio commercials had a soft edge. All of the ads had a chatty, conversational tone, a quality that made the speakers sound reasonable and moderate—two attributes that Feldman and others felt were crucial to persuading swing voters.

Candice Bergen: I find political advertising very confusing. Take Proposition 209. They say it prohibits discrimination, but 209 will eliminate affirmative action for women and people of color. That's like the Ku Klux Klan calling itself "The Martin Luther King Society." Anyone who depends on a working woman's wage should listen carefully. If 209 passes, we could lose maternity benefits. . . . 209 will cut funding for rape crisis centers. . . . Don't make a permanent change to the constitution that will hurt young girls, women, and minorities. Vote No on 209.[31]

Dolores Huerta: I am Dolores Huerta, co-founder of the United Farmworkers. Proposition 209 is a lie. It aims to take away our civil rights. It aims to close the doors of opportunity that have opened for us. . . . Many people gave their lives so that we could better ourselves—César

Chávez, Rubén Salazar. Together, we can defeat this
Proposition 209. Sí Se Puede!

Bruce Springsteen: This is Bruce Springsteen. Working men
and women are the backbone of California, and their
livelihoods and their opportunities to compete fairly in
the work place and at school are in serious jeopardy if
Proposition 209 passes this November. . . . Proposition
209 will eliminate affirmative action programs for
women and people of color. Proposition 209 will legalize discrimination against women and girls in jobs, in
education, and in sports. . . . If you count yourself
among the Californians who support civil rights for
all people, then you'll join me in voting NO on
Proposition 209.

Alfre Woodard: This is Alfre Woodard with five reasons to
vote No on Proposition 209: Newt Gingrich, Pete
Wilson, Pat Buchanan, Jesse Helms, and David Duke.
They're all for 209. Here are some people I trust a little
more when it comes to defending equal opportunity.
Jesse Jackson asks that you vote NO on 209 to keep
the dream alive. . . . The League of Women Voters,
the NAACP, the National Organization for Women,
and the Rainbow Coalition are all against 209. . . .
This message was paid for by Stop Prop 209. I'm talking for free.

Ellen DeGeneres: Hi, I'm Ellen DeGeneres. Don't you think
it's odd that the people most against a woman's right to
choose are usually men. Turns out the same anti-choice
boys are trying to wipe out affirmative action for
women and people of color. That's right: Pat Buchanan,
Newt Gingrich, David Duke—all anti-abortion—all
supporting Proposition 209. . . . The religious right has
donated about half a million dollars to Proposition 209.
I guess they figure, once they stop those young girls
from playing softball, they're gonna march right over

and sign up for prayer in schools. Yeah, it's all kind of
funny, till you realize they might get away with it.

Jesse Jackson: This is the Reverend Jesse Jackson. We've
fought too hard, bled too much, and died too young, to
see the precious gains of the civil rights movement
snatched away. Vote No on Proposition 209. It's misleading. It is not civil rights. It's civil wrongs. They tried
to manipulate Dr. King's words and make him stand
against us with David Duke, Pat Buchanan, and Pete
Wilson. How vulgar. . . . Protect affirmative action in
education, jobs, and contracts, for women and people
of color. . . . This is a majority issue for all, not a minority matter for a few. . . . Keep Hope Alive—Vote
November Five.

The ads tested the power of the gender argument.
Feldman's June poll showed that women had yet to buy the arguments that Proposition 209 would end maternity leave,
girls' sports, tutoring, and girls outreach. However, the
Feminist Majority believed that with a long enough campaign,
voters could be convinced.

On the final weekend before the election, the Feminist
Majority and NOW put on their only television commercial.
The ad, conceived and produced in twenty hours by a group
of volunteer screenwriters, producers, and editors orches-
trated by Lorraine Sheinberg, was designed to be provocative,
and it didn't disappoint. If the other opposition ad insinuated
that the Klan was behind Proposition 209, the Feminist
Majority's ad suggested that women might fare better under
Afghanistan's Taliban than under 209. It showed male hands
stripping a woman of a diploma, a stethoscope and medical
lab coat, a police officer's cap, and a hard hat.

Chorus of Male Voices: Take it off. Take it all off.
Female Announcer: Want to be a doctor? Police officer? Hard
hat? Forget it.

Chorus of Male Voices: Take it off. Take it all off.

Female Announcer: How about women business owners? Forget it! Want your daughter going into math, science, or sports? Counting on a pension? Or just a job? Well, there's always . . .

(cut to woman in black lingerie, a black jacket dangling from her right shoulder, while a man's hand reaches in and yanks her chin sideways)

Female Announcer: Don't strip away our future. Vote No on Proposition 209. Save affirmative action for women.

Like the Duke ad produced by Shrum, this commercial left little to the viewer's imagination. Unlike the Steinberg ads, which invited the viewer to "Bring us together," this commercial took an "us against them" direction. Also, like the Duke ad, it appeared to be aimed more at getting out people who'd already made up their minds rather than trying to convince undecided or swing voters.

The ad was intended to reframe affirmative action from an issue of race to one of gender. Coming so late in the campaign, the Feminist Majority and the National Organization for Women wanted the ad to call attention to itself and to amplify its message through any controversy it might spark. The problem was that its play was so brief, viewers were as unaware of the controversy as of the ad.

The Duke and stripper ads were desperate tactics, but, given the polls and the opposition's lack of money, desperation was understandable. Less fathomable was the lack of leadership from a popular Democratic presidential candidate who had said he believed affirmative action was still necessary. Since the early 1960s the Democratic Party had championed civil rights, but Clinton held his beliefs on Proposition 209 so closely that there was no chance he would inspire anyone to follow his lead. Clinton's reluctance to reveal his opposition to Proposition 209 was abundantly clear a few days before the election, when he appeared in Oakland. It was a beautiful evening at the city's Jack London Square, and the crowd—a mixture of black, white, and Latino supporters—had waited hours to go through the security and emerge on the square. Most people seemed pleased when Clinton arrived. But when he brought up Proposition 209 near the end of his speech—his first mention of the initiative in California—the disappointment in what he had to say was palpable.

"My problem with this 209," said Clinton, "I know it's maybe popular, maybe not. But, let me tell you . . ." He hesitated as he heard the crowd boo. Supporters who had been ready to hoist banners held back and Clinton continued. "Let me tell you what I know. I'm old enough to remember in my home state when I could go into county courthouses and the restrooms were divided between white and colored. I'm old enough to remember when people had to buy a poll tax to vote. I'm old enough to know that if my skin were a different color I could not have been born to a widowed mother in a tiny town in Arkansas who married my stepfather, who did not have a high school diploma, and become president."

These were vivid memories of discrimination, and Clinton believed that affirmative action was still needed to combat ongoing discrimination. Nevertheless, he could not bring himself to denounce an initiative that would end state affirmative action programs. Instead he reminded the crowd that he was against quotas—that he'd actually gotten rid of some affirmative action programs. "We've got to get to the point in this country where we can let some of this stuff go." It was typical Clinton—he managed to leave light footprints in both camps.

Election Day

On November 4, the day before California voters would decide whether the state still needed affirmative action programs, local television stations featured a story that might have been scripted by the opponents of Proposition 209.[32] It was the painful illustration of racism in mainstream America that their campaign had so lacked. The story focused not on the predictable racism of David Duke, but on the surprising hatefulness in Texaco, the giant U.S. oil company. It revealed a picture that looked a lot different than that of the inclusive new society Ward Connerly had drawn in debates and speeches. At a secretly taped meeting Texaco managers had derided their African American employees and colluded to destroy evidence to protect Texaco from a discrimination case.

If the story had an impact on California voters, however, it was not apparent at the polling places. By the end of the day 9,657,195 California residents had split their votes in favor of Proposition 209, 54.6 percent to 45.4 percent; the initiative won by 9.2 percent or 879,429 votes. The wedge issue that had so frightened the Democrats in 1995 and so empowered the Republicans during 1995 didn't put a nick in Clinton's support. The state favored the president over Dole 51 to 38 percent. Neither presidential candidate was directly helped or hurt by Proposition 209, but Clinton and the Democrats got plenty of indirect help. The minority vote in California surged, and it voted overwhelmingly Democratic.

Californians for Justice

At 4:40 A.M. at the Oakland headquarters of Californians for Justice, Jan Adams contemplated the bad start of a worse day: no one had made coffee to offer volunteers before they drove out to their precincts to slip door hangers on the homes of potential voters. In the last year and a half, Californians for Justice had become active in 1,350 precincts, close to Adams's goal of 1,500. "We did what we could," she said, predicting accurately that the precincts CFJ had worked would vote against 209, but that the state overall would not. "We had an opportunity in this election to occupy the middle ground, and we were screwed by Clinton and the donors; we couldn't amplify the message," Adams said flatly. She and Anthony Thigpen had been right, however, that minority neighborhoods could be energized.

Although Proposition 209 failed to play as a wedge issue, the vote broke down along racial lines. The *Los Angeles Times* exit poll showed that 74 percent of African Americans, 76 percent of Latinos, and 61 percent of Asians voted against Proposition 209. In these numbers were two surprises. The first was California's Latinos, who finally showed some measure of their potential strength and increased their share of the voting bloc to 13 percent from 10 percent. The second was the Asian vote. Most analysts had expected Asians to support Proposition 209 because affirmative action hurt them in competitive admissions at the top public schools. But most analysts don't read or see the ethnic press, said Kathay Feng, a lawyer for the Asian Pacific American Legal Center. The ethnic media—print and cable stations in Chinese, Vietnamese, and Korean—stressed the employment rather than the education value of affirmative action.

Asians, she said, understood that they were affected much more by the many jobs they failed to get because of discrimination than by the few spots in colleges or top high schools that they might miss because of affirmative action.[33] And although U.C. Berkeley Chancellor Chang-Lin Tien had failed to convince the regents to retain affirmative action in July 1995, he was more persuasive with Asians, Feng said. "He is so high up on the academic ladder that in several Asian communities he is a household name," said Feng. "So when he came out opposed on 209 and explained the benefits of affirmative action, it had a very strong impact." The Asian Pacific American Legal Center's exit poll in Los Angeles showed an even greater Asian turnout against Proposition 209 than the *Los Angeles Times* exit poll: 76 percent of the Asians polled by the Legal Center rejected Proposition 209. Asians registered as Democrats voted against it by 78.5 percent, and Asian Republicans rejected it by 73 percent. Even in conservative Orange County a majority of Asians voted against the initiative.

The white vote reflected the predictions of pundits: 63 percent supported Proposition 209. But it was not as high as the 70 percent in earlier polls, and it was not as high as the 66 percent who supported Proposition 187.

The South Los Angeles Affirmative Action Project

More than 350 miles to the south Anthony Thigpen shared Adams's state of mind—optimistic about his own precincts, resigned to statewide defeat. As he prepared boxes of campaign literature and tally sheets for volunteers to take to churches to set up get-out-the-vote centers for nearby precincts, the phone rang. A voter wanted to know what Thigpen had been trying to make clear for nearly two years: If he voted for Proposition 209, was he voting for or against affirmative action? The look of pain on Thigpen's face was noticeable as a volunteer patiently explained Proposition 209.

The caller wasn't the only mystified voter. The *Los Angeles Times* exit poll asked voters whether they supported affirmative action programs "designed to help women and minorities get better jobs and education." Fifty-four percent said yes, and 46 percent said no—nearly the reverse of Proposition 209's vote.

Even early in the day Thigpen knew the opposition would not win, and he was already trying to figure out what the coalition could have done better. "The original gender strategy campaign should have continued," he said. He was disappointed that the two women's groups had been asked to leave the main coalition. African Americans in California are not going to beat "racist initiatives without alliances," he said. The returns bore him out: the vote in the precincts where the Metropolitan Alliance had worked overwhelmingly opposed 209. And just as Thigpen, Rice, and Ridley-Thomas had told volunteers on that very first morning at St. Brigid's, it did not change the outcome.

Ewing and the Coalition

Most members of the coalition went their own way on election day and then gathered in the evening at the downtown Biltmore Hotel for a celebration. Molly Munger took the day off from work at the NAACP Legal Defense and Education Fund and returned to the Pasadena neighborhood where she had grown up. She was there as the polls opened, at lunch time, and again in the evening. For two hours at each turn she stood the legal distance from the polling place—a converted garage—wearing a sandwich board asking voters to reject Proposition 209. "I would like this to never happen again," she said. To her, opposing Proposition 209 was a "big tent issue" with an "obvious centrist opposition." Yet it had slipped away. Why? The Democrats, she said, "ran screaming from the room." How could the opposition have kept the Democrats in? She had no answers.

Munger's colleague Rice found cause for optimism in the final numbers. The issue had divided the Republican Party, and the worst had not happened: blacks had not supported Proposition 209. "We did better than we thought," said Rice. "They did not get the minority vote." Like the others, she felt betrayed by the Democratic Party. "The advocacy groups ran the campaign because no one else would," she said. "We would have gladly handed this over." But after a long tradition of taking on civil rights causes, the Democratic Party took a pass. "The Democrats," she said, "would rather have Republican women than blacks. They have no principles, no integrity."

Ewing put her own unique spin on the vote. "What 209 did and what 209 accomplished was outstanding and amazing," she said, referring to the opposition campaign. Although it might have been news to others in the coalition that they had any goal other than defeating the initiative, Ewing claimed victory on "all but one goal."

"We created an environment in which people are going to look at affirmative action twice before attacking; the Democrats took back the assembly and it was not the steam-roller that Pete Wilson had expected," she reported enthusiastically.

The Feminist Majority and NOW

On the third floor of the Bubble Factory, the Feminist Majority's president, Eleanor Smeal, was in the kitchen. When she had finished up the dishes from the election eve meeting, she walked out onto the open floor that had been transformed into an election day war room. It was a classy war room, with large flower bouquets atop television sets tuned to CNN, computer printouts on the walls, and a bag of gourmet lemon drops spilling out onto one of the tables.

By the end of the day Smeal and Katherine Spillar would be forced to concede that the Feminist Majority and NOW had failed to turn Proposition 209 into a rallying point for white women: 58 percent of white women (compared with 66 percent of white men) had supported Proposition 209, according to the Voter News Service Poll.[34] The Clinton Administration, as it turned out, had been right. The women's rights groups could get the vote of many professional women, but the majority of white women were unwilling to back affirmative action. Spillar, Smeal, and Ireland had been unable to change their minds.

Never one to accept defeat, Spillar still insisted they had been right. The campaign's tactics, she argued, had been too little too late. "I wish that women had been included all along, and instead we were treated as an add-on or an afterthought," Spillar said. "There was a tone that somehow the attempts to get the debate on gender was just a tactical decision to offset the race issue, and that was never the intention. We are impacted by what happens with affirmative action. Women had benefited significantly by affirmative action. We should not be treated as an add-on, but as an equal partner in this debate."

Custred, Wood, Connerly, and the
Proposition 209 Campaign

The Proposition 209 campaign closed up shop early on election day. The fact was, there was no grassroots campaign. The staff headed up to Sacramento for the victory celebration, held in a large ballroom at the Raddison Hotel. Nearly everyone who had helped along the way was there. Wood and Custred, the initiative's two authors, were agog, buzzing around the ballroom in constant motion, hardly able to believe they had won. The campaign's petition gatherer, Bill Arno, was there, and Connerly had made sure Steinberg was invited. Even Gelman, the campaign manager who had been fired in December 1995, had flown in from Las Vegas for the occasion. "It's kind of creepy," he said jokingly as he surveyed the mostly male, mostly white crowd. "We're a lot of white men in suits." Indeed, one of the strangest lines of the evening came from Ward Connerly, who asked the nearly all-white crowd to indulge him for a moment as he had "a conversation with my fellow black Americans."

Connerly's speech on November 5 was a measure of how far the politics of affirmative action had changed in the last ten years. Connerly said he had had no doubt that he would be giving a victory speech. "The reason lies in an editorial endorsement of one of this state's most important newspapers— U.C. Berkeley's *Daily Californian*," he said, referring to the campus paper that had once been a dependable liberal voice. Later in the speech, he drew not on Senator Dole's argument against affirmative action, but on President Clinton's. "I do not often quote President Clinton, but last week, speaking to a predominantly black audience," Connerly said, referring to the president's speech in Oakland, "the president said something which was extremely significant. In reaffirming his support of affirmative action, the president reminded the audience that there comes a time to let go. For black people and our reliance on affirmative action, the time has, indeed, come to let go."

Twelve hours after the polls closed ACLU lawyer Mark Rosenbaum filed a lawsuit in federal court in San Francisco asking for an immediate order blocking Proposition 209. The ACLU attorney argued in the lawsuit, which was joined by other opposition groups, that Proposition 209 violated the Fourteenth Amendment's equal protection clause by singling out minorities and women. On December 23 Judge Thelton Henderson, chief U.S. District Court judge for the Northern District of California, granted a preliminary injunction that prevented state government entities and the University of California from implementing the initiative until the conclusion of a trial or a final ruling from a higher court. The ACLU, he argued in a sixty-seven-page ruling, had a "probability of success" in proving their claim that the initiative was unconstitutional. "It is not for this or any other court to lightly upset the expectations of the voters. At the same time, our system of democracy teaches that the will of the people, important as it is, does not reign absolute but must be kept in harmony with our Constitution."

Henderson's decision was overturned on April 8, 1997, by a three-judge panel of the U.S. Court of Appeals for the Ninth Circuit. "A system which permits one judge to block with the stroke of a pen what 47,736,180 state residents voted to enact as law tests the integrity of our constitutional democracy," wrote Judge Diarmuid F. O'Scannlain. On Monday, November 3, 1997, without comment the U.S. Supreme Court let O'Scannlain's decision stand. The following day Houston voters rejected an initiative to ban affirmative action, and that same week the House Judiciary Committee killed federal legislation to end affirmative action.

Afterword

This is the first time I have followed an American election so closely. And up close it is both a more interesting and a more disturbing event. As a casual observer I've watched the polls and advertising, the ancillary apparatus of a campaign. This time I watched the campaigners: men and women who acted in brave, cowardly, idealistic, and opportunistic ways. Heaven help us.

With the best of intentions—to give ordinary citizens the ability to change laws—the initiative process instead permits wealthy special interest groups to bypass the deliberative process and change laws in their narrow interest. As the Proposition 209 campaign demonstrated, it is a process that desperately needs reform.

When individuals vie for office, the system tempers the extremes of a campaign by tossing the winner into a deliberative pool where promises and human shortcomings are held in check by the give and take of the legislative process. An initiative campaign is different: it promises and often delivers radical change.

The impact of initiatives in the 1996 election was dramatic. Not only did California voters reject affirmative action, but also voters in California, Florida, Nevada, and South Dakota approved measures to make tax increases more difficult to enact; voters in Maine rejected a ban on clear-cutting; Floridians turned down a sugar tax to pay for restoration of the Everglades; and California and Arizona voters agreed to legalize the medicinal use of marijuana. In all, voters in twenty-four states considered nearly one hundred initiatives.

Although it makes sense for voters to decide whether or not to spend tax money for a new ballpark, leaving central questions of social policy up to a popular vote is nonsense. Issues regarding discrimination, welfare, and immigration are emotional and complex. They can be manipulated all too easily by politicians to win votes in a manner that tramples on the rights of vulnerable minorities and disregards the long-term interests of the majority.

Proposition 209 was a case in point. Watching the campaign in motion was like witnessing democracy in free fall. Any safety nets that might have kept the dynamic of a campaign in control had gaping holes. Proposition 209 and the issue of affirmative action did not have to be particularly urgent with voters because money put it on the ballot. It could be cleverly written to confuse and still make it past elected officials and appointed judges because too many are driven by politics rather than any thoughtful vision of policy or fairness. And if the baffled voters looked to the country's highest leaders for counsel, they found politicians so wedded to polls or so personally ambivalent that they were better off looking elsewhere.

The initiative process was first envisioned as a populist tool. Indeed, Glynn Custred and Thomas Wood became interested in the issue of affirmative action for personal reasons that motivate many people to participate in our society in a way that is healthy and desirable. Custred didn't like what he saw happening at his campus in Hayward and at the universities nearby, and he participated in the debate that questioned multiculturalism and affirmative action. Thomas Wood had had bad luck trying to find a job in academia, and he blamed it on unfair competition from women and minority candidates. He too sought to change something through a system that was open to his grievances.

What is clear in following Custred and Wood's campaign is that on their own these two men could widen the debate on campus and within their communities, but neither would have put the California Civil Rights Initiative on the ballot without the self-interested support of Governor Pete Wilson.

CCRI did not get on the ballot because of the salience of affirmative action with voters—less than 1 percent of the electorate mentioned it as a pressing concern. Nevertheless, it is one of those issues that, if used correctly, has the potential to pit white middle-class interests against those of blacks, Latinos, and Asians. For Republicans looking for a way to retain the white male vote that had fueled the party's sweep in 1994, affirmative action looked like a good bet. No one knew this better than Wilson. Fresh from his success in using illegal immigration as a wedge issue, Wilson believed that CCRI could take him to the White House. When the CCRI petition campaign ran out of steam, Wilson stepped in to raise money for it and returned the signature gatherers to the streets. Similarly, George Soros, the New York billionaire financier, forked out the money necessary to put Proposition 215 on the ballot, and, thanks to securities lawyers, Proposition 211 went before the voters. In short, anyone with a million dollars to pay for the signatures necessary to put an initiative on the ballot can attempt to enact laws or change a state constitution.

As distasteful as this may be, it's unlikely to change. Colorado tried to ban paid signature gatherers, but in 1988 the U.S. Supreme Court unanimously agreed that such a restriction violated the right of free speech. It seems that initiatives put on the ballot by special interest groups are here to stay. The Proposition 209 campaign illustrates, however, that there are ways to make the process fairer to the voter.

Custred and Wood frequently talked about CCRI's impact on affirmative action; it was explicitly designed to end affirmative action programs upheld by the U.S. Supreme Court. But polls showed that voters tended to support affirmative action by a slim margin while they abhorred "preferences." To take advantage of the powerful emotional reaction against the latter, Custred and Wood wrote an initiative to end race and gender preferences and omitted any reference to affirmative action. The semantic games that gave CCRI an advantage are not unusual in initiative campaigns. Rather, they are considered smart politics. Such cleverness is presumed to be held in check by the state attorneys general who write the ballot language explaining initiatives to the voters. By law, the attorney general's title and summary in California is to be a "clear and impartial statement on the purpose of the measure in such language that the ballot title shall neither be an argument nor be likely to create prejudice for or against the proposed measure."

Attorney General Dan Lungren was, as is his right, a partisan of the Proposition 209 campaign, but it's clear that he had difficulty keeping politics out of his official obligations. Chief Deputy Attorney General David Stirling met with the proponents and talked about the language of the title and summary in the summer of 1995. Generally, according to Rosemary Calderon in the attorney general's office, the office does not meet with the proponents of any initiative becuase it must remain impartial. Nevertheless, the rules were ignored for Proposition 209, and Lungren's final title and summary for Proposition 209 reflected the campaign's wish to omit any mention of affirmative action. One judge took objection to that. "The Court is satisfied by clear and convincing evidence that the Attorney General has not fully stated the main purpose or chief point of the initiative, and, accordingly, the Court will remand it to the Attorney General for revised language to reflect a determination by this Court that the chief purpose of the initiative is to effect changes or stop the affirmative action programs within the state of California," concluded Judge James T. Ford of the Sacramento Superior and Municipal Court District in Sacramento County. Ford's decision, however, was overruled by Judge Robert Puglia of the Court of Appeals, who concluded that the Attorney General had merely repeated the language of the initiative. "The electorate can hardly be deceived by this essentially verbatim recital of the straightforward text of the measure itself," Puglia wrote.

No text put together with the help of polls and focus groups can be considered straightforward. Exit polls on election day—echoing earlier polls available to the courts—underscored the continuing confusion over the initiative's impact. It's unclear if voters would have rejected Proposition 209 had the attorney general included mention of its impact on affirmative action. At least, however, the electorate would have understood what it was voting on. California voters must make decisions on dozens of initiatives. Enacting a new law or changing the state constitution is too important to permit the manipulative use of deliberately ambiguous language.

The importance of language was underscored a year later in Houston, when voters there rejected Proposition A to "end the use of affirmative action for women and minorities" in employment and contracting. The 1996 California and the 1997 Houston votes illustrate what polls have shown for years— that voters are favorably disposed toward the words *affirmative action* and repelled by the notion of preferences.

Supporters of Proposition 209 argued that the words *affirmative action* were confusing, but, as Steinberg said in his memos, they would be hard-pressed to come up with any affirmative action programs that did not take race and gender into account. When Texans voted against banning affirmative action, the initiative told them they would be upholding existing programs in Houston that, like the vast majority of current affirmative action programs, explicitly consider race and gender. In contrast, when Californians voted to ban preferential treatment, exit polls showed that they remained confused about exactly what the initiative would do and that the attorney general's summary failed to clarify its purpose.

The Presidential Campaign

The need to clarify what was at stake in Proposition 209 was all the more urgent given the lack of leadership Californians encountered. This was the first time a significant segment of the American electorate voted on a civil rights initiative, yet political leaders with any mainstream cachet—most notably the presidential candidates—refused to lead. "Affirmative action has not always been perfect, and affirmative action should not go on forever," President Clinton said in July 1995. "It should be changed now to take care of those things that are wrong, and it should be retired when its job is done. I am resolved that that day will come. But the evidence suggests, indeed, screams that that day has not come." Clinton ignored the screams, however, never publicly and unequivocally urging voters to reject Proposition 209.

President Clinton's campaign team said that voters were more concerned about jobs and the environment. Although this was true, the electorate in California was voting on the future of affirmative action. In early 1995, when Clinton's political prospects appeared bleak, his timidity might have been pardonable. However, even as his popularity increased, Clinton never mentioned Proposition 209 on the campaign trail. The only instance in which it came up during his trips to California was less than a week before the election, in his visit to Oakland's Jack London Square. There he seemed as determined to understand why voters might support it as to explain why he personally was against it. Five days later he beat Senator Dole by a margin of 13 percent in California. Many of the president's supporters voted for Proposition 209.

Clinton now promises to make civil rights a legacy of his administration. As he concluded in his inaugural address, "The divide of race has been America's constant curse." He has started a year-long conversation on race, but when it counted in California in 1996 his legacy was silence.

Clinton's challenger, Senator Dole, was equally evasive. Having supported affirmative action for years, candidate Dole decided it was time to end it, but demurred at endorsing Proposition 209 vigorously. As late as June, when there was a slim prospect that General Colin Powell might join the ticket, Dole softened his stance, suggesting that he, like Clinton and Powell, supported affirmative action but felt that "there are some changes that should be made." Ultimately, Dole waited until the last minute to speak out for Proposition 209, making his argument for the initiative seem all the more shallow by its lateness and by publicly considering the initiative's potential as a wedge issue. His running mate, Jack Kemp, was just as slippery, cynically modifying his position depending on which constituency he was addressing. He knew the national press had neither the time nor the inclination to nail him on his numerous reformulations. To this day it is impossible to say where Jack Kemp stands on the issue. Vice President Al Gore made clear his commitment to preserving affirmative action, but he generally spoke out against Proposition 209 at small minority events, far from the television cameras and the national spotlight.

As I watched Clinton and Dole fudge the issue time and time again, I began to long for any political leader with convictions strong enough to withstand political pressure. General Colin Powell offered some leadership. Even from the sidelines, Powell's public statements supporting affirmative action in interviews with reporters and at Bowie State carried visible weight. In the summer of 1996 he cowed Dole and helped derail legislative action in Congress. He was the only public figure with something to lose to stand up at a national party convention and endorse affirmative action. However, in the final months of the campaign—except for one brief visit to Sacramento, which was barely covered in the press—Powell stayed away from California.

The Opposition Campaign

From the start, the opposition to Proposition 209 overestimated the support for the measure. Opponents had two opportunities to defeat it. The first came in the months before the measure qualified for the ballot, when the campaign was seriously behind schedule and close to going broke. At that point the opponents might well have tripped up the signature gathering effort by educating voters on what they were signing or by trying to collect signatures for an alternative initiative. The months between November 1995 and February 1996 represent a lost opportunity. Once the initiative made it onto the ballot, the cost of a campaign to defeat it and the odds of it winning rose astronomically.

With CCRI on the ballot, the opposition had its second opportunity. In early 1996 leaders had two strategies on the table: They could follow their polls and pursue a mainstream message that appealed to men and women, or they could follow their instincts and try a gender strategy.

Initially it appeared that, with the Feminist Majority in the lead, the opposition would attempt a media strategy emphasizing gender combined with targeted outreach to black, Latino, and Asian voters. Because California doesn't have enough minority voters to defeat any statewide initiative, it seemed logical to pursue a larger group of voters—women— who had benefited from affirmative action. The polls showed that this would not be easy. White women in particular were unconvinced that they needed affirmative action, but a consistent and prolonged campaign might have persuaded them otherwise. The grassroots get-out-the-vote drives by Jan Adams and Anthony Thigpen might have put them over 50 percent. The Feminist Majority, however, failed to raise the money to make this strategy work.

Once the opposition split, the traditional civil rights advocates had the freedom to try the second tactic: Clinton's poll-tested mend-it-don't-end-it message. Voters liked it, the slogan was already well known, and it was closely identified with the winning candidate. Instead, the opposition permitted the campaign manager, Patricia Ewing, to get trapped by the race issue. In trying to make Klansman David Duke the poster boy for Proposition 209, Ewing missed a key political principle: Negative advertising often backfires, especially with liberals. Equating voter ambivalence toward affirmative action with the explicitly racist sentiments of David Duke was not just silly, it was offensive. Ewing and others defended the choice of Duke as a means of spurring black and Latino voters to go to the polls. I believe that their own polling data, focus groups, and the work of Thigpen and Adams demonstrated that Pete Wilson's support of Proposition 209 was more than enough to animate minority voters. In addition, polls showed that many white voters were disgusted by Wilson's willingness to exploit racial tensions for political gain. His association with Proposition 209 would have damned the initiative with at least some of them.

In their defense, the civil rights and women's rights lawyers and advocates who took up the opposition campaign were the only ones willing to do so. The state Democratic Party and the national party, both of which depend on women and minorities for their winning margins, refused to take up the challenge.

In contrast to the California campaign, the opposition to Proposition A in Houston had the support of local political and business leaders. The opposition's commercials were sharply different also. Instead of David Duke, the Houston opposition's commercials featured the popular white mayor, seventy-two-year old Bob Lanier. The wealthy developer asked viewers if the city really wanted to turn back to the time when "guys like me" got all the city's contracts. Voters said no.

The Proposition 209 Campaign

Patricia Ewing was no match for Arnold Steinberg. Governor Wilson's critical financial support in getting the initiative on the ballot and its language made the Proposition 209 campaign an easier one to run, but Steinberg also had deep roots in the California political community. He understood the issues, the players, and the electorate. Steinberg believed that voters were upset by the divisiveness of the Proposition 187 campaign, and he sought to run a campaign that appealed to unity. Just how successful he had been hit home on election day, when I asked an African American woman working for the opposition how she felt about the Duke ad. "I wished we had nicer ads," she said. "Theirs, you know, had that nice line at the end, bring us together."

Having Ward Connerly as a spokesperson was icing on the
cake. Even if the great majority of African Americans opposed
Proposition 209, Connerly's black face blunted charges that the
initiative was inspired and driven by white males. He gave whites
looking for solace the embrace of a successful black American.

Connerly said in the early days of the campaign that he
wanted to have a conversation about race and that if that did-
n't happen, he would have failed. He failed. Connerly offered
no solutions to ongoing discrimination and even dismissed
the notion that government has any role in leveling the playing field. Voters looking to Connerly as a sure-footed leader instead got a man full of contradictions. In the days following
the vote, Connerly established a national organization—
launched on Martin Luther King, Jr.'s, birthday—to take his
initiative to other states. At the same time, he wondered
whether "he was going too fast" in ending all race and gender
preferences. Even after the election, Connerly seemed more
interested in press coverage than exploring solutions to the
country's race problems.

The Proposition 209 campaign also benefited from far
greater and more consistent financial support from the state
Republican Party and the RNC than the opposition campaign
got from the Democrats. During the full campaign year,
Proposition 209 raised $3.6 million in cash and in-kind con-
tributions. The California Republican Party was responsible
for nearly $1 million of the total, and large Republican donors
were responsible for close to another $1 million. In addition
the state Republicans paid for their own Proposition 209 commercial.

In comparison the women's rights and civil rights groups
raised $3.1 million in cash and in-kind contributions. The state
Democratic Party and party officials contributed nearly
$200,000 to the opposition, and the Democratic National
Committee wrote a $100,000 check to keep the Duke commer-
cial on the air. The majority of these funds came at the close of
the campaign, when the opposition was already doomed.

Neither the state Democrats nor the Clinton-Gore campaign produced a separate commercial opposing Proposition 209.

The Impact

At least a half-dozen other states are considering similar initiatives, and Connerly has formed a national organization to help them and to push Congress for federal legislation. Majority Leader Newt Gingrich put aside earlier temerity and endorsed federal legislation to end affirmative action. But after the California and Houston votes, other Republicans remain divided over the issue. Four Republicans and thirteen Democrats voted in the House Judiciary Committee in November 1997 to kill federal legislation that would have ended all federal affirmative action programs aimed at women and minorities.

The campaign in California, however, should continue to serve as a cautionary tale: undoing affirmative action here was more politically complex than many expected in 1994. The most prominent advocates of Proposition 209, Governor Pete Wilson and Pat Buchanan, gained little from their advocacy. Their presidential campaigns failed, and Wilson's party lost control of the California Assembly.

In fact, Proposition 209 and Proposition 187 had a totally unforeseen—and for state Republicans, dismaying—effect. The 1994 vote on Proposition 187 helped to inspire a 6 percent increase in the number of Latino immigrants who became citizens between 1994 and 1996. Proposition 209 sent them to the polls in unprecedented numbers, increasing the Latino share of the vote to 13 percent. This surge ended Republican Bob Dornan's congressional career and returned the assembly to the Democrats. Michael Schroeder, the new chair of the Republican Party, said that "it would take years" for the state Republicans to recover from the damage Propositions 209 and 187 had done to the party's image.

The political battles for California's minority voters will go on for years, but because of Proposition 209, they will do so in a far different environment. If upheld, Proposition 209 will end programs that have helped to diversify one of the most socially stratified states in the union. Meanwhile, its precursor—the decision by U.C. regents to end affirmative action at the University of California—is already making itself felt. Latino residents represent more than 30 percent of the population, yet in 1997 only thirty-nine Latinos—down from eighty—were offered admission to Boalt Hall School of Law, the state's premier public law school. Black admissions dropped by 80 percent to fourteen. Only one African American entered Boalt in the fall of 1997.

Both proponents and opponents of Proposition 209 declared their commitment to overcoming the pernicious effects of discrimination. In the days and years to come, they will have ample opportunity to prove their sincerity.

Appendix A

Cast of Characters

In the Proposition 209 Campaign

Larry Arnn, president, Claremont Institute and chair of the campaign until December 1995

Ward Connerly, University of California regent and chair of the campaign after December 1995

Glynn Custred and Thomas Wood, co-authors of Proposition 209

Joe Gelman, Los Angeles office manager for Proposition 209 until December 1995

Gail Heriot, law professor, University of San Diego, and co-chair of the campaign

Pamela Lewis, private lawyer and co-chair of the campaign

Arnie Steinberg, pollster and campaign strategist

Proposition 209 Campaign Supporters and Advisors

Howard Ahmanson, a conservative Christian and leader of the Allied Business PAC

Michael and Bill Arno, co-owners, American Petition Consultants

Louis W. M. Barnett, member, California Unemployment
    Appeals Board

William Bennett, co-director, Empower America

Clint Bolick, vice president, Institute for Justice

Linda Chavez, president, Center for Equal Opportunity

Jerry Cook, statistician and the father of James Cook, a
    sixteen-year-old graduate of University of California,
    San Diego, who was rejected by five University of
    California medical schools

Dinesh D'Souza, author

Richard Epstein, law professor, University of Chicago

Richard Ferrier, professor, Thomas Aquinas College

Lino Graglia, law professor, University of Texas

Darrell E. Issa, founder and president,
    Directed Electronics

William Kristol, publisher, *Weekly Standard*

Michael McConnell, law professor, University of Chicago

Bernie Richter, Republican assemblyman from Chico

Thomas L. Rhodes, publisher, *National Review*

William Rusher, distinguished fellow, Claremont Institute,
    and former publisher, *National Review*

Ron Unz, gubernatorial candidate in 1994

Eugene Volokh, law professor, University of California,
    Los Angeles

In Governor Pete Wilson's Presidential Campaign

Dick Dresner, pollster

George Gorton, campaign manager

Dan Schnur, press officer

Pete Wilson, governor

In the California Attorney General's Office

Dan Lungren, attorney general

David Stirling, chief deputy attorney general

In the California Republican Party

George Deukmejian, former governor

John Herrington, former energy secretary and chair of the
California Republican Party

Michael Schroeder, treasurer

In the Republican National Committee

Haley Barbour, chair of the RNC

Pat Buchanan, presidential candidate

Newt Gingrich, speaker of the House of Representatives

Phil Gramm, presidential candidate

General Colin Powell, one of the few prominent Republicans
who supported affirmative action

Scott Taylor, liaison between the state Republican Party and
the Republican National Committee

In the Dole Campaign

Bob Dole, presidential candidate

Tony Fabrizio, pollster

Jack Kemp, vice-presidential candidate

Scott Reed, campaign manager

Dennis Shea, advisor

In the California Democratic Party

Willie Brown, mayor, San Francisco

Bill Lockyer, Senate president pro tempore

Bill Press, chair through 1995

Mark Ridley-Thomas, city councilman, Los Angeles

Steve Smith, political director

Darry Sragow, political consultant

Art Torres, chair after December 1995

In the Clinton Campaign

Bill Carrick, senior advisor

Bill Clinton, president

Al Gore, vice president

George Stephanopoulos, senior advisor

Tom Umberg, California campaign manager

Bill Wardlaw, private lawyer and 1992 and 1996 campaign advisor to Bill Clinton

In the Opposition to Proposition 209

Jan Adams, grassroots organizer

Hari Dillon, director, Vanguard Foundation

Patricia Ewing, campaign manager

Dorothy Erlich, executive director, ACLU of Northern California

Diane Feldman, pollster

Jeff Gordon, lawyer

Rebecca Gordon, grassroots organizer

Louis Harris, pollster

Mary Hughes, political consultant

Aleita J. Huguenin, manager, governmental relations division, California Teachers Association

Patricia Ireland, president, National Organization for Women

Jesse Jackson, chairman, Rainbow Coalition

Martha Jimenez, lawyer, Mexican American Legal Defense and Education Fund

Jerome Karabel, professor, University of California, Berkeley

Judy Kurtz, lawyer, Equal Rights Advocates

Philip Monrad, lawyer, Remcho, Johansen and Purcell

Molly Munger, lawyer, NAACP Legal Defense and Education Fund

David Oppenheimer, law professor, Golden Gate University

Eva Jefferson Paterson, executive director, Lawyers' Committee for Civil Rights

Constance Rice, Western Legal Director, NAACP Legal Defense and Education Fund

Ramona Ripston, executive director, ACLU of Southern California

Lorraine Sheinberg, major donor and advisor

Bob Shrum, media advisor

Eleanor Smeal, president, Feminist Majority

Katherine Spillar, national director, Feminist Majority

Anthony Thigpen, grassroots organizer

Elizabeth Toledo, president, National Organization for Women in California

Ted Wang, lawyer, Lawyers' Committee for Civil Rights

Peg Yorkin, co-founder, Feminist Majority

Appendix B

Time Line

1964. President Lyndon Johnson signs the Civil Rights Act of 1964. It prohibits discrimination in employment and education on the basis of race, color, religion, sex, or national origin.

1965. President Johnson signs an executive order requiring federal contractors to "take affirmative action" to ensure that applicants are employed and that employees are treated equally without regard to race.

1969–72. The Department of Labor under Presidents Johnson and Nixon begins requiring federal contractors to keep track of their workforce and to set goals and timetables for ending the underrepresentation of minorities and women.

1971. In *Griggs v. Duke Power*, the U.S. Supreme Court approves a statistical approach to discrimination law.

1978. In *Regents of the University of California v. Bakke*, the U.S. Supreme Court rules against quotas but, to foster diversity in education, approves the consideration of race and ethnicity as a "plus factor" in admissions.

1979. In *United States Steelworkers v. Weber*, the U.S. Supreme Court rules against a white steelworker's claim of reverse discrimination and holds that employers have an "area of discretion" to employ minority preferences to eliminate imbalances in their workforce.

1988.   Thomas E. Wood, a 1975 Ph.D. recipient from Berkeley's philosophy department, fails to find a tenure-track teaching job and began to believe that affirmative action was part of the problem.

1988.   A group of professors form the National Association of Scholars to "reclaim the academy" from multiculturalism and affirmative action programs that they believe result in the hiring of unqualified faculty and the admission of unqualified students.

1989.   In *Richmond v. Croson*, the Supreme Court narrowly restricts the ability of state and local governments to use preferences in contracting.

1988–90.   Glynn Custred, a tenured professor at the California State University, Hayward, helps to organize the California Association of Scholars, a chapter of the National Association of Scholars.

1991.   Tom Wood and Glynn Custred meet through the California Association of Scholars.

1993.   Under pressure to diversify the Board of Regents, Governor Pete Wilson appoints Ward Connerly, a financial contributor to the governor's campaigns and an African American.

October 1993.   Custred and Wood file the California Civil Rights Initiative with the state attorney general for the first time but fail to collect enough signatures to put it on the ballot.

August 1994.   University of California regent Ward Connerly questions the fairness of affirmative action at hearings held by the assembly's judiciary committee.

November 1994. The Republicans sweep Congress, and pollsters begin writing about the white male voting bloc. On the strength of this bloc and the popularity of the anti-immigrant Proposition 187, California Governor Pete Wilson comes from behind to beat challenger Kathleen Brown.

December 1994. Wood and Custred name a campaign team that includes Joe Gelman, Arnie Steinberg, and Larry Arnn.

January 1995. Connerly questions the fairness of affirmative action at the mid-January University of California regents meeting.

January 1995. Members of the opposition to the California Civil Rights Initiative begin meeting and polling.

February 1995. Governor Wilson reverses his earlier support for affirmative action and comes out in support of the California Civil Rights Initiative.

February 1995. President Clinton calls for a review of all federal affirmative action programs.

March 1995. Senator Dole, the leading Republican presidential challenger, reverses his long-time support of affirmative action.

March 1995. Governor Pete Wilson announces that he has a "duty" to explore the possibility of running for president.

April 1995. President Bill Clinton attends the California Democratic Party's convention, where he says he supports affirmative action but asks minorities and women to recognize that "this is a psychologically difficult time for a lot of white males."

May 1995. The opposition to the California Civil Rights Initiative splits into two groups. One group, led by Eva Jefferson Paterson in the north, pursues an alternative initiative strategy. The other group in the south, led by Katherine Spillar of the Feminist Majority, plans to confront the initiative straight on.

June 1995. In *Adarand Constructors v. Peña* the Supreme
Court rules that "all racial classifications" are "inherently suspect and presumptively invalid."

June 1995. Jack Kemp says he opposes the Republican
stand against affirmative action.

July 1995. President Clinton defends affirmative action and
calls for a policy of "mend it, don't end it."

July 1995. Led by Governor Pete Wilson and Ward
Connerly, the U.C. regents vote to end affirmative action
at the University of California.

July 1995. Wilson jumps in the polls and has his most successful fund-raiser to date.

July 1995. Senator Dole introduces legislation in the
Senate to end federal affirmative action.

August 1995. For the second time, Custred and Wood file
the California Civil Rights Initiative with the state attorney general.

September 1995. Wilson, failing to attract financial backing, drops out of the campaign for president.

October 1995. The northern California opposition files an
alternative initiative—Equal Opportunity Without
Quotas—with the attorney general's office.

October 1995. Unable to pay its bills, the California Civil
Rights Initiative campaign halts its signature drive.

December 1995. The northern California opposition drops
the alternative initiative after the legislative analyst's office concludes that it will eliminate magnet schools and
programs for minority students.

December 1995. Ward Connerly takes over as chair of
CCRI; Wilson's fund-raising effort for the California
Republican Party pours nearly $500,000 into the cam-
paign, and the signature drive resumes.

January 1996. The opposition to CCRI regroups while CCRI struggles to collect enough signatures before its February deadline.

February 1996. The CCRI campaign turns in more than a million signatures to the attorney general's office.

February 1996. The Feminist Majority assumes leadership of the statewide coalition to oppose CCRI and hires Patricia Ewing to run the campaign.

February 1996. The presidential primary season begins, with every Republican presidential candidate running against affirmative action.

March 1996. In the week before the California primary Ward Connerly refuses to attend any press conference with Pat Buchanan, a contender in the Republican primary and an early supporter of CCRI.

March 1996. Dole plans and then fails to give a major policy address on affirmative action, but he endorses CCRI.

March 1996. In *Hopwood v. Texas*, the U.S. Circuit Court of Appeals in New Orleans strikes down an admissions policy at the University of Texas law school giving preferences to blacks and Hispanics, saying that public universities may not justify affirmative action programs based on the benefits of diversity.

May 1996. General Powell makes his first public statements attacking the California Civil Rights Initiative.

June 1996. House Speaker Newt Gingrich questions the wisdom of eliminating affirmative action.

June 1996. Dole pulls back in his opposition to affirmative action.

July 1996. CCRI is given a ballot number, Proposition 209.

July 1996. Attorney General Dan Lungren issues a title and summary for Proposition 209 that omits the initiative's impact on affirmative action.

August 1996. Sacramento County Superior Court Judge James T. Ford orders the attorney general to rewrite the ballot language because the omission of "affirmative action" is misleading.

August 1996. Judge Ford's decision is overturned on appeal.

August 1996. Dole chooses Kemp as his vice-presidential running mate. Kemp comes out in support of Proposition 209.

August 1996. The Feminist Majority and NOW are forced out of the anti–Proposition 209 coalition.

September 1996. Former Klansman David Duke visits California State University at Northridge to speak in favor of Prop 209.

October 1996. Falling in the polls, Dole decides to launch a major media campaign in California and to run commercials in support of Proposition 209.

October 31 1996. President Clinton visits Oakland, California, and makes his first public statement about 209.

November 3, 1996. Racial discrimination at Texaco becomes front-page news.

November 5, 1996. Voters in California approve Proposition 209, 54.6 percent to 45.4 percent.

November 6, 1996. The anti–Proposition 209 coalition files suit in the U.S. District Court for Northern California, alleging that the proposition violates the Equal Protection Clause of the Fourteenth Amendment.

December 23, 1996. Chief U.S. District Judge Thelton Henderson grants a preliminary injunction preventing the state from implementing Proposition 209 until the conclusion of a trial or a final ruling from a higher court.

April 8, 1997. A three-judge panel of the U.S. Court of Appeals for the Ninth Circuit overturns Henderson.

June 1997. In the first year after Wilson and Connerly led the battle to end affirmative action at the University of California, the university's Boalt Hall School of Law announces that only one African American and eighteen Latinos plan to enroll in the incoming class of 270 students for Fall 1997.

August 21, 1997. The U.S. Court of Appeals for the Ninth Circuit reaffirms its earlier ruling that Proposition 209 is constitutional.

September 4, 1997. The U.S. Supreme Court refuses to block enforcement of Proposition 209 but postpones the decision of whether to take up the opposition's appeal until the fall.

September 9, 1997. Governor Pete Wilson asks the California legislature to remove or amend thirty state statutes that he says grant illegal race or gender preferences.

November 3, 1997. Without comment, the U.S. Supreme Court lets stand the decision by the U.S. Court of Appeals for the Ninth Circuit that upholds Proposition 209.

November 4, 1997. Houston voters reject an initiative to end the city's affirmative action program by a vote of 55 to 45 percent.

November 6, 1997. The House Judiciary Committee kills federal legislation to end affirmative action.

Notes

Chapter 1

1. Richard Morin and Mario A. Brosard, *Washington Post,* June 17, 1996, p. Al.

2. In the next two years President Bill Clinton would become the first Democratic president to "feel the pain" of white males and reflect their wishes by declaring the "era of big Government" over.

3. Glynn Custred, interview, July 25, 1995.

4. Institutional Research and Analysis, California State University, Hayward.

5. Only one California State University campus—San Luis Obispo—is oversubscribed.

6. California Department of Finance, Demographic Research Unit, *Population Projections by Race/Ethnicity for California and Its Counties, 1990–2040.* Sacramento: 1993.

7. Glynn Custred, interview, July 25, 1995.

8. Robert S. Portillo, *ACACIA,* Spring 1979, p. 4.

9. Barbara Paige, interview, February 20, 1996.

10. Glynn Custred, interview, September 26, 1996.

11. Gayle Young, interview, January 22, 1996.

12. Glynn Custred, interview, July 25, 1995.

13. Custred's views drew on writing by Arthur M. Schlesinger, Jr., who published *The Disuniting of America* (Knoxville, TN: Whittle Direct Books) in 1991.

14. Glynn Custred, interview, July 25, 1995.

15. Gayle Young, interview, January 22, 1996.

16. Glynn Custred, interview, July 25, 1995.

17. Gayle Young, interview.

18. Glynn Custred, interview, September 26, 1996.

19. Glynn Custred, interview, July 25, 1995.

20. Barbara Paige, interview.

21. Glynn Custred, interview, July 25, 1995.

22. Ibid.

23. "The Stanford Mind," *Wall Street Journal,* December 22, 1988, p.14.

24. John Searle, "The Storm Over the University," *New York Review of Books*, December, 6, 1990, p. 39.

25. Ibid.

26. California Legislature, 1991–1992 Regular Session. Assembly Bill No. 2150. Introduced by Assembly Member Brown, March 8, 1991.

27. Ibid.

28. Glynn Custred, interview, January 17, 1996.

29. Bruce Vermazen, interview, January 11, 1996.

30. Anita Silvers, interview, February 16, 1996.

31. *Washington Post*, December 27, 1994, p. A3.

32. Tom Wood, interview, June 1995.

33. I found the memo in a large book of CCRI team memos that Joe Gelman, CCRI's campaign manager, kept until December 1995.

34. Tom Wood to Glynn Custred, Joe Gelman, and Arnie Steinberg, memorandum, April 1995.

35. Ibid.

36. Anatole Anton, interview, 1996.

37. *Regents of the University of California v. Bakke*, 438 US 265 (1978).

38. Ibid., p. 74.

39. Ibid., p. 83.

40. Robert Post, "Introduction: After *Bakke*," *Representations*, Vol. 55, Summer 1996, p. 3.

41. David A. Hoekema, "Issues in the Profession," *APA Proceedings*, Vol. 65, No.7, June 1992, p. 39.

42. Thomas E. Wood, Memo to Joe Gelman, head of CCRI's Los Angeles office, April 7, 1995. The one-page memo included five points on miscellaneous items.

43. Tom Wood, interview, June 1995.

44. *Newsweek*, December 24, 1990.

45. Ibid., p. 49.

46. Ibid.

47. Ibid.

48. Eugene C. Lee, "Representative Government and the Initiative Process." In *California Policy Choices*, Vol. 6, edited by John Kirlin and Donald Winkler. Los Angeles: University of Southern California, 1990. See bibliography for other sources on the initiative process.

49. Ibid.

50. Louis Barnett, interview, January 1996.

51. Paul Craig Roberts and Lawrence M. Stratton, *The New Color Line*. Washington, DC: Regnery Publications, 1995, p. 107.

52. *United Steelworkers v. Weber,* 443 US 193 (1979).

53. Ibid.

54. "Key words influence stands on minorities; polls find whites favor remedial programs—until quotas or preferences are mentioned." John Brennan, *Los Angeles Times*, August 21, 1991, p. A5.

55. Ibid.

56. Ibid

57. Paul M. Sniderman and Thomas Piazza, *The Scar of Race*. Cambridge, MA: Harvard University Press, Belknap Press, 1993, p. 130.

58. This was the language of the initiative filed with the attorney general in October 1993. The same paragraph was revised slightly in 1995 to read: "The state shall not discriminate against, or grant preferential treatment to, any individual or group on the basis of race, sex, color, ethnicity, or national origin in the operation of public employment, public education, or public contracting."

59. Richard Epstein, interview, March 1996.

60. Thomas Wood to Michael McConnell, June 26, 1995. Wood's conversations with McConnell began in 1993.

61. Lino Graglia, interview, February 16, 1996.

62. Glynn Custred, memo to Larry Arnn, November 17, 1994.

63. Thomas Wood, memo to Larry Arnn, November 18, 1994.

64. Charles Geshekter, interview, February 2, 1996.

65. Michael Biechler, interview, March 4, 1996.

66. William Rusher, *National Review,* November 1, 1993, p. 55.

67. Patrick Buchanan, *San Francisco Examiner,* February 3, 1994.

68. Wayne Johnson, interview, January 18, 1996.

69. Thomas Wood, interview.

70. The quote continues: "And I made it anyway—high school, college, my own big business, important friends. If I could make it, anybody can, because the playing field is a lot closer to level now. The truth is that preferences at this point are not just reverse discrimination, they're degrading to people who accept them. They've got to go." B. Drummond Ayres, "Fighting Affirmative Action, He Finds His Race an Issue," *New York Times,* April 18, 1996, p. A1.

71. In the retelling of even these details to the press, Connerly changed some of them. To a reporter at the *Sacramento Bee,* he said that both his parents had died by the time he was four years old. He told me in 1995 that his parents had divorced, that his father was still alive, and that his stepfather had pursued custody. When he talked to a *New York Times* reporter in the summer of 1997, he never mentioned his stepfather or a custody battle and expressed surprise at learning that his father was still alive and had filed a custody suit.

72. The details on the custody suit come from papers filed by Roy Connerly and Mary Soniea in the 11th Judicial District Court, Vernon Parish, Louisiana, December 1945.

73. Ward Connerly, interview, August 30, 1995.

74. Ibid.

75. A. Lin Neumann, "I Am Not African-American," *San Francisco Focus Magazine,* May 1997, p. 58.

76. Elizabeth Stansberry, interview, September 16, 1997.

77. Arthur Soniea, interview, September 19, 1997.

78. Elizabeth Stansberry, interview, September 16,1997.

79. Ward Connerly, interview, August 30, 1995.

80. Ward Connerly, interview, May 7, 1996.

81. Ibid.

82. Ward Connerly, interview, August 30, 1995.

83. Ibid.

84. Connerly said when he went to work for the housing department, he reregistered to vote and declined to state any party affiliation.

85. Ward Connerly, interview, August 30, 1995.

86. The housing plans are referred to as housing elements and are one of seven elements cities and counties must include in their general plan.

87. The condition for an affordable housing plan is one of eight elements, including transportation and schooling, that are required in local housing plans.

88. Policy analyst Kim Alexander, Common Cause.

89. Louis Freedberg, *San Francisco Chronicle,* February 28, 1993, p. A13.

90. Dana Wilkie, *San Diego Union-Tribune,* February 24, 1993, p. A4.

91. Stephanie Rubin, a consultant to the Select Committee on Higher Education, interview, October 1996.

92. Ward Connerly, interview, May 7, 1996.

93. Editorial, *Los Angeles Times,* January 9, 1994.

94. Clair Burgener, interview, June 10, 1996.

95. Fahizah Alim, "A Different Minority," *Sacramento Bee,* July 12, 1991, p. 81.

96. Terry Lightfoot, University of California spokesperson.

97. Jerry Cook, interview, 1996.

98. Ibid.

99. Ibid.

100. Field poll, March 1993.

101. "California's Growing Taxpayer Squeeze," California Department of Finance, 1991.

102. Henry Muller and John F. Stacks, *Time*, November 11, 1991.

103. In 1985 64 percent of the population was white, 20.4 percent was Latino, 6.7 percent was black, and 8.9 percent was listed as "other." By 1994, whites accounted for 52.8 percent, blacks 5.9 percent, Asians 9.3 percent, and Latinos 31 percent. *Current Population Survey Report*, California State Census Data Center, March 1994 and March 1995.

104. *Los Angeles Times*, October 30, 1994.

105. The numbers do not add up to 100 percent because some Latinos are also counted as white. *Los Angeles Times* exit poll.

106. In the 1992 presidential election, 60.5 percent of the state's white population was registered to vote and 55.9 percent voted; 64 percent of the black population was registered and 56.1 percent voted; 25.4 percent of the Latino population was registered to vote and 20.9 percent voted. Bureau of the Census, Statistical Information Office, Population Division.

107. Bill Stall and Amy Wallace, *Los Angeles Times*, October 29, 1994, p. A1.

108. *Supplement to the Statement of Vote—November 8, 1994 General Election*, compiled by Bill Jones, Secretary of State, pp. 2, 104.

109. Bill Stall and Cathleen Decker, *Los Angeles Times*, November 9, 1994, p.1.

Chapter 2

1. *Los Angeles Times* exit poll.

2. Peter Schrag, *Sacramento Bee*, November 16, 1994, p. B6.

3. *San Francisco Chronicle*, March 20, 1995, p. 1.

4. John Boudreau, *Washington Post*, December 27, 1994, p. 3.

5. Ibid.

6. Tom Wood, interview, June 1995.

7. Scott Taylor, interview, April 1995.

8. Larry Arnn, interview, February 27, 1996.

9. Joe Gelman, interview, August 24, 1996.

10. Arnold Steinberg, interview, 1995.

11. Arnold Steinberg, *The Political Campaign Handbook.* San Francisco: Lexington Books, 1976, p. 53.

12. Larry Arnn, memo to Joe Gelman, January 9, 1995.

13. Ibid.

14. Ibid.

15. Larry Arnn, interview.

16. Ibid.

17. Joe Gelman, interview, January 29, 1996.

18. Arnold Steinberg, interview, January 25, 1996.

19. Scott Taylor, interview.

20. Ibid.

21. Arnn to Gelman, memorandum, January 1, 1995.

22. Joe Gelman, interview, January 29, 1996.

23. Ron Unz, *Los Angeles Times*, March 12, 1995, p. 5.

24. A Gallup/CNN poll done in March 1995 showed 55% of those polled favoring affirmative action while 63% opposed quotas (*USA Today*, March 24, 1995, p. 3A).

25. Gerald C. Lubenow, ed., *The 1990 Governor's Race.* Berkeley, CA: Institute of Governmental Studies Press, 1991, p. 169.

26. George Gorton, interview, 1995.

27. Ward Connerly, interview, 1995.

28. Amy Wallace, *Los Angeles Times*, January 20, 1995, p. A1.

29. Ralph Carmona, interview.

30. Steinberg to Arnn, memorandum, February 28, 1995.

31. Bill Stall, *Los Angeles Times*, February 26, 1995, p. A3.

32. *The New Orleans Declaration: A Democratic Agenda for the 1990s*, endorsed by the Democratic Leadership Council in New Orleans, Louisiana, March 22–24, 1990.

33. Linda Chavez, interview, October 10, 1996.

34. Paul Richter and Doyle McManus, *Los Angeles Times*, March 4, 1995, p. A1.

35. *Congressional Record*, March 15, 1995, p. S3929.

36. Frank Swoboda, *Washington Post*, March 16, 1995, p. A1.

37. Dave Lesher and Bill Stall, *Los Angeles Times*, March 24, 1995, p. A1.

38. Wood to Steinberg, memorandum, April 12, 1995.

39. Tom Wood, interview, June 1995.

40. Duanne Garrett committed suicide in July 1995.

41. Mary Lynne Vellinga, *Sacramento Bee*, April 30, 1995, p. A1.

42. Tom Wood, interview, June 1995.

43. Ibid.

44. The $1 million would pay for the direct-mail campaigns, signature gatherers, and office expenses.

45. Bill Lockyer, interview, February 6, 1996.

46. Ibid.

47. Glynn Custred, interview, September 26, 1995.

48. Joe Gelman, interview, 1995.

49. Scott Taylor, interview.

50. *Adarand Constructors v. Peña*, 115 Sup. Ct. 2097, 2113 (1995).

51. Ibid.

52. Thomas E. Wood, memo to Joe Gelman, July 26, 1995.

53. Arnold Steinberg, memo to Larry Arnn, May 13, 1995.

54. Arnold Steinberg, memo to Larry Arnn, May 24, 1995.

55. George Gorton, interview.

56. Dick Dressner, interview, January 5, 1996.

57. Amy Wallace and Dave Lesher, *Los Angeles Times*, July 20, 1994, p. 3.

58. Thomas Edsall, *Washington Post*, October 2, 1988, p. C1.

59. *Overview of the Policies and Procedures Governing Undergraduate Admissions*, Attachment B, Fig. 7.

60. Ibid.

61. These numbers do not add up to 100 percent because 1.8 percent were listed as unknown and 1.5 percent as Filipino American. In addition, the U.C. administrators break Latino into two categories: Chicanos, who comprised 28.8 percent of the total, and Latinos, who accounted for 8.1 percent of the total.

62. Ibid.

63. The U.S. Office for Civil Rights concluded in March 1996 that the University of California, Berkeley, was in "compliance with Title VI with regard to the undergraduate admission policies and procedures for the College of Letters and Sciences."

64. Dave Lesher and Bill Stall, *Los Angeles Times*, March 24, 1995, p. 1.

65. Jackson often described his constituency with these words. *Chicago Tribune*, April 12, 1994.

66. Roy Brophy, interview, September 29, 1995.

67. Ibid.

68. Interview, 1995.

69. The regents' votes remained the same, except for Bagley, who abstained, and Velma Montoya, a Latino and a Wilson appointee, who voted against ending the consideration of race in admissions. Montoya had voted for ending the consideration of race in employment and contracting.

70. David G. Savage, *Los Angeles Times*, July 28, 1995, p. 20.

71. Attorney General Daniel E. Lungren and initiative coordinator Kathleen F. DaRosa, Initiative Title and Summary, December 8, 1993.

72. Arnold Steinberg, memo to Joe Gelman, May 16, 1995.

73. Joe Gelman, interview, January 3, 1997.

74. Dick Dressner, interview, January 5, 1996.

75. In September 1995 a Gallup poll showed Powell with a favorable rating of 64 percent, compared to 55 percent for Clinton and 42 percent for Dole.

76. *Wall Street Journal*/NBC News poll, September 1995.

77. R. W. Apple, Jr., *New York Times*, September 4, 1995, p. A1.

78. Robert Shogan, *Los Angeles Times,* September 17, 1995, p. A1.

79. The attorney general returns a title and summary for every initiative filed. In the summary, the legislative analyst assesses the financial impact of the initiative. Both the title and the summary must appear on the petitions that voters are asked to sign.

80. Initiatives to change the state constitution require a number of signatures equaling 8 percent of the last gubernatorial vote, and an initiative statute requires a number of signatures equaling 5 percent of the last gubernatorial vote. *Blueprint for Our Future: Increasing Voter Participation and Reforming the Initiative Process.* Senate Office of Research, Sacramento, January 1991.

81. Arnold Steinberg, letter to General Colin Powell, August 3, 1995.

82. Colin L. Powell, note to Arnold Steinberg, August 5, 1995.

83. Thomas E. Wood, memo to Arnold Steinberg, October 17, 1995.

84. For more information on initiatives, see Daniel H. Lowenstein, "California Initiatives and the Single Subject Rule," UCLA Law Review, Vol. 30, No. 5, June 1993; Eugene C. Lee, "Representative Government and the Initiative Process," in *California Policy Choices.* Vol. 6, edited by John Kirlin and Donald Winkler. Los Angeles: University of Southern California, 1990 and Jim Shultz, *The Initiative Cookbook,* San Francisco, Democracy Center Advocacy Institute West, 1996.

85. John Bunzel, interview, January 22, 1996.

86. Michael Arno, interview, January 18, 1996.

87. Ibid.

88. Ibid.

89. George Gorton, interview, September 19, 1996.

90. Tom Wood, interview, 1995.

91. Thomas Wood, memo to Ward Connerly, October 22, 1995.

92. Thomas Wood, memo to Arnold Steinberg with copies to Larry Arnn, Glynn Custred, Joe Gelman, and Darrell Issa, October 31, 1995.

93. Joe Gelman, interview, January 5, 1997.

94. Arnold Steinberg, interview, January 1996.

95. Ballot Measure Committee Campaign Disclosure Statement—Long Form, Registrar of Voters, 1996.

96. Glynn Custred, interview.

97. *The Hotline*, July 24, 1995.

Chapter 3

1. Kathleen Brown's campaign focused early on crime and the economy, but neither issue took off for her, and her stand on Proposition 187 became one of the points on which she differed sharply from Wilson. For a complete look at the 1994 race, see Gerald C. Lubenow, ed., *The 1994 Governor's Race*. Berkeley, CA: Institute for Governmental Studies Press, 1995.

2. After the 1994 elections, Republicans held four out of six state offices and had virtual control of the assembly for the first time since 1970.

3. The NAACP and the NAACP Legal Defense and Education Board are separate nonprofit entities.

4. Many nonprofits were involved in the early stages of the campaign against the California Civil Rights Initiative, including the Equal Rights Advocates and Vanguard.

5. When people were asked, "Thinking about the words *affirmative action*, what is your general opinion of affirmative action?" 13.9 percent said it was very favorable, 35.5 percent said it was somewhat favorable, 21.4 percent said it was somewhat unfavorable, and 17.5 percent said it was very unfavorable (Project 5002, California Medium Propensity Voters, CCRI, 1995).

6. Charles Whalen and Barbara Whalen, *The Longest Debate: A Legislative History of the 1964 Civil Rights Act*. Cabin John, MD: Seven Locks Press, 1985.

7. *The Polling Report*, March 1995, p. 2.

8. Cathleen Decker, *Los Angeles Times*, February 19, 1995, p. A1.

9. Cathleen Decker and Daniel Weintraub, *Los Angeles Times*, November 10, 1994, p. 1.

10. Eleanor Smeal, interview, October 12, 1996.

11. Peg Yorkin, interview, March 22, 1996.

12. Molly Munger, interview, January 24, 1996.

13. Project 5002, California Medium Propensity Voters, CCRI, February 1995.

14. Molly Munger, interview, January 24, 1996.

15. *Washington Post*, February 4, 1995, p. 1.

16. Connie Rice, interview, January 23, 1996.

17. Darry Sragow, interview, February 2, 1996.

18. Ibid.

19. Molly Munger, interview, January 24, 1996.

20. Ibid.

21. Ibid.

22. Steve Smith, interview, May 2, 1996.

23. Steve Smith, interview, January 18, 1996.

24. Molly Munger, interview, January 24, 1996.

25. Ibid.

26. Gil Ray, interview.

27. Molly Munger, interview.

28. Molly Munger, Gil Ray, and Peg Yorkin, interviews.

29. Molly Munger, interview.

30. Peg Yorkin, interview.

31. Molly Munger, interview.

32. Ibid.

33. Elizabeth Toledo, interview, March 11, 1996.

34. Katherine Spillar, interview, March 22, 1996.

35. Amy Chance, *Sacramento Bee*, April 7, 1995, p. A26.

36. Elizabeth Toledo, interview, April 24, 1996.

37. Ibid.

38. Amy Chance, *Sacramento Bee*, April 9, 1995, p. A1.

39. Ibid.

40. Ken Chavez, *Sacramento Bee*, April 10, 1995, p. A1.

41. George Skelton, *Los Angeles Times,* April 10, 1995, p. 3.

42. Aleita Huguenin, interview, February 1, 1996.

43. Ibid.

44. Ibid.

45. Martha West, a law professor at U.C. Davis, wrote a draft of a legislative proposal for state Senator pro Tempore William Lockyer's office in 1995 that essentially addressed the same issues of quotas and the hiring of unqualified prospects.

46. Joe Duff, interview, March 20, 1996.

47. Louis Harris poll, April 1995.

48. Anthony Thigpen, interview, March 23, 1996.

49. Steve Smith, interview.

50. Katherine Spillar, interview.

51. David Oppenheimer, interview, January 8, 1996.

52. Steve Smith, interview.

53. Philip Monrad, interview, March 4, 1996.

54. Ted Wong, interview, March 6, 1996.

55. Office of the Press Secretary, The White House, transcript, July 19, 1995.

56. Jim Moore, memorandum, September 1, 1995.

57. Ibid.

58. David Oppenheimer, interview, November 27, 1995.

59. The official title of the initiative was Equal Opportunity and Non-Discrimination Without Quotas, but the lawyers who drafted it referred to it as the Equal Opportunity Without Quotas initiative.

60. Aleita Huguenin, interview, February 1, 1996.

61. Jim Moore, interview, March 14, 1996.

62. Anthony Thigpen, interview.

63. Connie Rice, interview.

64. Judy Kurtz, interview, January 5, 1996.

Chapter 4

1. Ward Connerly, interview, May 7, 1996.

2. Kathleen Hall Jamieson, *Dirty Politics.* New York: Oxford University Press, p. 81.

3. Ward Connerly, interview, May 7, 1996.

4. Patrick Buchanan, *San Francisco Examiner,* February 3, 1994.

5. Alan Keyes also competed in the Louisiana primary, but in deference to New Hampshire's primary as the first in the nation, the other Republican challengers declined to participate.

6. Wayne Parent, interview, May 8, 1996.

7. In the 1991 runoff for governor, David Duke won 38 percent of the votes, including 55 percent of the white vote.

8. Tyler Bridges, *Times-Picayune,* July 28, 1995, p. A1.

9. Wayne Parent, interview, May 8, 1996.

10. *Dallas Morning News,* January 17, 1996.

11. Courtesy of Charles Rand, curator of the Commercial Archive, University of Oklahoma.

12. Exit polls showed that more than half of those who voted identified themselves as part of the religious right. They went two to one for Buchanan.

13. James Llorens, interview, May 9, 1996.

14. Jonathan Atler and Michael Isikoff, *Time,* March 4, 1996, p. 28.

15. Paul Gigot, *Wall Street Journal,* April 12, 1996.

16. Ken Chavez, *Sacramento Bee,* March 7, 1996.

17. Dennis Shea, *Washington Post,* February 16, 1993, p. A13.

18. Ibid.

19. *Congressional Record,* March 15, 1995, p. S3929.

20. Ibid.

21. Kevin Merida, *Washington Post,* March 17, 1995, p. A4.

22. Ibid.

23. Bob Dole, opinion, *Los Angeles Times,* November 19, 1995, p. M5.

24. William Schneider, interview, April 24, 1996.

25. Linda Chavez, interview, July 10, 1996.

26. Bill McGrath, interview, April 19, 1996.

27. *Christian Science Monitor,* June 14, 1996.

28. Deukmejian to author, August 26, 1996.

29. Ibid.

30. Doug Willis, Associated Press, April 18, 1996.

31. Ken Chavez, *Sacramento Bee,* June 27, 1996, p. A1.

32. *Los Angeles Times,* June 13, 1996.
33. Ibid.
34. Fred Barnes, *Weekly Standard,* May 27, 1996, p. 21.
35. Ibid.
36. Scott Taylor, interview, August 21, 1996.
37. Dave Lesher, *Los Angeles Times,* June 13, 1996, p. A1.
38. Ward Connerly, interview, May 7, 1996.
39. Ibid.
40. Amy Chance, *Sacramento Bee,* August 9, 1996, p. A1.
41. Arnold Steinberg, interview, August 12, 1996.
42. *San Diego Union Tribune,* July 16, 1996.
43. Copy of a letter from Governor Pete Wilson to Stanley Skinner, August 2, 1996.
44. Arnold Steinberg, interview, October 29, 1996.
45. Ibid.
46. Arnold Steinberg, interview, August 12, 1996.
47. Ibid.
48. Arnold Steinberg, interview, November 19, 1996.
49. Arnold Steinberg, interview, October 29, 1996.
50. The 1996 Republican platform, *Individual Rights and Personal Safety,* adopted August 12, 1996.
51. Ward Connerly, public remarks at a GOPAC meeting, San Diego, August 14, 1996.
52. Joyce Price, *Washington Times,* July 23, 1995.
53. Godfrey Sperling, *Christian Science Monitor,* August 8, 1995.
54. Ibid.
55. Jack Kemp, *Washington Times,* September 3, 1995, p. B4.
56. Ibid.
57. Arnold Steinberg, interview, November 19, 1996.
58. Richard Cohen, *Washington Post,* August 14, 1996.
59. "The Jack Kemp Reverse," lead editorial, *New York Times,* August 15, 1996, p. A26.
60. Arnold Steinberg, interview, October 29, 1996.
61. Ward Connerly, interview, August 14, 1996.
62. Ibid.
63. Arnold Steinberg, interview, October 29, 1996.
64. Bob Dole, speech presented at the Republican National Convention, San Diego, August 1996.

65. Ronald Brownstein, *Los Angeles Times*, August 14, 1996, p. A1.

Chapter 5

1. Jim Shultz, *The Initiative Cookbook*. San Francisco: Democracy Center, Advocacy Institute West, 1996.

2. Polling by Jim Moore, Sacramento, California.

3. Author attended the meeting.

4. Although the money officially came from the state Republican Party, party officials said that it was raised by Wilson with the understanding that it would go to CCRI.

5. The campaign needed fewer signatures, but wanted one million to ensure that there were enough valid signatures.

6. Bill Arno, interview, November 8, 1996.

7. Connie Rice, interview, October 18, 1996.

8. Campaign Plan, California Civil Rights Initiative for November 1996 (Arnold Steinberg, Arnold Steinberg and Associates, Inc.), pp. 68–70.

9. Patricia Ireland, interview, December 6, 1996.

10. Robert W. Welkos, *Los Angeles Times*, August 25, 1996, p. A1.

11. Peg Yorkin, interview, October 19, 1996.

12. Patricia Ewing, interview, September 28, 1996

13. Ibid.

14. Ibid.

15. Ibid.

16. Ellie Smeal, July 9, 1996.

17. Molly Munger, interview, September 29, 1996.

18. Eva Paterson, interview, December 27, 1996.

19. Researcher Mark Rabine, interview, October 9, 1996.

20. Interview in Los Angeles, October 19, 1996.

21. Connie Rice declined to comment on her letter to Powell or on her meeting with him. The details of this meeting come from sources in the coalition, and the meeting was confirmed by General Powell.

22. Campaign plan, California Civil Rights Initiative for November 1996, Arnold Steinberg, p. 41.

23. Author attended the breakfast. October 18, 1996.

24. Dozens of books document the role that race has played in contemporary politics. The following have been published most recently. Please see the bibliography at the end of the book for more.

Thomas Byrne Edsall with Mary D. Edsall, *Chain Reaction.* New York: W.W. Norton & Co., 1991.

Dan T. Carter, *The Politics of Rage.* New York: Simon & Schuster, 1995.

Kenneth O'Reilly, *Nixon's Piano.* New York: The Free Press, 1995.

Kevin B. Phillips, *The Emerging Republican Majority.* New York: Arlington House, 1969.

25. Theodore H. White, *The Making of the President 1964.* New York: Antheneum Publishers, 1965.

26. Thomas Byrne Edsall with Mary D. Edsall, *Chain Reaction.* New York: W.W. Norton & Co., 1991.

27. Ibid., p. 79.

28. Stanley Greenberg, *Middle Class Dreams: The Politics and Power of the New American Majority.* New York: Times Books, 1995, pp. 41–42.

29. David Moraniss, *First in His Class.* New York: Simon and Schuster, 1995.

30. *The New Orleans Declaration: A Democratic Agenda for the 1990s.* Washington, DC: Democratic Leadership Council, 1990.

31. Stanley B. Greenberg, *Middle Class Dreams: The Politics and Power of the New American Majority.* New York: Times Books, 1995.

32. Ibid.

33. Remarks by the President on affirmative action (transcript), The White House, Office of the Press Secretary, July 19, 1995.

34. Ibid.

35. Ibid.

36. Poll by the Feldman Group, Washington, DC, June 1996.

37. Jean Merl, *Los Angeles Times*, June 7, 1996, p. A1.

38. Connie Rice, interview, November 19, 1996.

39. Ibid.

40. Interview, September 17, 1996.

41. Bob Shrum, interview, November 22, 1996.

42. "A Strategic Analysis of the Anti-CCRI Campaign," prepared by Louis Harris, July 1996. Based on an in-depth survey conducted by the Feldman Group, June 1996.

43. Ibid.

44. Analysis by the Feldman Group, Washington, DC, June 1996.

45. Interview, December 27, 1996.

46. Peg Yorkin, interview, October 19, 1996.

47. Ralph Neas, interview, September 20, 1996.

48. Interview, September 1996.

49. Anthony Thigpen, interview, September 28, 1996.

50. Patricia Ewing, interview, September 28, 1996.

51. Peg Yorkin, interview, October 19, 1996.

52. Bill Carrick, interview, November 15, 1996.

53. Bob Shrum. interview, November 22, 1996.

54. Ted Rohrlich, *Los Angeles Times*, January 1, 1995, p. E1.

55. Ibid.

56. Joe Gelman, interview, December 21, 1996.

57. Arnie Steinberg, interview, November 19, 1996.

58. Bill Wardlaw, interview, January 5, 1997.

Chapter 6

1. Sandy Banks, *Los Angeles Times*, November 10, 1994, p. B1.

2. Steve Smith, interview, May 2, 1996.

3. Exit Polls Field, "A Summary Analysis of Voting in the 1994 Election," *California Opinion Index*, January 1995. Popu-

lation figures from Stephen Green, ed., *California Political Almanac*. Sacramento: California Press, 1995.

4. William Glaston and Elaine Ciulla Kamarck, "The Politics of Evasion: Democrats and the Presidency," *Progressive Policy Institute*, September 1989, p. 7.

5. Ibid., pp. 8–9.

6. The promise to end welfare was made repeatedly during Bill Clinton's 1992 campaign, and his declaration about big government was made in his 1996 State of the Union address.

7. Research by Councilman Mark Thomas-Ridley's office.

8. Ibid.

9. *Los Angeles Times*, August 30, 1992, p. A1.

10. Jan Adams, interview, December 16, 1996.

11. James Thigpen, interview, December 14, 1996.

12. *Understand the Riots*. Los Angeles: Los Angeles Times, 1992, p. 10.

13. James Thigpen, interview, December 14, 1996.

14. Ibid.

15. Ibid.

16. Mike Davis, *City of Quartz*. New York: Vintage Books, 1992.

17. Ibid., p. 272.

18. Ron Thigpen, interview, December 12, 1996.

19. Richard Walker, "California Rages Against the Dying of the Light," *New Left Review*, Vol. 209, 1995, p. 46.

20. *Understand the Riots*. Los Angeles: Los Angeles Times, 1992, p. 26.

21. Davis, *City of Quartz*.

22. Anthony Thigpen, interview, December 29, 1996.

23. Ibid.

24. Councilman Mark Ridley-Thomas, interview, December 23, 1996.

25. Interview, December 30, 1996.

26. Anthony Thigpen, interview, December 29, 1996.

27. Steve Smith, interview, May 2, 1996.

28. Anthony Thigpen, interview, November 8, 1996.

29. Anthony Thigpen, interview, December 29, 1996.

30. Anthony Thigpen, interview, June 6, 1996.

31. Ibid.

32. Jean Merl, *Los Angeles Times*, June 7, 1996, p. A1.

33. Jan Adams, interview, December 16, 1996.

34. Ibid.

35. Jan Adams, *Resist*, April 1995, p. 1.

36. Ibid.

37. Jan Adams, interview, December 16, 1996.

38. Jan Adams, interview, September 17, 1996.

39. Ibid.

40. Ibid.

41. Ibid.

42. Jan Adams, interview, January 8, 1996.

43. "Overview," Californians for Justice Field Organizer Binder, September 1996, p. 1.

44. Marshall Wilson, "U.S. Welcomes 11,000 Citizens," *San Francisco Chronicle*, September 19, 1996, p. A1.

Chapter 7

1. Arnold Steinberg, interview, November 19, 1996.

2. Thomas Rhodes, the publisher of the *National Review*, and Governor Pete Wilson—not Dole—had been responsible for raising most of the money, according to Steinberg.

3. Arnold Steinberg, "Campaign Plan, California Civil Rights Initiative for November/1996," Arnold Steinberg and Associates, Inc., p. 21.

4. Transcript, Arnold Steinberg and Associates, Inc., September 1996.

5. In most cases, these commercial transcripts come from scripts produced by the campaigns. Italicized words are used to signal emphasis or stage direction in a script, and the ellipsis is used to signal a pause rather than an excision.

6. Rick Orlov, *Los Angeles Daily News*, September 7, 1996, p. 1.

7. Ibid.

8. Arnold Steinberg, interview, November 19, 1996.

9. Gov. Pete Wilson, letter to Stanley Skinner, chairman and chief executive officer of Pacific Gas and Electric, August 2, 1996.

10. Thomas Wood, interview, February 21, 1997.

11. Mayor Willie Brown, interview, January 1997.

12. Jonathan Tilove, *Plain Dealer*, September 29, 1996, p. 1C.

13. President Bill Clinton, letter to Eva Paterson, August 22, 1996.

14. Jerome Karabel, interview, December 23, 1996.

15. Miriam Komaromy, Kevin Grumbach, et al., "The Role of Black and Hispanic Physicians in Providing Health Care for Underserved Populations," *New England Journal of Medicine*, Vol. 334, No. 20, May 16, 1996, pp. 1305–1328.

16. Gary Yates, interview, March 6, 1997.

17. Arnold Steinberg, "Campaign Plan, California Civil Rights Initiative for November/1996," Arnold Steinberg and Associates, Inc., p. 30.

18. Thomas Wood, interview, February 21, 1996.

19. Herb Gunther, interview, December 1996.

20. H. Chester Horn, Jr., to General Counsel, California Wellness Foundation, September 16, 1996.

21. Greg Colvin, interview, March 11, 1997.

22. Gary Yates, interview, March 6, 1997.

23. Herb Gunther, interview, December 1996.

24. Gregory Colvin, interview, March 11, 1997.

25. Pamela Burdman and Edward W. Lempinen, *San Francisco Chronicle*, September 5, 1996, p. A1.

26. William Claiborne, *Washington Post*, September 26, 1996, p. A3.

27. Arnold Steinberg, interview, November 19, 1997.

28. Ward Connerly, interview, March 31, 1997.

29. Sharon Bernstein, *Los Angeles Times*, September 11, 1996, p. A3.

30. Ibid.

31. Dan Walters, *Sacramento Bee*, September 27, 1996, p. A3.

32. Peg Yorkin, interview, October 19, 1996.

33. Lorraine Sheinberg, interview, February 25, 1997.

34. Ibid.

35. Justine Andronici, interview, February 25, 1997.

36. Town Hall Debate, October 22, 1996.

37. Bob Sipchen and Jonathan Peterson, *Los Angeles Times*, September 28, 1996, p. A15.

38. Ibid.

39. *The Hotline*, October 7, 1996.

40. Arnold Steinberg, interview, November 19, 1996.

41. Ibid.

Chapter 8

1. Dan Schnur, interview, March 13, 1997.

2. Lyn Nofziger, interview, March 18, 1997.

3. Tony Fabrizio, interview, March 18, 1997.

4. Transcript 96101501U68, Cable News Network, Special Campaign '96 Event, October 15, 1996.

5. Michael Schroeder, interview, March 19, 1997.

6. Arnold Steinberg, interview, November 19, 1996.

7. Thomas Wood, interview, February 21, 1997.

8. Interview, December 1996.

9. Michael Schroeder, interview, March 19, 1997.

10. The field poll showed that one-third of those who supported Proposition 209 and one-quarter of those undecided on 209 also planned to vote for Clinton.

11. Dave Lesher and Bettina Boxall, *Los Angeles Times*, October 23, 1996, p. A3.

12. Ken Chavez, *Sacramento Bee*, October 25, 1996, p. A1.

13. Connerly made this comment in response to a question I asked when the U.C. regent visited a U.C. Berkeley course on March 31, 1997. Connerly also said that Steinberg was upset because he would not get the 15 percent commission from the

television commercials. However, Steinberg had turned down earlier offers to do commercials that included Dole and Clinton.

14. Edward W. Lempinen, *San Francisco Chronicle*, October 31, 1997, p. A15.

15. Eric Brazil and Annie Nakao, *Fresno Bee*, November 2, 1996, p. A5.

16. Ibid. In the final two days of the campaign, Steinberg's Proposition 209 television ads began running in the Los Angeles market. Their run, however, was very limited, and the main 209 ad continued to be the one produced by Russo. Steinberg's ads highlighted the themes of equal opportunity without quotas—once the opposition's slogan for the alternative initiative. They ended with the "bring us together" tag line and were strictly nonpartisan. The ads featured Connerly, Janice Camarena, and Pam Lewis, a white woman who was one of the co-chairs.

17. Tom Umberg, interview, March 6, 1997.

18. Tony Fabrizio, interview, March 18, 1997.

19. Harold Ickes, "1996 Ethnic Constituency Proposed Outreach Plan," February 27, 1996.

20. Connie Rice, interview, October 18, 1996.

21. Mayor Willie Brown, interview, December 1996.

22. Rogers Wilkins, interview, September 11, 1997.

23. Connie Rice, interview, October 18, 1996.

24. Diane Feldman, "Strategic Memorandum, No on CCRI Campaign," The Feldman Group, Inc., June 1996, p. 7.

25. Stephen Ansolabehere and Shanto Iyengar, *Going Negative: How Political Advertisements Shrink and Polarize the Electorate*. New York: The Free Press, 1995.

26. Jerome Karabel, interview, December 23, 1996.

27. Dorothy Erlich, interview, January 10, 1997.

28. Eva Paterson, interview, December 27, 1997.

29. Harold Ickes, "African American Working Group, Principles for African American Outreach."

30. Ibid.

31. Because these ads are straightforward expositions of the No position, only excerpts are presented here for illustrative and thematic purposes. In these ads the ellipses signal where cuts have been made.

32. The story was first published on November 4 by the *New York Times*.

33. Kathay Feng, interview, March 4, 1997.

34. The Voter News Service Poll differed slightly with the *Los Angeles Times* poll in finding that Proposition 209 was supported by 52 percent of all women and rejected by 48 percent. The margin of error in both polls is plus or minus 3 percent, so the split between all women was probably close to 50-50.

Suggested Reading

"Affirmative Action Lawsuit, Dismantling Race- and Gender-Based Preferences in California." Report. Office of Governor Pete Wilson, August 10, 1995.

American Bar Association. "The Challenge of Direct Democracy in a Republic: Report and Recommendations of the Task Force on Initiatives and Referenda." February 1993.

Bennett,William J. "A Report on the Humanities in Higher Education." Washington, DC: National Endowment for the Humanities, November 1984.

———. *The Index of Leading Cultural Indicators: Facts and Figures on the State of American Society.* New York: Simon and Schuster, 1994.

Bergmann, Barbara R. *In Defense of Affirmative Action.* New York: Basic Books, 1996.

Bloom, Allan. *The Closing of the American Mind.* New York: Simon and Schuster, 1987.

Brody, Michael. "Congress, the President, and Federal Equal Opportunity Employment Policymaking: A Problem in Separation of Powers." *Boston University Law Review,* No. 239, 1980.

Brown, Edmund G. *Reagan and Reality: The Two Californias.* New York: Praeger, 1970.

Bureau of National Affairs. *The Civil Rights Act of 1964: Text, Analysis, Legislative History.* Washington, DC: Bureau of National Affairs Operations Manual, 1964.

California Department of Finance, Demographic Research Unit. *Population Projections by Race/Ethnicity for California and Its Counties, 1990–2040.* Sacramento, CA: Demographic Research Unit, 1993.

California Secretary of State March Fong Eu. "California Ballot Initiatives." Report. 1990.

———. "A History of the California Initiative Process." Report. 1989.

Carnoy, Martin. *Faded Dreams: The Politics of Economics and Race in America.* New York: Cambridge University Press, 1994.

Carter, Dan T. *The Politics of Rage: George Wallace, the Origins of the New Conservatism, and the Transformation of American Politics.* New York: Simon and Schuster, 1995.

Cronin, Thomas E. *Direct Democracy: The Politics of Initiative, Referendum, and Recall.* Cambridge, MA: Harvard University Press, 1989.

Curry, George E., ed. *The Affirmative Action Debate.* Reading, MA: Addison-Wesley, 1996.

Davis, Mike. *City of Quartz.* New York: Vintage Books, 1992.

Democracy by Initiative: Shaping California's Fourth Branch of Government. Report and Recommendations of the California Commission on Campaign Financing, 1992.

Dillon, Roger. "Blueprint for our Future: Increasing Voter Participation and Reforming the Initiative Process." Senate Office of Research, California State Senate. Sacramento, CA: Joint Publications, 1991.

Discrimination and Affirmative Action. Assembly Committee on Judiciary. California State Legislature. Report of the Hearing of May 4, 1995. Sacramento, CA: Assembly Publications Office, 1995.

Donohue, John J. III, and James Heckman. "Continuous versus Episodic Change: The Impact of Civil Rights Policy on the Economic Status of Blacks." *Journal of Economic Literature*, Vol. XXIX, No. 4, December 1991, pp. 1603–1643.

D'Souza, Dinesh. *Illiberal Education: The Politics of Race and Sex on Campus.* New York: The Free Press, 1991.

Dubois, Philip L., and Floyd F. Feeney. *Improving the California Initiative Process: Options for Change.* Berkeley: California Policy Seminar, University of California, 1992.

Edsall, Thomas Byrne, and Mary D. Edsall. *Chain Reaction: The Impact of Race, Rights and Taxes on American Politics.* New York: Norton, 1991.

Frady, Marshall. *Wallace.* New York: World, 1968.

The Furor over Affirmative Action and Practices. Documents on Affirmative Action Compiled by the California Senate Office of Research, 1995.

Glazer, Nathan. *Affirmative Discrimination: Ethnic Inequality and Public Policy.* New York: Basic Books, 1975.

Graham, Hugh Davis. *The Civil Rights Era: Origins and Development of National Policy, 1960–1972.* New York: Oxford University Press, 1990.

———. *Civil Rights and the Presidency: Race and Gender in American Politics, 1960–1972.* New York: Oxford University Press, 1992.

———. "The Origins of Affirmative Action: Civil Rights and the Regulatory State." *Annals of the American Academy of Political and Social Science,* Vol. 523, September 1992, pp. 50–62.

Greenberg, Stanley B. *Middle Class Dreams: The Politics and the Power of the New American Majority.* New York: Times Books, 1995.

Higginbotham, A. Leon, Jr., *Shades of Freedom.* New York: Oxford University Press, 1996.

Hughes, Robert. *Culture of Complaint: The Fraying of America.* New York: Oxford University Press, 1993.

Jamieson, Kathleen Hall. "Context and the Creation of Meaning in the Advertising of the 1988 Presidential Campaign." *American Behavioral Scientist,* Vol. 32, No. 4, March/April 1989, pp. 415–424.

———. *Dirty Politics: Deception, Distraction and Democracy.* New York: Oxford University Press, 1992.

Jaschik, Scott, and Douglas Lederman. "Appeals Court Bars Racial Preference in College Admissions: Experts Say That

Ruling in Suit Involving Law School at the University of Texas, If Upheld, Could Force Many Colleges to End Affirmative Action." *Chronicle of Higher Education*, Vol. 42, No. 29, March 29, 1996, pp. A26–36.

Kahlenberg, Richard D., *The Remedy: Class, Race, and Affirmative Action.* New York: Basic Books,1996.

Kazin, Michael, *The Populist Persuasion: An American History.* New York: Basic Books, 1995.

Kinder, Donald R., and Lynn M. Saunders, "Mimicking Political Debate with Survey Questions: The Case of White Opinion on Affirmative Action for Blacks." *Social Cognition*, Vol. 8, No. 1, Spring 1990, pp. 73–103.

LA 2000: A City for the Future: Final Report of the Los Angeles 2000 Committee. City of Los Angeles, 1988.

Lee, Eugene C. "Representative Government and the Initiative Process." In *California Policy Choices*, Vol. 6, edited by John Kirlin and Donald Winkler. Los Angeles: University of Southern California, 1990.

Lee, Eugene C., and Willis D. Hawley, eds. *The Challenge of California.* Boston: Little, Brown, 1970.

Levine, Lawrence W. *The Opening of the American Mind: Canons, Culture and History.* Boston: Beacon Press, 1996.

Lowenstein, Daniel. "California Initiatives and the Single-Subject Rule." *UCLA Law Review*, No. 936, June 1983.

———. *Election Law: Cases and Materials.* Durham, NC: Carolina Academic Press, 1995.

Lubenow, Gerald C., ed. *California Votes—The 1990 Governor's Race.* Berkeley, CA: Institute of Governmental Studies Press, 1991.

———, ed. *California Votes—The 1994 Governor's Race.* Berkeley, CA: Institute of Governmental Studies Press, 1995.

Maharidge, Dale. *The Coming White Minority.* New York: Times Books, 1996.

Maraniss, David. *First in His Class.* New York: Simon and Schuster, 1995.

McGinniss, Joe. *The Selling of the President, 1968.* New York: Trident Press, 1969.

McWilliams, Carey. *California: The Great Exception.* Westport, CT: Greenwood Press, 1971, 1949.

Novak, Michael. *The Rise of the Unmeltable Ethnics: Politics and Culture in the 1970s.* New York: Macmillan, 1972.

O'Reilly, Kenneth. *Nixon's Piano.* New York: The Free Press, 1995.

Phillips, Kevin P. *The Emerging Republican Majority.* New Rochelle, NY: Arlington House, 1969.

———. *Boiling Point: Republicans, Democrats, and the Decline of Middle-Class Prosperity.* New York: Random House, 1993.

Platt, Anthony M. "Beyond the Canon, with Great Difficulty." *Social Justice,* Vol. 20, No. 1-2, Spring/Summer 1993, pp. 72–81.

Polsby, Nelson W., and Aaron Wildavsky. *Presidential Elections: Strategies and Structures of American Politics.* 9th ed. Chatham, NJ: Chatham House Publishers, 1996.

Post, A. Alan, chairperson. "Report and Recommendations on the Statewide Initiative Process." *Citizen's Commission on Ballot Initiatives.* California Legislature, January 1994.

Post, Robert, and Michael Rogin, eds. "Race and Representation: Affirmative Action." *Representations,* No. 55, Summer 1996.

Reid, David, ed. *Sex, Death and God in L.A.* Berkeley: University of California Press, 1994.

Schlesinger, Arthur M. *The Disuniting of America.* Knoxville, TN: Whittle Direct Books, 1991.

Searle, John. *"The Storm over the University." New York Review of Books,* December 6, 1990.

Sedmak, Nancy J., and Chrissie Vidas. *Primer on Equal Employment Opportunity,* 6th ed. Washington, DC: Bureau of National Affairs, 1994.

Sherman, Richard B. *The Republican Party and Black America: From McKinley to Hoover, 1896–1933.* Charlottesville: University Press of Virginia, 1973.

Shultz, Jim. *The Initiative Cookbook.* San Francisco: The Democracy Center Advocacy Institute West, 1996.

Skrentny, John David. *The Ironies of Affirmative Action: Politics, Culture, and Justice.* Chicago: University of Chicago Press, 1996.

Sowell, Thomas. *Race and Cuture: A World View.* New York: Basic Books, 1994.

―――. *Inside American Education: The Decline, the Deception, the Dogmas.* New York: Maxwell MacMillan International, 1993.

Southern California's Latino Community. Los Angeles: Los Angeles Times, 1984.

Steele, Shelby. *The Content of Our Character: A New Vision of Race in America.* New York: St. Martin's Press, 1990.

Takaki, Ronald. *Strangers from a Different Shore.* Boston: Little, Brown, 1989.

Understanding the Riots. Los Angeles: Los Angeles Times, 1992.

Walker, Richard, "California Rages Against the Dying of the Light." *New Left Review,* No. 209, January/February 1995, pp. 42–74.

Wallerstein, Immanuel. "The Agonies of Liberalism: What Hope Progress?" *New Left Review,* No. 204, March/April 1994, pp. 3–17.

Whalen, Charles, and Barbara Whalen. *The Longest Debate: A Legislative History of the 1964 Civil Rights Act.* Washington, DC: Seven Locks Press, 1985.

White, Theodore H. *The Making of the President 1960.* New York: Atheneum Publishers, 1961.

Wilkins, Roger. "Racism Has Its Privileges." *The Nation,* Vol. 260, No. 12, March 27, 1995, pp. 409–414.

Woodward, Bob. *The Choice.* New York: Simon and Schuster, 1996.

Works Progress Administration. *The WPA Guide to California.* New York: Pantheon Books, 1939.

Index

Compositor: Publication Services
Text: New Aster 10/13
Display: Universe Condensed 67 Bold
Printer: Haddon Craftsmen
Binder: Haddon Craftsmen